Rate of Profit, Distribution and Growth: Two Views

J. A. KREGEL
Lecturer in Economics
University of Bristol

MACMILLAN

First published *1971* by
THE MACMILLAN PRESS LTD
London and Basingstoke
Associated companies in New York Toronto
Dublin Melbourne Johannesburg and Madras

SBN 333 12600 9

Printed in Great Britain by
ROBERT MACLEHOSE AND CO LTD
The University Press, Glasgow

Ellen L. Kregel

9.xii.1919 – 3.viii.1969

CONTENTS

LIST OF ILLUSTRATIONS

PREFACE

The analysis presented in the following pages is by no means orthodox, nor will it be easily accepted by all readers. Much of the argument is well known to only a few economists and even fewer students are objectively exposed to it. Likewise only a few will feel it necessary to object violently to the method of approach to the subject and the conclusions drawn. Most probably the majority of students and economists will be uncertain as to where they stand between the two extremes. It is to these students and economists that the book is directed.

The subject has, unnecessarily, at times been made excessively difficult and is often obscured by the semi-religious fervour with which some writers approach their particular point of view. It is also made up of several seemingly unconnected branches which has served to complicate understanding further.

It is hoped that by presenting the various subjects of current economic controversy in relation to economic growth, and to long-run growth models in particular, the deeper implications involved in the current growth theory controversy may be more readily appreciated. This contemporary dispute is something more than competing logical consistency of the models in question, and extends right down to first principles. Thus it is a field of study that cannot be ignored as a speciality and should be the concern of all students of economics. Its effects will eventually be felt in all aspects of economic theory.

The method of presentation and integration used below is felt to be a useful method for the further acceptance of the main propositions contained in the study. It also provides a convenient way so present new approaches to old concepts and allows a sufficient introduction to extensions of the subject as outlined in the last chapter. The book, in this context, searches the current body of theory to find the most fruitful directions for further extensions. Only time and further research will determine the full extent of their feasibility. This, however, cannot be accomplished until the basic questions are understood. If this book can interest and expose more economists and students to the field and enable them to cast a more searching and objective eye on what they are currently taught, I believe it will have more than achieved its goal.

The references cited in the text and notes should not be considered exhaustive. When new work by an author has appeared subsequent to the final revision of the text, it has been appended to footnotes with indications of its bearing on the general line of analysis taken in the text.

In addition some sources were available to me in draft form. These are cited, where possible, with their subsequent or expected place of publication and date. It remains for me to deal with some indebtedness which notes and references cannot reflect.

Gratefully, I initially acknowledge the aid and guidance of Professor Paul Davidson who first awakened my interest in the subject. His comments and criticisms have considerably improved both the exposition and the argument. While there is still disagreement on some points, much error has been avoided by beneficial discussions and his unflagging interest in the project.

The completed work quite obviously reflects the influence of Professor Joan Robinson, to whom I owe the greatest thanks and appreciation as both teacher and friend. Discussions with Mrs Robinson have provided an appreciation of the subject that would have been impossible without her aid and interest. No one could ask for more attention and guidance (not to mention patience with my oft-times slow process of thought) in a teacher. It is doubtful that the book could have existed in its present form without her tutelage. This is not, of course, meant to imply her agreement with all that is contained herein. One cannot hope fully to attain the standards of competence and exposition Mrs Robinson sets for herself and expects from her students.

The first draft of the book was completely written during my stay in the Faculty of Economics and Politics, University of

Cambridge, 1968–9. Final revisions were completed there in the summer of 1970. Any acknowledgement to the academic and environmental stimulus of Cambridge would be redundant.

Portions of the manuscript were read by Professor Nicholas Kaldor and discussions on Kaldor–Pasinetti models and technical progress are acknowledged.

In terms of less academic, but none the less intellectual, appreciation the camaraderie of the Sidgwick Site group must be mentioned. In particular T. R. Haigh and his wife Nuria, A. S. MacDonald, P. D. Balacs (now of Queen Elizabeth House, Oxford), R. T. Naylor, K. C. R. and Susan D'Arcy (now of the University of Toronto) and N. L. G. Eastman, as well as many others who provided excellent company and discussion both of economic and uneconomic issues.

Students at New Hall, Cambridge, and the University of Bristol deserve mention for submitting to the testing of the teaching use of some of the material. Jonathan Stern has been especially helpful in reading the various drafts of latter chapters. Hopefully their personal success is reflected in the final version.

Miss Marjorie Lunt deserves special praise for transforming an illegible hand into finished typescript. It is doubtful that the final draft could have been completed without her aid.

I must also thank Joan and Fred Hines of The Chequers, Fowlmere, for providing quiet relief at all times and summer accommodation away from a tourist-infested Cambridge!

To this vast group I give my complete expression of gratitude on the implicit assumption that this in no way implicates them in the final product. In any success they may receive as equals, for error of fact or logic I must stand alone.

The page of dedication stands to my mother who did not live to see the completion of this work. Her satisfaction would have been its greatest reward. Her unselfish devotion to her children cannot be adequately expressed in word or dedication.

J. A. K.

incorporated by Marx in *Capital*. Marx's approach to the problem of distribution, however, was slightly different. By extracting surplus value from labour the capitalist could, according the Marx, exploit labour and make a profit. Marx defines the rate of exploitation in terms of the economy-wide ratio of net profits to wages in value added.[1] Given net output and a uniform rate of profits for all lines of production in the system, the distributive shares and the pattern of prices can be determined. Nevertheless the transformation problem still remained unsolved, even though the system of distribution is logically consistent.

The problem still had not been solved when the neoclassical *laissez-faire* reaction to Marx developed. To justify the existence of interest and profit the neoclassicists did not emphasise the question of the measure of value (which was Ricardo's initial question); rather they searched for the cause of value. If labour caused value then so did capital, the neoclassicist argued, and therefore the capitalist received his profits as justly as the worker received his wages. Thus the neoclassicists were not interested in measuring the value of output in terms of the value of inputs, but were satisfied merely to prove that inputs cause value and that value was therefore divided among the inputs in accordance with their contribution to output. Their reaction to Marx's social theory caused them to miss the crucial problem in Marx's economic theory.

There are two distinct streams of thought stemming from the neoclassical approach. This dichotomy of views still maintains a stranglehold on most aspects of modern economic theory, even on models of economic growth. These distinct views are connected with the names of Walras and Alfred Marshall. Walras, enamoured at a young age of the harmony of the spheres,[2] attempted to produce a similar harmony of the economic sphere. The tale of the Walrasian auctioneer and the process of *tâtonnement* need hardly be retold at this stage. It is logically incontrovertible that the Walrasian system required

[1] See Joan Robinson, *An Essay in Marxian Economics* (London: Macmillan, 1952).

[2] See A. Leijonhufvud, *On Keynesian Economics and the Economics of Keynes* (London: Oxford University Press, 1968) 394 n.

perfect foreknowledge and equilibrium prices in terms of satisfaction and market clearing.[1] The question that Walras does not explain or explicitly treat is, who owns the initial stocks of commodities that are traded and who earns the prices received?[2] The pattern of prices is set by the ethereal auctioneer, the equilibrium that exists is merely for a trading day. There is no theory of distribution in the Walrasian system because there is no theory to set the rate of profit and thus determine how the system sets its pattern of prices. Indeed the system can be utilised in terms of allocative efficiency, but it cannot be used to distribute the output once the value is determined. Its application will be seen more expansively below in terms of problems of growth.[3]

The other half of the neoclassical development is carried forth under the name of Alfred Marshall. Marshall's intellectual offspring are probably just as numerous as the students of Walras, but seldom do they display the same degree of accuracy to the master. The fault, admittedly, lies partially with Marshall. It is said that a complete and separate theory can be evolved solely from his footnotes and appendices. In addition there is in Marshall both the analysis of a dynamic system and the stationary state. It is not always clear which case is being considered. Joan Robinson has commented that the more she learns about economics the more she respects Marshall as an economist and less as a man.[4] This view stems from Marshall's admitted

[1] This is not to mention the problems of fixed capital resources and their accumulation. See also Joan Robinson, 'Stationary States', and 'Interest and Profits' in *Economic Heresies* (New York: Basic Books, 1970; London: Macmillan, 1971) 3–15 and 25–51.

[2] And what happens to the chap whose good yields a zero price?

[3] It should be noted that we have not here delved into the mathematical neoclassical postulates that have been derived from the basic Walrasian system: the contentions surrounding the production function, e.g. the marginal product of capital is equal to the rate of interest, labour is paid a wage equal to its marginal product, etc. At this point we shall be satisfied just to present the development and primary nature of the necessity of the rate of profits. The truth or falsity of the postulates will be dealt with below. If the argument is logical we should not expect an approach without the posed crucial variable to yield satisfactory distributional statements.

[4] See Joan Robinson, 'A Lecture Delivered at Oxford by a Cambridge Economist', in *On Re-reading Marx* (Cambridge, England: Students' Bookshops Ltd, 1953) 14.

defence of pure competition and capitalism to the extent of rejecting or rationalising away results and paradoxes that Marshall the economist had presented. As a consequence there is some difficulty in finding a concise statement on profits and distribution in Marshall's writings.

Marshall has a normal rate of profit that rules in the long period where competitive entrants force the rate to uniformity in all lines of production. The normal prices in the system are then cost of production prices – long-run supply prices covering labour costs and a normal profit on the capital committed to the production of output. Sometimes Marshall views the economy as moving along dynamically and at other times grinding towards a stationary state. In the latter case the normal rate of profit is explicitly defined as the discount of the future. But in the stationary state the process of growth is completed; while in the case where the economy is rolling along with net investment continually being made and earning the normal rate of profits there is no explanation of what determines the normal prices or the normal rate of profits.[1] In both cases, however, it is clear that the demand blade of the Marshallian scissors is not the crucial factor.

In both the Walrasian and Marshallian neoclassical systems the problem of the determination of the rate of profits is left unsolved. Many modern neoclassical economists, however, when treating problems of long-run growth and distribution[2] seem to think that either the problem has been overcome or that it is inconsequential. Although modern neoclassicists claim Wicksell as a precursor, Wicksell admitted that he had not got the problem sorted our properly.[3]

The Keynesian revolution interrupted the study of these

[1] It should be noted that Marshall was openly suspicious of the above-cited neoclassical propositions on the marginal properties of distribution (D. H. Robertson's 'Wage Grumbles' notwithstanding). See A. Marshall, *Principles of Economics*, 8th ed. (London: Macmillan, 1920) bk v, chap. 8, and D. H. Robertson, *Economic Fragments* (London: P. S. King & Son Ltd, 1931) 42–57. Marshall's doubts were also held by Keynes; see *The General Theory of Employment, Interest and Money* (London: Macmillan, 1936) 139–40.

[2] See Solow's comment on the long period, Chapter 5 below.

[3] K. Wicksell, *Lectures on Political Economy*, I (London: Routledge & Kegan Paul, 1934) 148, 268, 296.

problems of capital theory for a time, but the application of Keynes's approach outside the short period was taken up again in the 1950s. The questions that will be focussed on in this volume are (1) whether the classicists, the neoclassicists, or the Keynesians have solved the problem of the determination of the rate of profits, and (2) which group has been able to utilise the concept of the rate of profits in a consistent theory of distribution in the context of economic growth.

C. RECENT DISCUSSION OF THE PROBLEMS

The real *raison d'être* for developing the problem of profits rates and distribution in the context of growth theory is more complex than historical disagreement. The controversy in distribution theory stems from the dual developments in extending macroeconomic theory to long-run problems after the *General Theory*.[1] In 1939 Harrod presented the first attempt at applying the basic *General Theory* analysis to problems of long-run growth.[2] In the late 1940s and early 1950s, on the other hand, the neoclassicists were fitting the concept of the production function into Ramsey–von Neumann models. Samuelson and Solow were the major contributors in this latter line. About the same time, Joan Robinson started pursuing the hint given by Harrod before the war and was further stimulated by Harrod's post-war *Towards a Dynamic Economics*.[3] Her express intent was a 'generalisation of the *General Theory*' to fit a wider range of long-run economic problems and to provide a theory of distribution. In the course of her work, which resulted in *The Accumulation of Capital*,[4] she launched a side analysis and attack on the existing neoclassical theory. This attack began in the literature with her exchange with Solow in the mid-1950s.[5] Initially this confrontation over the concept of the production

---

[1] J. M. Keynes, op. cit.

[2] 'An Essay in Dynamic Theory', *Economic Journal*, XLIX (Mar. 1939) 14.

[3] *Towards a Dynamic Economics* (London: Macmillan, 1948).

[4] *The Accumulation of Capital* (London: Macmillan, 1956).

[5] Joan Robinson, 'The Production Function and the Theory of Capital', *Review of Economic Studies*, XXI (1953–4), and R. Solow, 'The Production Function and the Theory of Capital', *Review of Economic Studies*, XXIII (1955–6).

function in neoclassical models and the distribution and growth theories stemming from the neoclassical view did not create the furore that was generated in the 1960s.

A major theoretical contribution to the conflict came with the appearance of Sraffa's *Production of Commodities by Means of Commodities*[1] in 1960. In that work, after some forty years' reflection, Sraffa was able to solve the old classical problem of the transformation of values into prices, and, in a short chapter on the choice of techniques, to show that the neoclassical proposition of increasing capital intensity resulting in low interest (profit) rates was not only false but misleading. The book, highly technical in nature, was not fully appreciated initially and it was not until Levhari, at Samuelson's suggestion, put forward the 'Non-switching Theorem'[2] that the value of Sraffa's work was fully appreciated. Pasinetti, using Sraffa's system and examples, disproved the non-switching theorem.[3] Both the Capital Measurement and Re-switching controversies should have been settled, at least in terms of the necessity of utilising the rate of profits to measure the value of capital and solve distribution, at this point. In 1966, however, Samuelson and Modigliani published a strong reaction,[4] in neoclassical terms, to a previous growth paper put forward by Pasinetti[5] which utilised the basic models of Kaldor and Joan Robinson. The question Samuelson and Modigliani posed was not the validity of the underlying determinants of the model (they accepted both types of approach as theoretically consistent), but which of the two approaches achieved the greatest generality of application.

[1] *Production of Commodities by Means of Commodities: Prelude to a Critique of Economic Theory* (Cambridge, England: Cambridge University Press, 1960).

[2] D. Levhari, 'A Non-substitution Theorem and Switching of Techniques', *Quarterly Journal of Economics*, LXXIX (Feb. 1965).

[3] As did Garegnani and others. For reference, see 'Paradoxes in Capital Theory: A Symposium', *Quarterly Journal of Economics*, LXXX (Nov. 1966) 503–83. In addition see P. Garegnani, 'Heterogeneous Capital, the Production Function and the Theory of Distribution', *Review of Economic Studies*, XXXVII (July 1970) 407–36.

[4] 'The Pasinetti Paradox in Neoclassical and More General Models', *Review of Economic Studies*, XXXIII (Oct. 1966).

[5] 'Rate of Profit and Income Distribution in Relation to the Rate of Economic Growth', *Review of Economic Studies*, XXIX (Oct. 1962).

This new battle line now moves under the guise of the 'Two Cambridges Controversy' with many economists unsure of where they stand between these two camps of giants.

D. THE NECESSITY OF THE STUDY

Many of the students of growth theory who are now faced with trying to analyse and understand the bifurcation that now exists in this area may not be fully aware of the ramifications of the many critical theoretical developments since the Keynesian revolution. It is the intent of this study (1) to present an analysis of the various views on growth; (2) to emphasise the crucial areas of theoretical evolution; (3) to point out the consequences of the various long-run models that do presently exist; and (4) to suggest further extensions and improvements in the analysis of economic growth. This can best be done by starting first with the problem of determination of the rate of profits. This will then provide a view of income distribution which is essential in understanding the consistency of the various models that have been applied to questions of long-run growth. The approach adopted in this study will enable the reader to raise a critical eye to the neo-Keynesian and neo-neoclassical models, analysing all the necessary theoretical propositions underlying these models rather than merely having to judge any particular formulation as something that can be viewed outside the context of these current theoretical developments in economic theory.

E. THE METHOD OF ANALYSIS

There are several different methods of presentation that could be adopted in the present study. A particular model associated with a particular economist could be taken as most representative of a particular school of thought and this model could be analysed for its strengths and weaknesses. The model could then be used as a benchmark and other models could be compared to it. Alternatively, the different major mechanisms at work in any model could be specified, such as transaction structure, aggregation structure, etc.[1] The various models could then be analysed under these headings, showing the implicit judgements involved in their assumptions about their structures. This latter approach would involve looking at and comparing pieces of different models.

The philosophy underlying the approach developed here is that it would be more useful if the model of each respresentative author is treated individually as a complete system. This approach may at times raise the problem of repetition when several writers use very similar approaches. Nevertheless, in what follows, each author's system will be presented separately, with comments where they are particularly relevant to an under-standing of the model. A critical appraisal of each author's work and his success in satisfying the criteria of profits and distribution theory will be presented.

Obviously, if the various models are primarily developed from two main sources, similarities are inevitable. To provide a common ground, for critical reference and appreciation of the subtleties involved in the controversies, particularly when these are not directly related to questions of growth, Chapter 2 will give a presentation of the most representative works concerned with the controversies. Initially von Neumann's classical model will be presented. This model of long-run growth provides, in a classical world, a consistent system with a defined rate of profit and distribution system. Following a discussion of the von Neumann model in Chapter 2, Sraffa's work will be reviewed. Sraffa was able to furnish a solution to the value–price problem without requiring a given subsistence wage. Simultaneously he supplied an analysis of the switching problem. Finally, in Chapter 2, the most recent neoclassical attempt, Samuelson's 'Surrogate Production Function,'[2] will be presented and compared in relation to the other two works. The conclusions reached in this chapter can then be used as the basis for criticism of the neoclassical models presented in the following chapters, thus avoiding repetition of the entire logical argument each time it becomes applicable.

[1] See the approach in Leijonhufvud, op. cit.

[2] 'Parable and Realism in Capital Theory: The Surrogate Production Function', *Review of Economic Studies*, XXIX (June 1962).

Chapters 3–11 will deal with modern growth systems. For purposes of consistency and ease in exposition these will be divided into two sections. First the modern neoclassicists will be treated, taking the most widely known models as representative: i.e. Chapters 3–6 will deal with the works of Meade, Tobin, Solow, and Samuelson–Modigliani. The reader approaching this area of analysis for the first time should not be startled by the fact that many of these modern neoclassicists are, in other areas of economics, often considered Keynesian authors. This particular appellation has very little relevance in the profession today, as will be seen when these works are compared with those of the second section which will be called Keynesian. Chapter 7 will present the basic work and underlying concepts of Kalecki and Keynes, the progenitors of this section.[1] Harrod's pioneering work will be treated in Chapter 8, followed by the systems set out by Kaldor, Pasinetti, and Joan Robinson in Chapters 9–11. These latter models in particular will be subject to searching analysis in terms of their treatment of the rate of profits, distribution and technical progress. Chapter 12 will present an analysis and extension of the basic Keynesian model developed by this latter group. One extension will be a model without the assumption of income class and class thriftiness differences. Another, a logical extension of the first, will present an outline of possible extensions of Keynesian distribution and growth theory to modern industrial systems. The analysis developed in Chapter 12 will free the so-called 'Cambridge' model from criticisms it has received on account of the classical savings assumptions, as well as to clarify the effects of the savings conditions on the functioning of the model.

It is hoped that this work will serve as an easy reference and explanation of the common threads developed in current long-run growth models while simultaneously providing critical appraisal of these structures by pointing out the crucial under-

---

[1] Although Marx, Marshall, Ricardo, and even Wicksell could be included as having made contributions of major importance that are acknowledged by various of the writers in this section. We shall restrict the chapter to Keynes and Kalecki, however, as the work is more straightforward and visible in their cases.

lying postulates and determinants. Moreover, the analysis of Chapter 12 should furnish direction to possible extensions and application of models of economic growth to modern institutions.[1]

[1] The particular authors chosen and omitted will not be further justified. Under the constraint of length there must be some excision. The works that remain do so because they are either representative or have achieved a degree of acceptance far in excess of their actual achievement or vice versa.

2 CLASSICAL AND NEOCLASSICAL APPROACHES

In striking contrast to the models developed by the modern neoclassical writers are two models of general equilibrium developed in the 1930s, one by von Neumann, the other by Sraffa.[1] Both are distinctly in the classical vein, but neither model involves recourse to marginal products, abstinence, rewards of waiting or the perfect substitutability of production functions that were later to be added by the modern neoclassicists.

(1) J. von NEUMANN
A MODEL OF GENERAL
ECONOMIC EQUILIBRIUM[2]

The first development of an economy, in equilibrium, expanding through time appears in a mathematical analysis by J. von Neumann. His purpose was to show (1) that such a growing equilibrium system can exist, and (2) what rate of expansion, prices, rate of interest, and production processes will obtain in such a perfectly competitive system.

[1] Sraffa's 1960 publication date is some forty years after his initial work on the model. See the Preface, P. Sraffa, *Production of Commodities by Means of Commodities: Prelude to a Critique of Economic Theory* (Cambridge, England: Cambridge University Press, 1960) vi.

[2] J. von Neumann, 'A Model of General Economic Equilibrium', *Review of Economic Studies*, XIII (1945–6) 1–9. The paper was first read in 1932 and published originally in German in 1938. See also D. G. Champernowne, 'A Note on J. v. Neumann's Article on "A Model of General Economic Equilibrium" ', *Review of Economic Studies*, XIII (1945–6) 10–18.

A. TECHNICAL PROPERTIES OF THE MODEL

In the system all goods are produced by each other in an infinite variety of combinations or productive processes. Thus there are n different goods in the system which can be produced by m different production processes. The number of possible processes may exceed the number of goods produced. Constant returns to scale and unlimited factor supplies (including labour) are assumed. One of the most significant aspects of the model is the treatment of the labour input. Consumption in the system can only take place through the process of production. Thus labour, as a factor of production (and an output of itself), is only allowed enough goods to maintain (and presumably reproduce) itself. That is, the real wage is unalterably fixed at subsistence. This, along with the assumption that all income in excess of subsistence is reinvested (if output exceeds inputs by more than replacement), gives the classic savings assumptions: workers do not (indeed cannot) save and profit-earners do not consume (except in production of themselves).

Capital goods are treated as both inputs and outputs of the production processes. A machine of a given age serves as an input and after the production process of unit time duration emerges as an output – a machine one time unit older. This treatment of capital necessitates the utilisation of the concept of joint products. The output of a production process is thus the produced good plus the new (older) capital good. Neumann shows the applicability of the system to joint production but does not appear to be fully aware of the implications and necessity of joint production as a result of the treatment of capital.[1]

Given the available processes, P_i, $(i = 1, \ldots, m)$, quantities of goods, a_{ij}, are used as inputs to produce quantities of goods, b_{ij}, as outputs, G_j, $(j = 1, \ldots, n)$. Thus:

$$P_i: \sum_{j=1}^{n} a_{ij} G_j \rightarrow \sum_{j=1}^{n} b_{ij} G_j. \qquad (2.1)$$

Goods need not be produced in similar amounts or intensities,

[1] See Sraffa's treatment of the same concept below.

x_i, but merely in constant ratios. Thus each process is multiplied by its intensity, x_i, $(i=1, \ldots, m)$, to yield total production E:

$$E = \sum_{i=1}^{m} x_i P_i. \qquad (2.2)$$

If $x_i = 0$ then the particular production process is not used. Given the processes and intensities there is a coefficient of expansion, α, at which the system not only reproduces itself but grows proportionately at the rate α. Still to be determined in the system are the prices, $y, \ldots, y_n$, of the goods, $G, \ldots, G_n$, which are used as both inputs and outputs, and the interest factor, β, where $\beta = 1 + z/100$ and z is the rate of interest in per cent per unit of time. With the restriction that intensities are non-negative:

$$x_i \geqq 0, \quad \text{and} \quad \sum_{i=1}^{m} x_i > 0 \qquad (2.3)$$

and that the prices are non-negative:

$$y_j \geqq 0, \quad \text{and} \quad \sum_{j=1}^{n} y_j > 0 \qquad (2.4)$$

von Neumann presents the economically meaningful conditions (2.5) and (2.6). Thus

$$\alpha \sum_{i=1}^{m} a_{ij} x_i \leqq \sum_{i=1}^{m} b_{ij} x_i \qquad (2.5)$$

which indicates that the system will at least produce its own replacement and a surplus available for reinvestment and expansion at a rate α. If the amount produced in any individual process is greater than that required for the equality, then y_j, its price, will equal zero and it will be a free good. In addition:

$$\beta \sum_{j=1}^{n} a_{ij} y_j \geqq \sum_{j=1}^{n} b_{ij} y_j \qquad (2.6)$$

which requires that any process must produce, at the given

prices, enough output to cover its replacement and interest in value terms. If the process does not meet this condition of profitability, then its intensity is zero and it is not considered for use.

In these price and production inequalities the a_{ij}s and the b_{ij}s are known for each process, P_i; while x_i, the intensities, y_j, the prices, α, the rate of expansion, and β, the rate of interest, are unknown. Thus there are m intensities and n prices and α and β, or $m+n+2$ unknowns. As equilibrium expansion only requires that the ratios of x_i and y_j are constant, there are then only $m-1$ intensities and $n-1$ prices to be determined or exactly $m+n$ unknowns to match the $m+n$ possible inequalities given in (2.5) and (2.6). Von Neumann mathematically (with the use of topology) demonstrated the existence of solutions for the inequalities, but the results are not unique in price and intensity proportions. With a given set of processes, however (here the system differs from Sraffa's), α and β are always unique for any given set of $x_i : x_m$ and $y_j : y_n$ solutions, given that $a_{ij} + b_{ij} > 0$. Thus it follows that the rate of interest is equal to the co-efficient of expansion of the system, and both rates are determined by the available processes of production used, irrespective of prices and intensities.

B. ECONOMIC CONTEXT OF THE MODEL

Translating this result into modern terminology gives the conclusion that when the real wage is set as a technical condition of production, the process of production will set the rate of growth in the system which will be equal to the rate of profit. The rate of profit is, of course, uniquely determined since the capital stock of the system is measurable in consistent prices for capital both as an input and as an output. The goods prices, once determined, are constant as the proportions $x_i : x_m$ and $y_j : y_n$ are unchanged as the system expands at the rate α, yielding a profit rate of β. The aggregate of profits is nothing more than the surplus produced over replacement (on non-zero-price goods) and it is also valued in consistent prices. The rate of profit is then merely the ratio of the surplus goods output to the goods input and it will be the same value whether measured in physical quantities or any consistent set of prices. Since recipients of profits do not spend (it is impossible under the assumptions) and workers cannot earn more than they consume, all the surplus (profit) is by hypothesis automatically invested and thus the rate of growth and the rate of profits are seen to be identical and uniquely determined by the coefficients of production.

C. SUMMARY: ANALYSIS OF RESTRICTIONS

The von Neumann system has been worked out, however, without any reference at all to consumer demand. Given the savings assumptions, however, this is logically correct since personal consumption is, in this model, technically determined by the people production process and, it must be supposed, this implies that consumables are determined by the coefficients of the diet. It is immediately seen that once consumption above this subsistence level is allowed, it is no longer possible to maintain the growth–profits equality. Once the profit-earners are allowed to consume part of the surplus, the growth ratio will fall as the entire surplus is no longer available for reinvestment. The rate of profits and the relative prices will, however, remain unchanged. If, for example, profits recipients decide to consume a proportion of the surplus, then the amount reinvested in each process is lower by the amount of the consumption. The rate of increase in total output will then be lower as the intensities of each process are lower. With the same production processes, however, the ratio of surplus over inputs (the rate of profits) will remain the same and hence the *ratios* of the intensities will also be the same. Thus relative prices are also unchanged, as are values. In this case, then, the rate of growth is below the rate of profit in the same proportion as consumption to surplus.[1]

---

[1] The case is not so simple when only one good is consumed rather than a proportion of all output. With consumption of single goods consumption must be restricted to a proportion (as 10 per cent) of the absolute surplus of that good. If an absolute amount (100 tomatoes) is involved, then the ratios of production intensities and prices will change and comparisons of quantities in the system at different points in time or across systems cannot

Additionally, if the assumption of the technically determined subsistence real wage is relaxed, the uniqueness of the solutions for the rate of profits and the rate of growth are lost, not only in terms of their equality, but also in their determination. Without the given real wage, the surplus in production is no longer exclusively profit and may be distributed as wages. An increase in real wages above subsistence would therefore lower the surplus available for reinvestment or consumption by profits recipients. Thus both β and α would fall by the same degree. There is no mechanism to deal with the level of real wages outside subsistence in von Neumann's paper, and thus when the subsistence real wage constraint is relaxed profits and consequently growth are no longer explicitly determined. In sum, the introduction of consumption by profits recipients collapses the equality proposition and the rejection of the technically determined real wage loses the solution for a determinant rate of profits in the von Neumann system.

The crucial proposition in von Neumann's system is the determination of the real wage as a given technical datum, similar to the fixed coefficients in the production processes used. The model turns on the fixity of the real wage rate which permits the relegation of consumer demand to a minor role except as it is technically determined as the inputs necessary for subsistence. Despite this limitation, von Neumann's approach is highly useful in exhibiting the operations of a purely classical model in the context of growth. It explicitly highlights the conditions for a determinate rate of profit and rate growth in such a system. The single efficient process approach and the fixed wage assumption, while necessary to the model, keep von Neumann from approaching other interesting properties that can emerge from this type of formulation. Some of these extensions will be seen in the next section.

---

be made in either physical or value terms. This is of course possible with the case given in the text.

It should also be noticed, in both the case given in the text and in this note, that labour supply is fully elastic – the redundant labourers that exist when the rate of growth (and labour force) falls with profits consumption simply disappear.

(2) PIERO SRAFFA: COMMODITIES, TRANSFORMATION AND SWITCHING

The basic format of the classical system set out by Sraffa in *Production of Commodities by Means of Commodities*[1] resembles the von Neumann construction. Sraffa, however, is primarily concerned with the Ricardian puzzle of measurement of value and the distribution of output. This problem, commonly known as the 'transformation of values into prices', is solved by Sraffa's proof of the possibility of the construction of a measuring rod that is invariant in price and value terms when the rate of profits and wages (distribution) changes. Besides the direct treatment of this problem, Sraffa's book furnishes an important insight into the determination of the value of capital and thus choice of technique considerations,[2] as well as an insight towards a critique of accepted economic theory in general.

A. SIMPLE REPRODUCTION

The development of the measuring rod is meticulous. Sraffa starts with the production equations of a self-reproducing system with a given price pattern. In the system all basic commodities appear as both inputs and outputs of the processes of production. The prices or exchange values of the outputs are such that each producer is able to replace his inputs exactly by the sale of his output. When the system produces more than replacement, i.e. a surplus of goods, then two problems arise. Not only must the exchange values be determined, but the surplus of production in excess of replacement needs must be

---

[1] P. Sraffa, *Production of Commodities by Means of Commodities: Prelude to a Critique of Economic Theory* (Cambridge, England: Cambridge University Press, 1960).

[2] In von Neumann's model there were an infinite number of techniques available but only one set could ever be chosen as economically feasible, on the criterion of cheapness, for the system.

apportioned over the various production processes. Since the system is classically competitive, the surplus must be allocated in proportion to the value of the means of production and be such that the ratio of surplus to means of production is uniform over all processes. This is merely specifying the familiar competitive condition of the equality of the rate of profits in all lines of production.

In order to determine the uniform rate of profits, an additional variable is added to the system which determines the rate of profits and the prices simultaneously. It would, of course, be meaningless to apportion the surplus either before or after prices themselves are set, as prices and profits are interdependent and the value of one will affect the other. In other words, prices are a reflection of the inputs' prices which include the rate of profits. Thus the production system takes the equational form:

$$
\begin{aligned}
(A_a p_a + B_a p_b + \ldots + K_a p_k)(1+r) &= A p_a \\
(A_b p_a + B_b p_b + \ldots + K_b p_k)(1+r) &= B p_b \\
\ldots \qquad \ldots \qquad \ldots \\
(A_k p_a + B_k p_b + \ldots + K_k p_k)(1+r) &= K p_k
\end{aligned}
\tag{2.7}
$$

where $A, B, \ldots, K$ are the quantities of commodities as inputs and outputs, $p_a, \ldots, p_k$ are the prices, and r the rate of profits. Thus $A_k p_a$ is the amount of commodity A used in the production of commodity K with p_a the price of A, or cost of a unit of A when used in production of K.

B. REPRODUCTION WITH SURPLUS

The existence of a surplus in production gives rise to the possibility of goods in the system that do not enter into the production of other goods. Such luxury goods, or non-basic goods, since they do not enter into the production of other goods in the system, do not have any effect on the determination of prices or the rate of profits for the system. Nevertheless, there must be at least one basic good used in all processes in the system to make the system determinate.

Up to this point Sraffa has viewed the real wage in a manner similar to von Neumann, namely, as the subsistence intake of a means of production. If, however, the possibility of some of the surplus being paid in wages as well as going to profits is admitted, then labour must enter into the equations explicitly. By assuming that the wage is paid after the process of production is completed, Sraffa eliminates the idea of a rate of profit to be paid on the wage fund. Thus, labour enters each process of production as the percentage of total labour employed such that with the addition of w, the price of labour or the wage bill, the system of production equations becomes:

$$
\begin{aligned}
(A_a p_a + B_a p_b + \ \ldots \ + K_a p_k)(1+r) + L_a w &= A p_a \\
(A_b p_a + B_b p_b + \ \ldots \ + K_b p_k)(1+r) + L_b w &= B p_b \\
\ldots \qquad \qquad \ldots \qquad \qquad \ldots \\
(A_k p_a + B_k p_b + \ \ldots \ + K_k p_k)(1+r) + L_k w &= K p_k
\end{aligned}
\tag{2.8}
$$

where $L_a + \ \ldots \ + L_k = 1$, and the system produces a surplus:

$$
\begin{aligned}
A_a + A_b + \ \ldots \ + A_k &\leq A \\
\ldots \qquad \ldots \qquad \ldots \\
K_a + K_b + \ \ldots \ + K_k &\leq K.
\end{aligned}
\tag{2.9}
$$

The wage is therefore free to vary as a proportion of the surplus produced (and the similarities with the von Neumann system cease).

If the surplus produced by the system in excess of reproduction is called the national income, then wages and profits will exhaust this national income. Thus it is possible to vary the rate of profits and the wage in order to isolate the resultant changes in the prices of produced goods. For example, if the wage is set equal to unity (the whole of the national income going to wages), then the relative values (prices) of goods are in direct proportion to the quantity of labour that has gone, directly or indirectly, into their production. In this case Marxian values rule unquestionably. Alternatively, if wages are zero, the whole of the national income is paid as profit. The maximum rate of profit that the system can produce is then the ratio of the total surplus to the aggregate means of production. In this case technical conditions of production set the rate of profits, and prices are proportional to the value of the means of production used to produce the output. The problem is to determine the reaction of prices to changes in the wage share in national income between zero and unity.

C. THE STANDARD SYSTEM

The key lies in the conditions under which the set of prices in the system would be unchanged when the proportion of national income going to wages changes. Prices will be constant only if the proportions of labour and means of production used in all processes in the system are exactly the same. Given this restriction, equal reductions in the wage over all processes would create equal additional amounts of net product to be paid as profits on the means of production in all processes. Thus the rate of profits would rise equally and remain uniform over all processes of production without any change in the set of prices.

If the proportion of labour to means of production is not equal across industries, it is seen that prices must change if the rate of profits is to remain uniform. Outputs with processes using a greater proportion of labour to means of production would have to have diminished prices and vice versa. There will exist, however, some critical proportion of labour to means of production in any given system which will exhibit constant prices at changing levels of the wage and rate of profits. The processes with more labour employed than this critical proportion will, at the existing prices, have a greater saving due to the wage reduction than is necessary to pay its below critical proportion means of production at the new, uniform, rate of profits. In this case the price of the good must fall (to reduce the value of its surplus) if the process is to have the uniform profit rate. This will be the general result unless the processes which produce the means of production for the process in question have a lower than critical proportion of labour such that the price of the output may indeed have to rise. This is necessary to offset the increased value of means of production in the process that produces the final good's means of production. It is then impossible to say exactly whether the price of a good will rise of fall unless all the past processes of the inputs are known. It is then also impossible to generalise the reaction of

B

prices with changes in the wage when processes exhibit a greater or lesser than critical proportion of labour to means of production. It is also necessary for a process which exhibits the critical proportions to have this proportion in all the layers of processes that may go into producing its inputs of means of production.

A commodity produced by a process with the critical ratio of labour to means of production would provide the properties necessary for a unique measuring rod of value as it would necessarily be invariant in price to changes in wages and the rate of profits. This commodity could then be used as a numeraire in which to measure the value of the net product and to compare price changes of the other commodities in the system.[1] Since it is unlikely that such a commodity exists, Sraffa proceeds to construct a 'composite commodity', made up of all basic goods in the system, which will exhibit the desired characteristics.

D. THE INVARIABLE MEASURE

The composite commodity will have to consist of all the basic commodities that go directly or indirectly as inputs into the production of all the basic commodities as outputs. Each basic must make up the composite in the same proportion as the individual commodities enter into the total means of production

---

[1] Ricardo laid numerous hints as to the ideal measure of value:

'I hope I have succeeded in showing, that there are no grounds for such an opinion and that only those commodities would rise which had less fixed capital employed upon them than the medium in which price was estimated, and that all those which had more, would positively fall in price when wages rose. On the contrary, if wages fell, those commodities only would fall, which had a less proportion of fixed capital employed on them, than the medium in which price was estimated; all those which had more would positively rise in price.' (46)

And:

'If on examining still more particularly into all the circumstances connected with the production of these various commodities, we find that precisely the same quantity of labour and capital are necessary to the production of the shoes, stockings, hats, iron, sugar, etc.; . . .' (18)

Both from *Principles of Political Economy*, in *Works*, ed. P. Sraffa, op. cit.

of the composite. Writing basics as means of production as $A_i, B_i, \ldots, K_i,$ and as outputs $A, B, \ldots, K,$ the ratios $\sum_{i=1}^{k} A_i : \sum_{i=1}^{k} B_i : \ldots : \sum_{i=1}^{k} K_i$ of the individual means in total means of production must be the same as the ratios $A:B:\ldots:K$ of individual outputs in total output. The same relation can be expressed as $\sum_{i=1}^{k} Ai / \sum_{i=1}^{k} X_i = A/Xo$ where X is the total means of production in the system and Xo the total output. This relation must hold for each individual basic that forms the composite.

The system that produces this commodity mix is called the Standard system. The problem is to derive this Standard system from any given initial system. Sraffa accomplishes this by taking fractions of the initial equations of production (reducing each by the same percentage) such that the remaining system uses commodity inputs, in the aggregate, in the same proportion as it produces commodities as outputs. The mix of commodities produced in these proportions is the Standard commodity. Since the original system has been fractionally reduced it will no longer utilise the total labour force used in the initial system. The full Standard system is achieved by expanding all production equations by a proportion that will bring the labour term back to unity. The net output of the system when the whole labour force is employed is called the Standard net product or the Standard national income and will, necessarily, bear the same proportions as the Standard commodity.

A standard system that produces goods in the same ratio as the goods enter into the overall means of production also exhibits the property that the ratio of net product to means of production for each process of production will be equal to the overall ratio of aggregate net product to aggregate means of production for the whole system. This ratio is called by Sraffa the Standard ratio, R, and is the maximum technically determined rate of surplus for the Standard system. It is possible to determine this ratio, which is composed of differing commodities, since both the composite of goods in the numerator (the net commodity surplus) and the denominator (the aggregate means of production) are made up of the same commodities in the same Standard proportions.

As the rate of surplus is the same for all processes there is no problem of aggregation. Thus the Standard ratio may be determined irrespective of the prices of the goods and the ratio is invariant even when all the commodities are multiplied by their prices. Because of the nature of the Standard system, the proportions of the component commodities of the ratio of aggregate net product to the aggregate means of production will be unchanged when the net product is divided in any proportions between wages and profits (despite the necessary concomitant changes in prices). Thus the rate of surplus is the same in both physical and value terms when the division of the surplus between wages and profits changes.

As the wage, measured in Standard net product, rises, the prices of some of the commodities in the Standard system which have a low proportion of direct labour to means of production will fall. Those commodities with a high proportion of direct labour to means of production rise. The proportional construction of the system guarantees that the price changes will just balance over the whole system to keep the rate of profit constant and thus leave the ratio of net surplus to means of production constant in value terms (quantities multiplied by prices). Thus the technically determined ratio of aggregate net surplus to aggregate means of production is equivalent in either physical or value terms and independent of the share of net surplus paid to wages and profits. *The system is thus simultaneously determinate given the technical production processes and either the wage or the rate of profits.* There are n given production equations for the n commodities. Taking the Standard net income as unity, or the numeraire, there are $n + 1$ equations for the n commodity prices, the wage and the rate of profits. Thus when the wage is fixed, the rate of profits is determined. Alternatively, given the rate of profits, the wage and commodity prices are soluble.

If the wage is set at zero, the entire standard income is paid as profit and the rate of profits is equal to the Standard ratio in both physical and value terms. If part of the net product is paid as wages, the ratio of the remaining net product, after deduction of the wage share, to the means of production will likewise be unaffected by the resulting changes in prices, for the ratio is still in Standard proportions.

Sraffa is thus able to make a general statement about the relation of the proportion of net product paid as wages and the rate of profit in the Standard system. When wages are deducted from the net surplus, and both are in the Standard proportions, the ratio of the resulting rate of profits to the Standard ratio will be equal to the ratio of the share remaining for profits to the whole net product. This can be seen by writing N for the total means of production, P for the share of profits, and S for the net product, such that:

$$\frac{P/M}{S/M} = P/S \qquad (2.10)$$

when $P/M = r$, the rate of profits, and $S/M = R$, the Standard ratio. The relation can be rewritten as

$$r/R = P/S. \qquad (2.11)$$

If the net product is taken as unity, P can be written as $(1 - w)$, where w is the share of wages, and the expression becomes

$$r/R = (1 - w) \qquad (2.12)$$

or upon further manipulation

$$r = R(1 - w) \qquad (2.13)$$

which is the form given by Sraffa. Thus, following Sraffa's example,[1] if the share of wages in net product is $\frac{3}{4}$ and the Standard ratio, R, is ·20, then the rate of profits, r, will be equal to $\frac{1}{4}$ of ·20 or 5 per cent. The general linear relation of (2.13) is similarly unaffected by changes in prices.

E. THE RELATION OF ACTUAL AND STANDARD SYSTEMS

This relation, which holds in the Standard system, can also be shown to apply to the actual system that generates the Standard system. Since the actual system provides the basic equations from which the Standard system is derived, the rate of profits, whether measured in quantities of Standard system commodities or values in the actual system, will be the same for both

[1] Sraffa, op. cit., 21.

systems provided the wage is given in terms of Standard net product.[1] When the equivalent of the wage in Standard net income is deducted from the actual net surplus, the prices in the actual system will, to yield the postulated uniform rate of profits, be such as to bring the remaining non-Standard pro-portion surplus quantities into equality with the ratio of quantities in the Standard system by means of price corrections. To obtain the uniform rate of profits in the actual system in value terms, prices must correct the actual non-uniform rate of surplus in physical terms to equality in value terms, since the actual system does not have the same proportions of physical quantities as both inputs and outputs. The rate of profits that is determined in the Standard sytem in physical terms can then be demonstrated to be the same that rules in the actual system in value terms.

Armed with this result, Sraffa is able to determine the rate of profit without constructing the Standard system that corres-ponds to the actual system. Since the linear relation between the rate of profits and the wage holds for both systems, and since the relation is true of the Standard system, then it rules in the actual system when wages and prices are expressed in terms of Standard net product. Consequently, the relation $r = R(1 - w)$ can replace the Standard commodity which was expressed as unity, without the compositions or proportions of the latter being known, since the proportional relation holds only when wages and commodity prices are expressed in terms of Standard net product. If the relation holds in the actual system, then it can replace the equation for the Standard net output and therefore the Standard system no longer need be determined, although it is still necessary as a measure of wages and commodity prices.

Given the proportionality relation and the uniform rate of profits in the actual system, the prices ruling there will correct the ratios of non-uniform physical quantities such that the ratio of the value of surplus to the value of means of production is uniform and the same as the ratio resulting from the physical quantities in the Standard system. If wages and prices are measured in Standard net product, then the rate of profits is

[1] Ibid., 23.

equal in both the actual and Standard system, for any actual system always produces the basic equations which must be used to make up the Standard system.

F. A VARIABLE LABOUR MEASURE

Sraffa, however, finds it possible to measure wages and commodity prices in another manner, with even less reference to the Standard commodity. This measure Sraffa calls 'the quantity of labour that can be purchased by the Standard net product'. This measure is based on the linear relationship between wages and profits. In both the Standard and actual systems, when the rate of profits is given the wage is also given, subject to the maximum rate of surplus possible. Thus a relation can be established between the quantity of labour expended and the proportion of the net product it receives. The quantity of labour equivalent to the whole net product can thus be determined without recourse to prices by setting the actual amount of labour used in the system equal to unity. The quantity of labour equivalent to the Standard net product can then be derived by manipulation of the linear relation derived above, i.e.

$$r = R(1 - w) \qquad (2.13)$$

to yield

$$1/w = R/(r - R). \qquad (2.14)$$

Thus when r and R are known, the labour equivalent of the net product is given by this relation. Prices can be expressed in terms of either (1) the Standard net product, or (2) the equivalent quantity of labour at the given rate of profit and technique.

Since the Standard system is not necessary to determine the relation, then the labour measure is likewise determinable without construction of the Standard system. Sraffa is, therefore, able to substitute a variable quantity of labour for the Standard net product as 'an invariable standard of value'. The labour measure is variable in the sense that, given equation (2.13), the equivalent labour unit varies directly with the rate of profits.

When the rate of profits is set at zero the measure is equal to the labour actually expended in production. As r becomes positive the variable labour measure increases and approaches infinity as r approaches R.

The Standard product, however, still must serve as the measuring rod for the wage. The only possible way to replace this relation would be to regard the wage as an index reflecting the quantity of labour in the production process. Sraffa suggests but rejects this possibility.[1]

G. DEPENDENCE ON THE STANDARD SYSTEM

The development of the labour measure permits Sraffa to extricate his system from complete reliance on the Standard commodity, for he is now able to treat his system in terms of a variable wage (determined within the system) related to the rate of profits. The rate of profits (not the Standard ratio or the maximum rate of profits) thus becomes the independent variable which is exogenously determined. This view of an exogenous rate of profits is, of course, the fundamental difference between the Sraffa model and both the previously discussed von Neumann approach and the neoclassical theories which will be developed in Chapters 3–4. Sraffa cites the major determinate of the rate of profits as the level of the money rate of interest,[2] a variable not determined in his actual system.

Sraffa has not only succeeded in constructing a measure of value that is invariant when the distribution of net product changes, but he has also eliminated the necessity of its actual construction. The proof of the possibility of constructing the

---

[1] See ibid., 32–3. It is possible to do without the Standard net product as the expression for the wage, but this involves viewing the value of w 'as a pure number' ranking quantities of labour, *given the rate of profits* and corresponding prices. Prices of commodities could then be given by the index of labour embodied. This would require, however, a new set of indices for every value of r between zero and R and thus the utilisation of the concept is extremely difficult. By this method, however, the commodity wage could be determined by taking the reciprocal of the commodity price. See Sraffa, op. cit., 21.

[2] Ibid., 33.

Standard system is necessary, but once armed with this proof Sraffa is able to analyse different economic problems without explicit knowledge of its nature.

H. APPLICATIONS OF THE COMMODITY APPROACH: REDUCTION TO DATED LABOUR

Sraffa initially applies his method of analysis to a system involving the labour measure of value, assuming that all productive processes are made up of direct or indirect (means of production) labour. Sraffa reduces the indirect labour in the production processes to direct labour values in order to explore the effect of differing applications of labour over time (the time pattern of production). This process of converting indirect labour to direct labour Sraffa calls reduction to dated labour. It is related to the Böhm-Bawerkian and Wicksellian concepts of capital measurement in terms of 'periods of production'.

For any production process the means of production can be reduced to their own means of production and direct labour. By netting out the direct labour input at each regressive step back through the layers of the production processes that went into the creation of the final means of production in the process under consideration, the remaining indirect labour input will eventually become infinitesimally small. The value of the means of production can then be represented by the summation of the collected labour terms. The value of the process's output will be the current direct labour plus the collected past (or dated) labour properly valued. At each step back through the layers of production the indirect labour netted out must have the rate of profits assigned to it for the time that it has been embodied in physical means of production, i.e. $1+r$ for the first indirect labour term removed, $1+r^2$ for the second indirect labour term involving means of production remaining, until $1+r^n$ for the final input of direct labour that combined with the infinitely small quantity of physical means of production. Thus over the regressive steps back in the process the indirect labour will be represented by $Lw(1+r)^n$ with no appreciable production term remaining.

The labour value of a commodity can then be expressed as

$$L_x w + L_{x_1} w(1+r) + (L_{x_2} w(1+r)^2 + \ldots + L_{x_n} w(1+r)^n = X p_x \tag{2.15}$$

where L is the proportion of total labour used in the particular production process, w the wage, and X the commodity output with p its price. Utilising the linear relation given above between the wage and the changing rates of profit, i.e.

$$w = 1 - r/R,\text{[1]} \tag{2.16}$$

the labour terms in the above relation can be rewritten as

$$L_x \left(1 - \frac{r}{R}\right) + L_{x_1} \left(1 - \frac{r}{R}\right)(1+r)$$

$$+ \ldots + L_{x_n} \left(1 - \frac{r}{R}\right)(1+r)^n = X p_x. \tag{2.17}$$

The value of each labour term at rates of profits from zero to R can therefore be determined. At zero the value is exactly the labour quantity, while at R each term is of zero value and disappears. At intermediate rates the value depends on the age or time pattern of the process; the higher the rate of profits and the higher the exponent on $(1+r)$, the larger the value of older labour terms. Thus it is possible for two similar outputs with dissimilar time patterns of production to have varying labour terms and different relative values at different rates of profit between zero and R. The prices will be equal (if the processes have the same physical requirements) at $r=0$ and $r=R$, the two extremes. The values may or may not be equal or may be of constant relative difference at intermediate rates of profit depending on the time pattern of their processes as the value of each labour term varies as r changes.

Thus with unchanged productive processes, it is possible to have varying relative prices between commodities when the real wage and the rate of profits change. This is due to the compounding effect on the labour terms of the rate of profits exponent in processes with different time distributions of inputs. It is therefore evident that it is impossible to speak of the

[1] This relation is derived from equation (2.13).

quantity or value of capital (which in this case is represented completely by labour) without reference to the rate of profits and the distribution of the product and prices-set that any rate of profits implies. Merely measuring capital by the length of the production process or the physical amount of labour or capital involved will not take account of the possible changes in relative prices (and thus changes in the value of means of production) that will result. 'The reversals in the direction of the movement of relative prices, in the face of unchanging methods of production, cannot be reconciled with *any* notion of capital as a measurable quantity independent of distribution and prices'.[1] Sraffa has, at this point, provided the first direct proof of the primal role of the rate of profits in the economic analysis of capital theory. In his exposition of reduction to dated labour, he has demonstrated that the valuation of capital is impossible without reference to the distribution implied in the rate of profits.

J. FIXED CAPITAL

In practice, however, it is impossible to reduce the means of production of any process or any system of processes completely to its labour value. Although the exposition of variable relative prices between any two commodities with fixed production processes is logically correct, Sraffa expands his approach to deal explicitly with the valuation of fixed capital. If Sraffa's solution to the valuation problem is to be completely general, the problem of valuing a physical capital stock with unbalanced age distribution is necessary.[2] To accommodate fixed capital to the commodity approach, Sraffa adapts the system to multiple product (joint product) processes. This approach expands the number of commodities produced and thus the number of price variables to be solved for in the system, since fixed capital

[1] Ibid., 38.

[2] With a stock of machines of balanced age and with no technical progress, the replacement of machines can be deducted from gross output in physical terms. Thus the machines in their final year of operation are deducted from the output of that type of machine in the current year, machines one year old become two-year-old machines, etc., and the age distribution stays constant over time.

is now an output as well as an input and therefore another equation is necessary to determine the price of fixed capital at any moment in its life. To keep the system soluble, additional equations are necessary to determine the increased number of variables. The number of production processes (all of which must be equally eligible)[1] must be expanded to match the number of commodities actually produced under joint production. Thus processes are no longer indentified by their outputs; rather they are specified by the proportions in which the processes use inputs to produce joint outputs in given proportions. This adaptation of the Standard system makes for some loss of purity from the single-process approach, as negative multipliers[2] will now appear, but does allow the system to be generalised for explicit consideration of fixed capital.

A machine enters the production process as a means of production of a specified age and at the end of the process emerges as a means of production of the same type but one period older and thus as a distinctly different means of production and joint product in every year of useful life. This treatment yields the additional complication that an industry using fixed capital will use a different process of production each successive time period.[3] Thus the determination of the

[1] This does not imply equal productiveness or profitability of the process. This can only be determined after the prices set is found. As seen above in the case of reduction to dated labour values, there may be one or more rates of profits at which processes have equal prices sets but one process cannot be said to be generally more profitable than another.

[2] With joint outputs the proportion in which the outputs are produced in any one process may not be in the proportion in which the outputs are required as inputs. Thus the correction will involve possible use of both processes to achieve the required amounts but with negative multipliers necessary to eliminate production excesses. Also some of the joint outputs may be non-basics and thus their effects on prices must be suppressed. Both occurrences will necessitate negative multipliers. In addition the definition of a basic good becomes much more complicated under joint production but is too lengthy to be treated here. See Sraffa, op. cit., 47–52.

[3] Save in the case where the capital goods are equally balanced over *all* possible ages and the sum of the ages of the means of production is constant over time as replacement of equipment is made. If machine life is five years, then at the end of the fifth year the number of five-year-old machines must

price of each age-differentiated capital product will require an additional process equation to keep the system soluble.

Utilising separate process equations for age-differentiated capital goods also allows explicit consideration of the allocation of depreciation over the life of capital goods. Moreover it permits analysis of changes in productivity and differing costs of maintenance and operation for similar capital goods used in differing processes of production.

Over the life of any capital good the amortisation fund must provide for the replacement of the capital good. In addition the ruling rate of profit must be earned on the finance committed to the capital good, at any point in time. Thus the total charge per period is the remaining unamortised cost of the capital good plus the rate of profit on this amount less the accumulated depreciation fund and interest on the fund. This charge must be met if the system is to continue to produce the same proportion of net product over time.

Assuming constant productive efficiency of means of production, the price of output must remain constant as the undepreciated value of means of production changes, if the system's production process does not change. At a zero rate of profits the problem can be approached in labour value embodied in the machine. If the production process lasts one year and the useful life is n years, the embodied labour expended in any one production period will be constant at $1/n_{th}$ of the embodied labour over the life of the machine. The depreciation charge is then $1/n_{th}$ of the embodied labour value for each period irrespective of the age of the means of production. The prices of identical outputs in different years will then also be constant and equal to the sum of direct labour expended in the process plus the embodied labour expended.

Once the rate of profits is greater than zero it is no longer possible to maintain constant prices for identical outputs if depreciation is constant over the useful life of fixed capital.

---

be replaced by new machines of the same kind. Last year's new machines are now one-year-old machines; the one-year-old machines are two years old, etc., such that the age distribution of the capital stock is constant and the production process is unchanged.

With equal yearly depreciation quotas the yearly charge on capital (depreciation allowance plus the rate of profits on the remaining committed finance) will be unequal as the machine ages. The older the machine, with constant depreciation, the smaller is the amount of the profit on the committed finance and thus the total annual capital charge is smaller. Prices will no longer be constant for the same output produced with fixed capitals of differing age compositions as the fixed charge is no longer constant independent of age. Therefore, when the rate of profits is positive the total annual charge must be constant to yield constant prices. This makes it necessary to re-arrange the depreciation allowance over the life of the machine to assure constant prices. Annual depreciation must be raised the older the machine and reduced the newer the machine, such that the changes positive and negative still sum to the original cost price of the machine.

Thus the value of machines, when a rate of profits exists, will not be independent of age and will change unequally over the life of a machine. Consequently, two stocks of machines with the same physical composition but differing age composition will not be of equal value. The higher the rate of profits the more unequal will be the difference in value, with differences small in the early years of life and large over the later years. The value of machines of a balanced age composition is dependent directly on the rate of profits but will not vary as the age distribution of machines is constant. Unbalanced stocks are affected by both the rate of profits and the age distribution.

When the age compositions of two different processes producing the same output are different, the value of machines will also be different even though the original costs and physical aspects of the machines are identical in both processes. At a zero rate of profit it is possible to speak of the value of capital per man in terms of embodied labour. Even if the physical and age compositions were different it would be possible, with a zero rate of profit, to identify which technique required the greater capital per man. As the rate of profits moves above zero, however, it is not possible to make any general statement about the relative capital intensities of the two processes. Changes in the rate of profits affect the book value of means of production no matter what the historical cost price.

In sum, Sraffa has analysed the effect of changes in the rate of profits on the problem of fixed capital valuation for the economic system and has demonstrated the impossibility of regarding capital, or value in general, without reference to the effects of the rate of profits and income distribution on value.

K. CHOICE OF TECHNIQUE

Sraffa reaches his most forceful conclusions concerning the effect of the rate of profits and distribution on the valuation problem by extending the results of the dated labour and fixed capital approaches to the problem of the choice of techniques of production. It is in this exposition that Sraffa's 'critique' of existing economic theory (as suggested by the subtitle of his book) is most explicit.

The problem of choice of technique arises if there exist two alternative methods of production for a single commodity. The relative prices of the outputs from the two differing methods should vary (just as in the dated labour case) as the rate of profits moves from zero to R unless the methods are exactly the same in all respects. There will then be some rate of profits at which prices will be the same despite the fact that the methods differ in technical nature. These points of price coincidence will be called *switch points*. In other words, at some rate of profits (or a switch point), the prices (values) of two alternative techniques will be equal. It is possible to compare techniques explicitly at the switch points, for with the same prices at the same rates of profits, the wage and price patterns will be the same even though each technique is different.

It is somewhat easier to approach the problem by viewing the outputs of the two competing processes as distinct commodities which can be utilised as basic commodities in either of two differing Standard systems, while they serve as non-basics when not eligible as basics, on the criterion of cheapness, in either system. Thus both are employed as non-basics in both systems while the cheapest, given the rate of profits, is used as the basic in both systems. The two systems, say A and B, will have a different value of R and different sets of wages and prices at different rates of profits. Thus the price ratios of the commodities will be different, at a given rate of profits, depending upon which system is used as the base for the comparison. No matter which system is chosen, however, the commodity that is the basic in the system with the highest value of R will be the cheapest and its process of production chosen for both systems starting from $r = R$. As r departs from R the price differential will change until a point is reached where the prices are equal. This is a switch point and at this point it will be more profitable in both systems, to switch to the second process.

There may be any number of such switches back and forth between the two processes depending on the technical difference between the two processes. Thus it is not possible to state with confidence which of the two processes will be used when the rate of profits is 'high'. In other words, it is not possible to state that a labour-intensive technique must be used when the rate of profits is low or vice versa. The only meaningful statement is that the process from the system with the highest value of R will be used when the rate of profits is between the differing values of R for the two systems.

Sraffa does derive the general statement that the prices of production of both processes must be equal to compare two differing methods of production, and that in order to make such comparisons, the rate of profits must be known to determine the wages and prices sets of the two systems. A switch may only occur when these variables are equal and the value of capital in the two systems may only be meaningfully compared when the variables are equal, for only then are the prices in the systems comparable.[1]

---

[1] This is one of the precise cases where capital can be compared in value terms. Sraffa states that he wishes to avoid use of the term 'capital' in his work to avoid confusion. 'This is because these terms have come to be inseparably linked with the supposition that they stand for quantities that can be measured independently of, or prior to, the determination of prices of the products'. Sraffa, op. cit., 9. It should be noted that this comparison is possible even though the production equations of the systems are non-identical.

L. SUMMARY

Sraffa's approach involves a much deeper analysis of the classical system than does von Neumann's. More importantly, Sraffa's analysis proves a basis for a critical approach to the neoclassical postulates.

The two classical systems presented in this chapter resemble each other in their utilisation of process equations and simultaneous system solutions. In the initial portions of Sraffa's work (Chapter 2) where he is dealing with a single-process system with a surplus, his model is indentical to von Neumann's. At this early stage the rate of profits is simply the ratio of the technical surplus over replacement to the physical means of production; the wage is given as a technical datum with labour as a technical factor of production. Von Neumann's system. however, stops at this level with a determinate rate of profit and value of capital, given the subsistence wage and the single set of economically feasible set of production equations available. For Sraffa, on the other hand, this system is merely the launching pad for a deeper analysis of the value of capital, the pattern of prices and the choices of processes of production when the wage and the profit rate vary. The first step for Sraffa is to free labour from its role as a physical factor of production with a technologically determined wage, and allow any portion of the net surplus to be paid as wages. Given the classical postulate that competition tends to bring the rate of profits to equality in all processes of production, the problem of spreading the remaining net surplus available over the capital stock involves Sraffa in an analysis of the effect on the pattern of prices of changes in the distribution of the surplus. These considerations would not represent a problem if the factor intensities of all processes were the same. Treating the problem of equal rates of profit in all processes when they differ in intensity, however, requires the construction of the Standard commodity. Once this invariable measuring rod of value is established, the analysis of the effects of differing rates of profit (and thus wages) on the prices of inputs and outputs is possible as the prices embodied in the measure are isolated from the effects of these changes. This permits the valuation of the capital stock and a comparison of different processes of production to determine the cheapest method of production at differing rates of profits.

Sraffa has therefore developed the system much further than von Neumann and has raised much deeper questions in tackling one of the persistently unsolved problems in classical theory. The remaining major difference in the two systems involves Sraffa's use of the rate of profits as the given variable from which, given the production coefficients, he determines the wage and, given the conditions of equality of profit rates, the system of prices and value of capital and factor shares. The von Neumann model simply utilises a technologically determined real wage to determine the rate of profit and relative prices.

Sraffa's approach brings the added benefit of providing the analysis of the time pattern of production on the prices of outputs and the capital stock via the demonstration that the rate of profits is the crucial variable in valuing the capital and labour applied to the process of production. Sraffa's analysis permits the possibility of analysing the switches in competing techniques whereas von Neumann avoids this by only allowing for one possible technique. Sraffa's work provides foundation for criticising the neoclassical contention of using a more labour- (capital-roundabout) intensive process as the rate of interest rises (falls). Sraffa's approach shows that switches need not be only unidirectional or of a given number. This conclusion is useful in approaching the neoclassical reaction to switching and the basic assumptions and restrictions that underpin their analyses which are carried over into the process of growth.

The Sraffa system, like von Neumann's, is, however, devoid of considerations of demand except as it affects the compositions of output of commodities in the Standard system. Although it would be possible[1] to introduce demand aspects explicitly into the model, this would greatly increase its complexity.

---

[1] Thus another system of equations would have to be introduced to take account of the composition of output when changes in the distribution of income cause changes in the consumption pattern of output. The fact remains, however, that demand equations have little effect in setting the ruling prices in the system. This is especially true of modern capitalism.

Finally, neither of the models makes any reference to either marginal utilities of consumers or marginal products of inputs. Sraffa was careful to avoid the term 'capital' completely.[1] His conclusions raise serious questions[2] about the contribution of marginal theory to economics. He claims that capital is a void concept outside the determination of the rate of profits and the prices of production that the rate of profit determines. Nowhere is the marginal product of capital necessary to determine the rate of profit on capital or the relative prices, although Sraffa's system is beyond doubt competitive and general equilibrium in nature.

The most important conclusion in the context of Sraffa's model is that it is impossible to determine capital as a value or a quantity independent of the rate of profits. It is therefore not possible to derive the rate of profits from an independently calculated quantity or value of capital. The neoclassical approach, which is considered in the next four chapters, on the other hand, is based on the firm belief that the rate of profit can be explained independently of the value of capital.

(3) P. A. SAMUELSON: MYTHICAL PRODUCTION FUNCTIONS

The impossibility of determining the rate of profit by the marginal net product of capital was one of the main implied points in Sraffa's 'Critique'. Nevertheless the applicability of marginal theory in approaching the problem of the rate of profit will be a crucial point in the modern neoclassical growth theory to be considered here. Thus it would be desirable to examine the reactions of a modern neoclassicist to the problems of extending and applying marginal theory to capital theory in the light of Sraffa's 'Critique' before the neoclassical models of growth are presented.

[1] See p. 36, n. 1 above.
[2] See Sraffa, op. cit., Preface, v.

A. MARGINAL THEORY AND FIXED COEFFICIENTS

Samuelson, recognising that the Sraffa system threatened the very foundations of the neoclassical marginal analysis, attempted to demonstrate[1] that the neoclassical and Sraffa approaches were in essence similar. Samuelson maintained that the same results could be reached by using either the classically defined (Sraffa) system or the neoclassical marginal productivity approach where the latter utilised a malleable (jelly) capital input and assumed smooth substitution in the production function between capital and labour.

The Samuelson comparison begins with the presentation of a model of the strictly classical type which contains any number of concrete, differentiated capital goods that can only produce output in fixed relations with other inputs. There is a fixed coefficient production process for each type of output. The system also exhibits constant returns to scale[2] and perfect competition.[3] Such a model will exhibit any number of definable equilibrium steady[4] or stationary states *given* the real wage and the rate of interest (which in neoclassical terminology is the same thing as the rate of profits when perfect certainty is postulated). Given this possible range of steady states, Samuelson contends that any steady-state position with a high wage and low rate of profit will show that society can 'afford' a more 'roundabout' (or more capital-intensive) method of production and vice versa. In other words, higher profit rates imply the use of more highly labour-intensive techniques of production.

---

[1] P. Samuelson, 'Parable and Realism in Capital Theory: The Surrogate Production Function', *Review of Economic Studies*, xxix (June 1962).

[2] As assumed in von Neumann but not strictly in Sraffa; see *Commodities*, op. cit., Preface, vi.

[3] Thus neglecting any optimum size problems that this juxtaposition may create in firm size and growth.

[4] The steady state of the Samuelson model is the same as von Neumann's equilibrium expansion where all variables in the system grow at a steady (or constant or stationary) rate. The concept is also the same as Marxian expanded reproduction at a constant rate and Harrod's 'Regular Advance'.

B. THE FACTOR-PRICE FRONTIER: CASE FOR SIMILARITY

Plotting all the possible steady-state positions of the wage and the rate of profits for a given set of available structural production equations results in what Samuelson labels the 'Factor-Price Frontier', i.e. the relation between the remuneration of factors at different equilibrium rates of steady advance. Systems with different available production equations will normally exhibit different factor-price frontiers, although the possibility exists that they may have a coincident frontier. The frontiers may or may not intersect. If two systems do have indentical frontiers, Samuelson contends that the two systems can be treated as similar for predictive purposes.[1]

In order to meet the requirements of strictly distinct non-homogeneous physical capitals, Samuelson chooses a 'special sub-class of realistic cases' in which each and every capital good is different and enters into the production process in fixed proportions with labour. Samuelson assumes that a fixed co-efficient production process can produce, not only any mix of final output, but also, alternatively, new capital goods of precisely the same kind as were used in the production process. Thus with one process capable of producing either consumption or capital goods the proportion of labour to means of production must be the same for all goods produced. Indeed, Samuelson's assumption of single processes producing all output assures that the proportions of inputs are the same for all output. This assumption is highly restrictive when the different technologies represented by different factor-price frontiers are made up of a single capital good and *not* heterogeneous capitals. Thus while claiming to treat distinct capital goods, only one particular process with one particular capital good–labour proportion enters any one technology and factor-price frontier in the Samuelson scheme.

---

[1] This, however, overstates the case of identity for, while the possibility of two distinct systems creating the same factor-price frontier at a single stage in their development is very plausible, there is no reason to expect that the changes in technology that the systems will exhibit over time will be at all similar. For them to be at all comparable, constant and exactly similar technical progress must be assumed for both systems.

When the factor-price frontier is constructed for a single capital-good technology, it therefore must result in a straight line showing the maximum remuneration of labour for the process in question at zero profits on the y axis and the ratio of technical surplus over replacement to means of production with a zero wage on the x axis. A straight line connects the two points, as only one possible process with one possible capital–labour ratio is being considered. Thus when a range of single capital-goods technologies is considered, each with either a higher

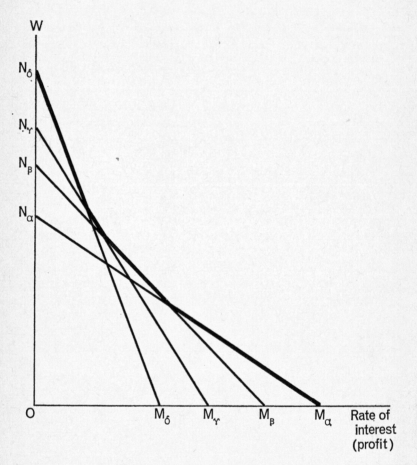

Fig. 2.1 The factor-price frontier

proportion of fixed capital to labour (or capable of producing a higher proportion of capital goods to consumption goods), the envelope of the outer portions of the straight-line factor-price frontiers shows the optimal single capital-good technology at any rate of profits given the available techniques. This envelope is shown as the heavy line in Fig. 2.1. In Sraffa's terminology this is the path of switches in technique. But these switches have the interesting neoclassical property of being all forward switches, i.e. the higher the rate of profits the lower the capital–labour ratio of the technique chosen (or the lower the rate of profit the more roundabout the technique).

The remainder of Samuelson's proof of the similarities of results of the classical and neoclassical approach involves (1) the possibility of deriving relative shares from the factor-price frontier without specifying in any sense the value of capital, and (2) proving that a neoclassical model using the marginal product of homogenous physical jelly capital will yield a Surrogate Frontier similar to the fixed coefficient factor-price envelope. The relevance of these conclusions, however, will stand or fall with the generality and validity of the 'special sub-class of realistic cases' and the resulting all forward-switching factor-price envelope. These latter results, however, appear to be direct contradictions to the results achieved by Sraffa; consequently an analysis of the relevance of these results must form the basis for the further investigation of Samuelson's contentions.

C. THE REALISM OF THE SPECIAL SUB-CLASS: A CRITIQUE

The fixed coefficient model developed by Samuelson specifically avoided the use of production functions or jelly capital or the measure of capital in any sense. This approach is very similar to Sraffa's attempt to construct a system which would be independent, in value terms, of changes in the distribution of the net surplus between wages and profits given a uniform rate of profit on the means of production. Indeed, this is precisely what Samuelson has done by applying his analysis in terms of a single capital-good technology that can produce either capital or consumption goods. Thus for any specified output in the goods basket produced by one technology in the Samuelson analysis, the ratio of capital to labour is uniform over all output. The linear relation of wages and profits is therefore given and the linear factor-price frontier is inevitable such that the value of capital is completely unaffected by changes in distribution. There can be only forward switches along the factor-price envelope for precisely the same reasons, since each technique is single valued in the capital–labour ratio that it contains. Samuelson has thus side-stepped the crucial double-switching problem by treating a case where, by definition, it cannot occur.

In addition Samuelson's Special Model of heterogeneous physical capitals is in reality no more non-jelly than his full jelly neoclassical system. While he posits that 'No alchemist can turn one capital good into the other',[1] this is really an unnecessary flourish, for under his assumptions any single capital good can produce anything desired in the desired proportions. The fact that capital must join labour in fixed proportions only allows Samuelson to avoid treating a *truly* fixed input and output coefficient model.

Sraffa indentifies a process by its proportions and he allows a specific process for every output proportion. Samuelson, on the other hand, defines his whole technology by a single capital good and its process by the input proportions, thus making all processes a single-valued capital–labour proportion for any desired outputs. This is, of course, very similar to the method used by Marx in positing uniform ratios of capital to labour to deal with the transformation problem. This Marxian approach has been criticised in another context by Samuelson himself.[2]

Thus little or no advance to the solution of the problems of the determination of the rate of profit, distribution and growth is provided by Samuelson's demonstration that the share of income can be determined independently of the value of capital, in the world of heterogeneous capital goods. The use of a stylised neoclassical jelly model equating the marginal product of jelly to the rate of profit irrespective of jelly measurement is not a

---

[1] Samuelson, op. cit., 196.

[2] 'Marxian Economics as Economics', *American Economic Association Papers and Proceedings*, LVII (May 1967) 619–20.

helpful tool for resolving the differences between the usual neoclassical results and the conclusions of a Sraffa-type model with distinct capitals and fixed processes. Whether there is perfect substitutability in the input mix or the output mix, the Samuelson model still maintains perfect substitution and jelly output simply replaces jelly capital. The results and defects must remain exactly the same.

D. GENERAL SUMMARY

The general results obtained from this chapter cover a broad range. In section 1 the possibility of generating a determinate rate of profit in a growing equilibrium system was outlined in the classical approach of von Neumann. The conclusion was dependent on a technically fixed subsistence wage with unchanging technique.

In section 2 Sraffa's research into the transformation problem brought to light the effects of changes in distribution on the values of the components of the economic system. This approach was also extended to choices of technique. In Sraffa's system the concept of change is defined as comparison of different values, not changes over time.[1] The Sraffa system also differs in that the rate of profit is given independently of the system rather than endogenously as in von Neumann. This is because Sraffa allows the wage to become variable and greater than subsistence.

The effect of the rate of profit and distribution on values in the economic system is Sraffa's main concern. His basic critique of Political Economy involves the conclusion that capital cannot be defined, nor can any economic variable be valued, independent of the rate of profits.

In the last section Samuelson's attempt to prove that the marginal approach to an undefined homogeneous substance, capital, would give exactly the same distributional results and the same determinate rate of profits as the classical fixed co-efficient approach used by Sraffa and von Neumann was reviewed. This result could only be achieved in the very special case where the value of capital is independent of the rate of

[1] The effects of time in economic analysis have often been overlooked but have considerable effect, as will be seen in later chapters.

profits and distribution, i.e. in a system similar to Sraffa's Standard system. Samuelson's results will not hold in a truly general case.

The logical errors in the marginal approach in the light of these conclusions can then be summarised. Capital in neoclassical analysis enters the production function as a known homogeneous input quantity. Since, in reality, all capital is physically different, its measurement is either left undefined or taken in value terms, i.e. the summation of the prices of the individual capital goods, in the typical neoclassical model. To obtain these values, however, the prices of all capital goods in existence must be known. If the value of capital could thus be determined, and all the prices could be shown to be consistent, then the marginal net product of this quantity would set the rate of profits. But, as Sraffa has shown, it is impossible to measure any economic quantity without first knowing the rate of profits. It is thus logically impossible to derive a rate of profit from a quantity that requires the rate of profit before its magnitude can be determined.

In the rest of this study the results of this comparison between the Sraffa-type classical and the neoclassical approaches to, and the determination of, the rate of profits will be often utilised. The results of the Sraffa analysis are particularly important in demonstrating that the value of capital is not independent of the rate of profit. This important conclusion implies that the marginal product of the thing called capital will always be meaningless until the thing capital has been determined in value terms. This crucial result remains unscathed, despite Samuelson's attempt to dislodge it with a Surrogate Production Function. The Sraffa result is additionally independent of the problems raised by time and space in comparing systems with a given rate of profit and similar technologies.[1]

In general, the failure of neoclassical analysis to recognise the fact that capital as a concrete good is a very different case from capital as representing the commitment of finance, expectation

---

[1] In Sraffa's work, change is not viewed as movement through time but as a simple way to indicate a comparison between two different positions or points in time. See also the concern over this problem expressed by Mrs Robinson, below, Chapter 11.

of profit, and risk in the future, has allowed the modern neo-classicists to neglect the influence of the distribution of the net product on how the finance is committed to concrete capital goods. In the following sections explicit examination of how these problems are handled in models of long-run economic growth will be developed always with reference to the general conclusions developed in this chapter.

3 J. E. MEADE:
AN ECLECTIC APPROACH TO
NEOCLASSICAL GROWTH

The analysis and conclusions of the preceding chapter on the treatment of the concept of the rate of profits and its implications for economic growth in mature capitalist economies can now be utilised in the discussion of the models of economic growth put forward by modern neoclassical theorists. The grouping of the following writters such as Meade, Tobin, Solow, Samuelson and Modigliani (many of whom prefer to wear the Keynesian label) as neoclassicists is in regard to their approach to the concept of capital and the rate of profits as the return to capital or more precisely as equal to the marginal product of that substance called capital.

A. SETTING OF THE MODEL

James Meade's *A Neo-Classical Theory of Economic Growth*[1] provides a good initial formulation of the views of this group. Many of the properties of Meade's model will also appear in the works of other authors who may be less explicit in admitting their reliance on neoclassical concepts. Nevertheless, Meade's labelling of his work as neoclassical is slightly misleading. Indeed, at one point in his discussion Meade calls his analysis classical. The neoclassical term is, however, more appropriate in that Meade's approach utilises purely competitive assumptions (including perfect foresight with no historical time involved) in a marginal productivity analysis of general equilibrium to determine the relative prices of the factors of production. In maintaining his equilibrium approach while later relaxing some restrictive initial assumptions, Meade's analysis relies on, indeed often overburdens, the possibility of

[1] J. E. Meade, *A Neo-Classical Theory of Economic Growth*, revised new edition (London: Allen & Unwin, 1965).

Keynesian employment and output adjustments preserving stability and equilibrium in conjunction with a mix of neoclassical postulates.

Meade's initial purpose is to provide a classical model of an economy in which all the variables that determine the system are allowed to change. It is his express intent not to deal with growth in the classical tradition of comparative statics.[1] This commitment to allow for change in all the variables of the system considered is, however, something of an overstatement as the determinants of growth are, by Meade's own definitions, immediately limited. The three reasons for growth in Meade's system are linked to the method and factors used to produce output. Growth may be caused by: (1) net savings, i.e. savings out of current income in the economy which permits additional capital formation and growth of output to occur; (2) population growth, that is, the working population (labour force) is increasing which, given equilibrium in the labour market, implies an increase in output as employment increases (given a relation to be specified below) with the growth of capital stock; and (3) technical progress, such that an increase in ouput over time can occur with a given fixed amount of factor inputs.[2]

B. THE ASSUMPTIONS

Meade thus restricts the variables that can induce growth. These growth factors are developed for a perfectly atomistic economy, under the following assumptions:

(1) A closed system.

(2) No government.

(3) A purely competitive economy with all the corresponding long-run marginal rules such as price = marginal cost = average revenue = marginal revenue, money wage = the value of marginal product. etc.

(4) Linear and homogeneous production functions.

[1] The method of comparative statics is, however, hardly most found among classical economists.

[2] On this particular type of technical progress see p. 61, n. 1 below.

(5) A two-commodity world consisting of a single unique consumption good and a plastic capital good which can either reproduce itself or produce consumption goods. Thus capital is an input for both types of good and an output of itself. In Meade's system the producing capital stock is called machines, while the flow of capital from itself is a capital good. The system's capital stock is, therefore, in terms of machines, and the output of these machines is either a capital good (to become a machine) or a unique multi-purpose consumption good. There is no provision for working capital in the Meade model.

(6) Three factors of production so that all output is produced by machines, land of a given amount, and labour.

(7) Identical production functions for the production of both commodities.

(8) Continual stability through equilibrium in the money and factor markets. Accordingly, (*a*) there exists a banking system under the control of a Central Bank, where the latter has perfect foreknowledge and is able to control the rate of interest in such a manner as to maintain a constant price level (i.e. the price of the unique consumption good or cost-of-living index does not change). Thus any change in the money wage implies a like directional change in the real wage. Moreover, the rate of interest is assumed to have perfect linkage with investment plans such that real incomes can be expanded (or lowered) by lowering (or raising) the rate at which investment projects can be funded. Thus, if an instantaneous Keynesian multiplier is assumed, the elasticity of investment in relation to the money cost of investment is unity. (*b*) In addition, the labour market always clears so that there is full employment and all the available land is fully utilised.

At this stage Meade deserts his dependence on Keynesian adjustments and explicitly posits the attainment of full-employment equilibrium in both the land and labour markets by means of a variable money wage per worker (which as seen above must imply a changing real wage given a constant price level) and money rent per acre of land. The wage per worker is always low enough to give entrepreneurs (facing a constant price for the unique consumption good) the incentive to hire all labour available, but never so low as to cause an excess demand for labour. These adjustments of relative factor prices are assured by the assumption of perfect foresight and, consequently, the possibility of a less than full-employment level of effective demand is prevented. Thus the demand for labour is a function of the money wage which is in turn dependent on the price level and the real wage.

Since prices are assumed constant, the demand for labour and effective demand both increase as the amount of goods produced increases. Meade does not treat the allocation of labour between the capital and consumption-good producing sectors, for all output may be either capital or consumption goods. Accordingly, the demand for labour is directly linked to the production of machines. Given a price for the consumption good and given the specification of the production function, there will exist a money wage which will always produce full employment at the given price of output.

Similarly the stock of machines will always be fully employed if the rate of interest is set to equilibrate the other two factor markets under the assumed conditions, i.e. classical smoothness in the production function.

(9) Perfect substitution between factors and capital malleability is assumed. There is only one form of machine which is measured in terms of tons of steel. This, of course, implies the same thing as perfect foresight on the part of entrepreneurs, for if their capital investment expectations are unfulfilled their capital equipment can be immediately switched into the proper type. Thus, in essence, Meade's two-commodity system is of a very singular nature with both output and capital capable of complete malleability.

(10) Depreciation is assumed to occur by evaporation. Each year, for example, 10 per cent of the existing machines will disappear regardless of age composition and the level of investment. With a given stock of machines, therefore, a disappearance rate of 10 per cent will leave an amortisation fund exactly equal to the cost of the evaporated machines. Accordingly, there is no problem of valuing capital stocks of unbalanced composition over time, as all existing machines can be reduced to the single unit of tons of steel.

C. PRODUCTION METHODS AND CHANGES IN OUTPUT

Given this set of highly restrictive assumptions, the production function in Meade's model takes the form

$$Y = F(K, L, N, t) \qquad (3.1)$$

where t, time, is the variable that takes technical progress into account. If the suitable land is limited, changes positive or negative in the other three variables utilised can induce an increase or decrease in output, Y. If there is saving in the community over time (given the classical assumption that all savings are automatically translated into physical assets), the stock of machines will increase by the value of net savings:

$$\Delta K = SY \qquad (3.2)$$

where S is the proportion of yearly net income saved. Given Y and S, the resulting ΔK will increase the value of Y in the next period by an amount equal to the marginal contribution of capital in the process of production, i.e.

$$\Delta Y = V \Delta K \qquad (3.3)$$

where $V \ (= \partial Y / \partial K)$ is the marginal product of capital. Substituting equation (3.2) into equation (3.3) results in

$$\Delta Y = VSY \qquad (3.4)$$

which implies that the increase in output is determined by the proportion of net income saved deflated by the marginal contribution to output of the capital produced from that saving. The value of V will determine the amount of increase in saleable output due to the marginal increase in tons of machines[1] and, given constant prices, the proportion of increased revenue from selling the extra output. Thus V could be called the rate of increase in value of output due to increased capital (saving) or, as Meade prefers, the rate of profit on capital where the

[1] Read 'marginal unit of savings'. Just exactly what a ton of machines involves is not specified, but is the value that enters the production function.

latter is equal to the marginal net revenue from additional capital.[1]

Growth in the available labour force can also raise output.[2] The contribution to output increase in a year due to increases in productively employed labour will depend on labour's marginal contribution, i.e.

$$\Delta Y = W \Delta L \qquad (3.5)$$

where $W = \partial Y / \partial L$. If the available land is fixed it cannot, by hypothesis, increase yearly output.

The remaining variable in the production function is t. The increase in output, with all other factors constant, due to a change in technology is viewed as an exogenous increase in output

$$\Delta Y = \Delta Y^t. \qquad (3.6)$$

The total increase in output is then the sum, positive or negative, of the three effects given in equations (3.3), (3.5) and (3.6), each weighted by their marginal importance:

$$\Delta Y = V \Delta K + W \Delta L + Y^t. \qquad (3.7)$$

This relation can be put into a dynamic context by viewing the changes with respect to the existing stocks of factors, thus:

$$\Delta Y / Y = VK / Y \; \Delta K / K + WL / Y \; \Delta L / L + \Delta Y^t / Y \qquad (3.7a)$$

where $\Delta Y / Y$ is the rate of growth of output, $\Delta K / K$ the rate of increase of machines, $\Delta L / L$ the rate of increase of the labour force and $\Delta Y^t / Y$ the rate of change of technical progress. Given competition and the production function, VK / Y is the share of profits in total income while the expression $VK / Y \; \Delta K / K$ is, of course, the rate of contribution of the extra unit of capital to the net national income. This yields Meade's basic formula for the analysis of growth:

$$y = Uk + Ql + r \qquad (3.8)$$

---

[1] The degree of coincidence with Samuelson's formulation will be outlined below.

[2] It is assumed that the marginal product of labour is positive. Since the model is long-run in nature, the gestation period of labour is viewed as instantaneous.

C

where the lower-case letters represent the rate of change of the upper-case factors and $U = VK/Y$ and $Q = WL/Y$.[1] Thus Meade outlines the determinants of growth, which is defined as an increase in output or net national income.

D. THE CAUSE OF INCREASING OUTPUT

Given the basic equation that embodies the determinants of growth, Meade moves on to analyse the factors that may cause the variables in the basic equation to vary. Equations (3.8) and (3.4) show that k, the rate of growth of machines, is $\Delta K/K = SY/K$ and thus may be affected by a change in S (a change in the proportion of national income saved) and/or a change in Y/K, the ratio of national income to the stock of machines. Y/K will rise ($\Delta Y > \Delta K$) either (1) if the rate of technical progress is high, (2) the rate of growth of the labour force productively employed is high, or (3) the proportion of income saved (rate of new capital formation) is low; for then the machine stock will increase at a relatively slower rate than national income. Even if S were unchanged it would still be possible for SY/K to rise in all three cases when k is rising or both income and the rate of accumulation are rising, for $SY = \Delta K$ and $k = \Delta K/K$. Alternatively, S may change if real income per head is rising or if there is an exogenous change in the method of production such that a larger proportion of national income is paid to rents and profits, both of which are assumed by Meade to have a lower percentage of income for consumption than wages income. This rise in S may come about more readily if a higher elasticity of substitution between land and machines and labour makes it

---

[1] Equation (3.4) should be recalled in this context. The relation in equation (3.8) could alternatively be derived:

$$\Delta Y = SY + \Delta L + \Delta Y^t$$
$$\Delta Y = VSY + W\Delta L + \Delta Y^t$$
$$\Delta Y/Y = VK/Y\, SY/K + WL/Y\, \Delta L/L + \Delta Y^t/Y$$

where the first independent term becomes $VK/Y\, SY/K = VS$ such that (3.7A) becomes

$$\Delta Y/Y = VS\, WL/Y\, \Delta L/L + \Delta Y^t/Y$$

and (3.8) becomes

$$y = VS + Q1 + r.$$

possible to replace labour with capital more easily. The rise in the value of S may also occur if technical progress is of a labour-saving nature, such that a fall in the marginal product of labour results in a rise in the profits share. This simply reduces to a change in the labour coefficient in the production function.[1]

E. STABLE RATES OF GROWTH

The technical properties of Meade's system have now been outlined as (1) the factors of production, (2) the manner in which changes in these factors affect the growth of output, and (3) the various ways in which the rates of change in factor growth may be achieved. Given these specifications, Meade attempts to determine (*a*) the various values of the growth rate that may result in a general equilibrium system, and (*b*) the conditions that must be imposed on the system to obtain a constant rate of economic growth. Meade's explicit objective is to show that the rate of growth of output in the economy will have a tendency to seek a constant rate which will signify a steady state of growth. The system as defined has linear homogeneous production functions, exhibits constant returns to scale, and unit elasticity of substitution between factor inputs. Technical progress, when it occurs, is assumed neutral towards all factors. Under these assumptions the percentages of national income paid to machines and labour (U and Q respectively) are unchanged even with changes in technology and changes in the relative amounts of factors used in production. This constant

[1] If, however, a change in income distribution has no effect on growth, Meade contends that the elasticity of factor substitution may cause a change in the rate of income growth if factors grow disproportionately. In a rather unrealistic case Meade posits a high elasticity of substitution between machines and other factors of production. If k is very high and l is very low, then, given $U = VK/Y$, the proportion of income going to profits will be increasing rapidly, for K will be growing faster than V may fall. Similarly, since $Q = WL/Y$, the rise in W is not fast enough to offset the slow rate of increase in L such that $U > Q$ (Q may even be falling if l is low enough). Thus profits will be receiving a rising proportion of income, machines will have more weight in total output and y will increase. Such an exercise, however, must be constrained by the possible level of capital intensity and the ability of the Central Bank to maintain full employment of the labour force. These problems are suppressed by Meade's stability assumptions.

distributional result follows from the unitary elasticity of substitution assumption, since an increase in any one factor relative to another will cause a drop in its marginal product, due to diminishing returns, which will exactly offset the increase in total product (or profit (wage) per machine (worker)), leaving the final distribution of total output unchanged.[1]

The final condition on the system is that the savings proportions of factor groups are constant. Thus if U and Q are constant due to the conditions just spelled out (and ignoring rent payments to landowners), then it follows that the proportion of total output which is saved will be constant. Thus, if S_w is saving from wages and S_p saving from profits, the conditions can be written as

$$S = S_p U + S_w Q \tag{3.9}$$

$$SY = S_p UY + S_w QY \tag{3.9A}$$

and from equation (3.2)

$$\Delta K = S_p UY + S_w QY. \tag{3.9B}[2]$$

Given the set of conditions on the basic growth relation specified in equation (3.8), and assuming (1) a constant and exogenously determined growth of the labour force, and (2) neutral technical progress (of a constant value) the only remaining variables which are endogenous to Meade's system are y and k. It follows that the rate of growth of output, y, will be constant if k, the rate of growth of capital, is constant. Over

---

[1] Given $U = VK/Y$, where $V = \partial Y/\partial K$, this relationship represents the total production due to capital weighted by its importance at the margin (V) as a proportion of total product produced. Thus as K rises by x per cent, with unitary elasticity of substitution, V will fall by x per cent and the marginal product of labour, W, will rise by x per cent as its contribution to Y falls by x per cent. Thus the changes offset each other and with constant return U and Q are unchanged with changing values for K, L, V and W. If the elasticity of substitution were greater than unity, then the increase in K would be greater than the decrease in the rate of change of V and machines would claim a larger proportion of total output.

[2] See Appendix A, pp. 201–2 below.

time k and y will, inevitably, approach equality as $\Delta K = SY$ while $k = \Delta K/K$ and therefore $k = SY/K$. Meade's assumptions force S to be a constant; accordingly, Y and K are Meade's only varying items. Since a ratio will be constant if both its numerator and denominator change at the same rate, and since $\Delta Y/Y$ and $\Delta K/K$, the rate of change of Y and K, are, by definition, y and k, then if, and only if, $y = k$ will Y/K be constant. SY/K, which is itself k, will then also be constant. Thus, moving in circuitous fashion, if k is constrained to a constant value then y will, over time, attain and hold that value which will be the constant rate of growth of output.

Given the production function and constant l and V, there is only one rate – Meade calls it the critical rate – a, which will achieve steady growth. Thus if $k = a$, then $y = a$, and $k = y$. Inserting a into equation (3.8) yields

$$a = Ua + Ql + r \tag{3.10}$$

$$0 = -a + Ua + Ql + r \tag{3.10A}$$

$$0 = -a\,(1 - U) + Ql + r \tag{3.10B}$$

$$a(1 - U) = Ql + r \tag{3.10C}$$

$$a = \frac{Ql + r}{1 - U} \tag{3.10D}$$

where $Q = (1 - U)$.

Equation (3.10D) gives Meade's expression for the critical rate. Meade never explains whether the ratio in this equation is an explanatory variable or simply a convenient way of expressing a rate. It would seem a bit awkward to explain k and y via a ratio in which labour and technical progress, which are predetermined constants, are presented as a proportion of the reciprocal of the profits share.[1]

Meade's expression is not the only one possible for a. If, for

---

[1] Fully expanded, (3.10D) becomes

$$S_p V + \frac{S_w WL}{K} = \frac{Ql + r}{(1 - U)} = \frac{WL/L \cdot \Delta L/L + \Delta Y^t/Y}{(1 - VK/Y)}.$$

example, constant returns $(U+Q=1)$ are assumed and land is ignored, it can be shown that[1]

$$a = l + \frac{Y^t}{(dY/dL)W} = l + \frac{Y^t}{VK} \qquad (3.11)$$

which gives another possible representation of a and indicates that a equals the ratio of the change in output due to technical progress, to profits. If k is assumed constant instead of l, then the steady-state equality implies that a and y must equal the value of l, the rate of growth of the labour force. Even without this restriction it would seem that a may be determined by different factors than indicated in equation (3.10D).

Exploring the relation further, in the absence of technical progress, i.e. $r=0$, the critical rate as expressed in equation (3.11) collapses to simply

$$a = l \qquad (3.12)$$

so that a is, by definition, the value that k must attain for y to be constant. Since Meade requires $y=k=a$ at the critical steady state, there is then an additional restriction to be added:

$$y = k = l \qquad (3.13)$$

---

[1] Derivation of equation (3.11) is as follows: Given $(1-U)=Q$, equation (3.10D) can be rewritten

$$a = y = k = \frac{Ql+r}{Q} = l + r/Q$$

$$= l + \frac{\Delta Y^t/Y}{Q}$$

$$= l + \frac{\Delta Y^t/Y}{WL/Y}$$

$$= l + \frac{\Delta Y^t}{WL}$$

$$= l + \frac{\Delta Y^t}{(\partial Y/\partial L)L}$$

which can also be derived in terms of k:

$$a = k + \frac{\Delta Y^t}{VK}.$$

which is the same thing as a natural or golden-age[1] growth path without technical progress and is no more certain of being reached under Meade's critical conditions than under any other.

Given the growth of factors at the rate of a, if technical progress occurs and is neutral then it should act to raise the rate of growth of output to a rate greater than a, i.e. $y > a = k = l$; for technical progress is increasing real output, y, at a faster rate than k is increasing. If a is a constant rate of growth under Meade's conditions, then the condition that

$$a = l = k = r \qquad (3.14)$$

must be added if steady-state equilibrium is to be maintained. The value of $y = k = l = r$, with Q and U constant, will consequently yield an unchanging rate of growth since all factors must initially be assumed to be growing at a constant rate.

Under Meade's determination of the critical rate, a, it can be shown that k will align itself with a. If, for example, $k = SY/K > (Ql + r)/(1 - U)$, i.e. $k > y$, then machines will be added to K more rapidly than output is increasing and the ratio Y/K will consequently be falling. With S assumed constant, k will fall until $k = y = l$. However, if l is outside its steady-state value as required by equation (3.13), i.e. $l \neq k = y$ or, utilising the manipulations that produced equation (3.11), $l > (Uk + r)/(1 - Q)$, then there is no neat formula that assures that the steady-state value of l will be achieved. As it turns out, with l taken as exogenous, given the condition of full employment and constant prices, k will collapse to the value of l.

---

[1] For Harrod the natural rate of growth is the maximum rate of increase in output possible given the rate of growth of the labour force and technical progress. Similarly, Mrs Robinson defines a golden-age rate of growth as one where output and the stock of capital (measured in commodities) grow at the same proportionate rate subject at the maximum to the rate of increase of labour and the rate of increase in output per head due to technical progress. For Mrs Robinson the golden age is a mythical construction, unlikely to be realised in any system. Harrod, likewise, devotes much of his writing on growth to showing that not only the attainment but the preservation of the natural rate is unlikely. See Chapters 8 and 11 below.

Likewise, a must adapt itself to the value of l. Therefore, if, and only if, l is of a constant value can there be any hope of attaining a steady state with full employment. Meade's proof of the existence of a steady state reduces to a proof that there is a possible value of k that will produce a steady rate of growth. There is nothing in Meade's system that makes the attainment of this value inevitable except the postulate that l is assumed to be constant and the assumption that all savings are invested at the assumed full-employment level of output. Thus Meade's entire stability analysis rests in (1) his assumption that l is constant, and (2) his initial assumptions of investment and full employment. There is nothing in the mechanism presented, even with malleable capital, that produces an explanation of his proposed inevitable stability.

Meade does, in fact, come very close to admitting this result when he states in another context: 'It is to be observed that this value of k (the critical rate) depends only on the constants Q, U, l, and r, and is quite independent of S, the proportion of income saved'.[1] It should be added that it not only depends on, but must be equal to, l and r, given the shape of the production function, which determines the constants Q and U, and are thus technical conditions.

F. REMOVAL OF CAPITAL MALLEABILITY

The first assumption Meade relaxes is the malleability of capital. Meade substitutes two possible types of fixed coefficient approaches for capital. It is assumed that production processes

---

[1] Meade, op. cit., 42. Meade's contention concerning S may not appear obvious. Following Meade's emphasis on k as the key balancing variable, if S were to rise then K must rise by the same amount, for $SY=K$ and $k=\Delta K/K=SY/K$. Thus k will grow faster than Y so that the ratio Y/K will fall until Y/K is lower (by the amount that S has increased) and becomes equal to $Ql+r/1-U$. Thus there is merely a shift upwards in K and Y due to increased savings while the same steady rate, a, is maintained unchanged. Therefore S does not affect the rate of accumulation, given the constants. It does, however, affect the level of the capital stock and the total (accumulated) wealth of the community. Any other possible effects of savings in the system are impossible given the equilibrium assumptions and the omniscient Central Bank.

may have either a fixed capital–output ratio or a fixed ratio of capital to labour. The introduction of fixed coefficients causes Meade to introduce the possibility of a system growing at different steady rates; for given the existence of fixed co-efficients there is no easy manner for a system to adjust to the critical rate. Meade introduces both a warranted rate of growth and a natural rate of growth. In the case of a system with a fixed capital–output ratio which is unchanged by neutral technical progress,[1] total output must grow at a rate equal to the rate of increase of the labour force plus the increase in output due to technical progress to preserve full employment of the labour force. Machinery must also then grow at this rate, for the capital–output ratio is fixed. This rate Meade calls the natural rate. The warranted rate is the the rate increase of machinery that occurs, given S, out of the increasing output due to l and r.[2] Meade does not say whether this rate is subject to his initial full-employment assumption; but he does assume that the warranted and natural rates may be unequal. The existence of inequality requires either unemployment or changing technical progress. This is, however, not discussed. Thus with a fixed capital–output ratio the warranted rate equals SY/K and the natural rate equals $l+r$.

With fixed capital–labour requirements output must grow at $l+r$ or $k+r$ (since K/L is constant: $k=l$) to preserve full employment of the labour force, and a natural rate of growth. The warranted rate, i. e. that which gives full employment of the available machines, is similar and will equal $k+r$, but k in this case does not necessarily equal the exogenous l, and thus unemployment must be inevitable if k is below l.

Under these assumptions of fixed coefficients Meade sets out to find the mechanism that might cause the warranted and natural rates to become equal if they are not initially so. If the

[1] Harrod defines neutral progress as that which keeps the capital–output ratio constant when the rate of profits is constant. Meade's use of Hick's neutrality criterion is quite unique. Formally the Hick's and Harrod measures may be considered equivalent, but not in the manner employed by Meade. See Joan Robinson, *Essays in the Theory of Economic Growth* (London: Macmillan, 1962) 111–15.

[2] It is immediately seen that these are not Harrodian warranted or natural rates. Cf. Chapter 8 below.

growth of capital, k, is less than the rate set by the growth of the labour force, l, there will, of course, be no tendency for k to increase to the value of l. In the fixed capital–output ratio case this will lead to over-employment of labour, while in the fixed capital–labour case unemployment will result. Meade argues that in either case a shift in the distribution of income can provide a mechanism to bring the warranted and natural rates together. This would necessitate a shift in the share of national income going to wages and profits respectively. In Meade's neoclassical model a change in the distribution of income implies a shift in the marginal products of capital and labour in the production relation. The model he is now discussing, however, involves fixed production coefficients which are independent of relative factor amounts. It would appear that with such a system of capital rigidity, equilibrium cannot be achieved through redistribution of factor shares. Indeed, Meade is ultimately forced to abandon his neoclassical system of income distribution and he states: "Where there are rigid ratios of the kind which we have been examining between machinery and output or between machinery and men, the marginal products of machinery and men lose their meaning.[1]

In other words, in the fixed capital–labour ratio case, for example, if there is not enough capital to provide full employment, the product at the margin of an extra unit of labour is zero, as there is no machine on which it might work and thus additional labour can produce no additional output. If there are excess machines, on the other hand, the addition of another unit of labour will cause the additional produce to be equal to the entire contribution of the extra machine brought into operation. If the growth of supply of labour and machines fit exactly to the requirements, then the value of any factor's contribution is indeterminate between zero and infinity. Thus Meade is no longer able to cope with the problem of distribution or the rate of profits.

To extricate himself from this puzzle as to the determination of the rate of profits and distribution, Meade appeals to another type of system, apparently not realising the extent to

[1] Meade, op. cit., 64.

which its use jeopardises his favoured neoclassical approach.[1]
Meade introduces the possibility of a disparity of factor supplies.
Then he stipulates that if there is an abundance of one factor
(and a dearth of the other), then the scarce factor will be paid
relatively more than the plentiful factor and consequently
there can be a redistribution of the share out of national
income towards the scarce factor. Finally, if there is a disparity
between the savings ratios of profits and wage incomes,
respectively, the level of aggregate saving will rise (fall) as more
(less) of the national income goes to profits, thus raising
(lowering) the rate of accumulation $(\varDelta K = S\varUpsilon)$ to align it with
the natural rate of growth.[2] Given Meade's previous assumptions
that savings from profits are higher than from wages, the
method will only work in a reasonable range when labour is the
abundant factor.

The similarities between Meade's adopted system of distribution and those presented by Joan Robinson, Kaldor and
Pasinetti will become more obvious as the analysis proceeds.[3]
Meade does explicitly note his debt to Kaldor, but draws no
significant conclusions from his indebtedness. The essence of the
matter is, however, that the profit rate, the rate of accumulation,
and the real wage are left undetermined and unexplained when
capital is no longer malleable as is normally assumed under the
neoclassical marginal productivity approach. Meade does,
however, assert that, given a possible level of S, neither too high
nor too low, the system will revert back to a rate that will
employ the expanding labour force. Whether this rate is the
same rate as the rate of capital increase that would be set by
marginal products, which are no longer capable of determination, cannot be resolved.

[1] At this point Meade again introduces a Keynesian mechanism to get
around an insoluble marginal problem. Once this method of distribution is
admitted, Meade must somehow rationalise Kaldor's statement: 'I am not
sure where "marginal productivity" comes in in all this . . .', after analysing
and formulating the method Meade finally adopts. See N. Kaldor,
'Alternative Theories of Distribution', *Review of Economic Studies*, XXVIII
(1955–6).

[2] This is precisely the mechanism of adjustment that Kaldor appends to
the Harrod model. See Chapter 9, section A, below.

[3] See Chapters 9–11 below.

G. SUMMARY AND CRITIQUE

The rate of profits in Meade's system is, of course, V, the marginal net product of capital. Assuming for the moment that the value of V is determinable, the marginal product is the direct result of the way in which capital and other factors are combined to produce output. Given all other factors constant, the change in output resulting from altering the amount of capital used in production will set the rate of profits or return per ton of steel. The reason why this particular rate exists can only be explained by the state of the arts or the method of production.

As Meade has shown in his two-commodity case with variable rates of factor increase, the returns to factors must change to achieve equilibrium. Thus the rates of profits and the prices in the system are continually changing as the system adjusts. It is therefore impossible to place a value, in terms of prices, on the quantity of capital, for the prices are never constant from one point in time to another. Meade avoids the problems of prices and values by measuring capital in tons of steel. Thus the rate of profit (in Meade's sense) at any point in time is a result of the availability of factors in the recent past, which, along with technical progress, influences the profitable possibilities for combining factors to produce output. Thus the forces that have determined the availability of factors must hold the causal clue. If natural resources are fixed (abstracting from altering rates of utilisation due to technical progress) and change in population is relatively free from Malthusian effects, then the only remaining endogenous factor in Meade's system is capital. Consequently, the problem resolves itself into determining that rate of capital increase which yields the equilibrium rate of profit. Meade's relation

$$\Delta K = S Y \qquad (3.2)$$

is helpful. Since Y is determinate in the system, savings must be the remaining key. Aggregate savings depend on the propensity to save out of wages and profits respectively; and therefore ultimately on the distribution of income. To determine aggregate savings, therefore, the relative shares between wages and profits must be determined. Given relative shares and savings propensities under the assumption of full employment, aggregate savings can be determined and from this the value of ΔK; for net savings must in equilibrium equal the growth in the stock of capital. Thus, with the quantity of capital, the required production function can be specified and the rate of profit derived. But in Meade's analysis the quantity of capital and the production function must already be known to determine the relative shares and thus aggregate savings. Thus Meade's solution requires that the values to be determined be known from the outset. This is true whether capital is measured in value terms or, as Meade prefers, in tons of steel. In order to value capital a method of distribution is needed which requires, as shown in Chapter 2, either the rate of profits or the level of real wages. There is no method of escape from Meade's circular reasoning other than relinquishing the production function, as he was forced to do on one occasion.

It should also be noted that Meade's two-commodity world is no more useful in solving the dilemma than Samuelson's analysis for capital in Meade's system can similarly produce jelly output as required: either more machines or more consumption goods. In addition Meade requires the use of the traditional assumption that all savings automatically become physical capitals, i.e. $SY = \Delta K$. What happens behind the scenes in the offices of the omniscient Central Bank is never detailed and the problem of labour markets and wage determination is likewise resolved off stage.

Meade has provided a system in which half of the relevant relations are never discussed. The theory of distribution is not analysed and without a concept for developing the value of capital, the rate of profits analysis is likewise ephemeral and of little real application. This, of course, Meade admits when faced with the problems of fixed coefficients of a greater degree of severity than those of Samuelson's 'sub-class of realistic cases'.[1] The fact is that the problem involves more than measuring capital but indeed valuing capital. It is impossible to do this without a theory of profits and distribution. Speaking of the rate of profit on a quantity of steel does not solve the problem or provide a measure of the rate of profits in terms of value (profits) on value (capital).

[1] See Chapter 2, section 3.

4 J. TOBIN:
MARGINAL PRODUCTIVITY, MONEY AND GROWTH

A novel attempt to blend a Keynesian and neoclassical growth system, complete with marginal analysis, is presented by James Tobin in a paper on 'Money and Economic Growth'.[1] As the title suggests, the paper is an attempt to analyse the role of money in a model of economic growth. Tobin attempts to monetise a standard neoclassical model by means of emphasising the Keynesian consumption–savings–money-holding decisions via his well-known concept of portfolio balance. The two-sided decision, to save or spend, and what form to hold savings, is the crux of the Keynesian format of the model. Unfortunately these savings and portfolio decisions are the only Keynesian aspects of the model. Tobin's model is neoclassical in all other aspects and it assumes full employment and the applicability of Say's Law.[2]

A. KEYNESIAN MARGINAL PRODUCTIVITY AND MONEY

Equilibrium capital intensity occurs in the model when the marginal product of capital is sufficient as a rate of return to induce savers to hold physical capital as concrete objects in their portfolios. Tobin alludes to the possible 'Keynesian' difficulties that may occur if savers allow more capital to be created than investors would desire to employ, given the marginal productivity of the then excessive amount of capital stock. Tobin, however, decries the neoclassical assumption that

[1] 'Money and Economic Growth', *Econometrica*, XXXIII (Oct. 1965) 671–84.

[2] For a slightly different critique of this model see P. Davidson, 'Money, Portfolio Balance, Capital Accumulation and Economic Growth', *Econometrica*, XXXVI (Apr. 1968) 291–321.

savings determine the accumulation of capital stock. Tobin avers that the savings decision and the investment decision should be separated;[1] nevertheless he ignores his own declaration.[2]

Tobin takes the concept of the required rate of profits as the key variable in modern Keynesian growth models.[3] In order to forge a place for portfolio balance in the analysis, money is introduced to compete with the required rate of profit on physical capital for a place in households' portfolio holdings. 'In a closed economy clearly the important stores of value are monetary assets. It is their yields which set limits on the acceptable rates of return on real capital and on the acceptable degree of capital intensity'.[4]

It is Tobin's treatment of the comparison of rates of return on real capital with the yield on money as finance that results in some crucial confusions within the Tobin model. First, the rate of return on real capital that Tobin uses is not the rate of profit on capital, but the marginal product of capital. In the real world it is the existence of profitable investment opportunities and an expected rate of profit that generates a demand for finance and thus allows a positive rate of interest on money to exist and not vice versa as Tobin's analysis assumes. Secondly, Tobin has no explicit treatment of the business sector; all accumulation is governed simply, in neoclassical fashion, by savings automatically invested in physical capital, and the portfolio demands of savers. In this respect the absence of placements (titles to physical capital) from the model is crucial. This neglect forces individuals to hold either (a) physical capital valued in terms of return by its marginal productivity; or (b) money, which in Tobin's case must necessarily have a positive yield in order to compete with physical capitals in portfolios.

Thus the Tobin model of growth ignores two important

[1] Tobin, op. cit., 675, section 7.

[2] Under Tobin's Keynesian view it hardly seems possible that the excess of capital referred to could ever occur.

[3] Tobin, op. cit., 675. In a rather drastic misinterpretation of the models of Harrod, Kaldor and Mrs Robinson, Tobin focuses on this concept as the key that separates their approach from the neoclassicists. As will be seen more clearly in Chapters 8–12, it is the *determination* of the rate of profits that is the key.

[4] Tobin, op. cit., 676.

aspects of the real world. For the individual, placements, representing titles to physical capital, are held for their rate of return as set by the supply and demand for these assets in the share markets. The expected rate of return on placements is unlikely to be closely related to the marginal product on the hard physical object (or part thereof) that the title represents. Similarly, for the entrepreneur, the investment in a piece of physical capital will not be primarily determined by the expected return to the title on the capital in the share market; rather it is related to the expected rate of profit he can realise on the sale of the future flow of output from the finance committed. Neither the portfolio decision of households nor the investment decisions of firms can be directly related to the marginal productivity of a particular piece of concrete capital. The two decisions may be related by the interest rate on finance, but this is necessarily a two-way causation between the two decisions.

In addition the form of money Tobin introduces into his model tends to negate even this causal connection, for without uncertainty as to the yield of other assets (the marginal product of capital is the yield on capital and thus certain over useful life once installed) money can serve no function in terms of off-setting capital risk and thus must, in the Tobin system, be made to carry an institutionally determined yield. With this form of money asset and no uncertainty as to the future it does, of course, stand to reason that the yield on money will determine the amount of capital and thus its marginal productivity. With a positive and certain yield on money, capital intensity can only be increased to the point where the marginal product of that amount of capital is equal to the yield on money. If any more capital is introduced savers will not accept it in their port-folios and will always prefer money with its higher rate of return.

Tobin's view of the world merely serves to reinstate the savings decisions to primary importance in accumulation and bind the savings–investment decision once again into a world where Say's Law prevails. This view explains the strange use of the savings function in the Tobin model. Savings for Tobin are not considered as a residual after the consumption decision has been made; rather it is an *ex ante* 'savings solely for investment in physical capital' function. In order to remedy Tobin's potential 'Keynesian' difficulties of *ex ante* savings (for physical capital) exceeding *ex ante* investment (production of physical capital), Tobin has the government introduce enough money with the proper positive rate of return to cause households to substitute money for their excess demand for (the non-existent) physical capital. Portfolio balance is thus made to be the main mechanism of adjustment.[1] This involves the necessity of assuming full-employment in the model, for if this were not the case one must inquire why the government would not find it feasible to increase the production of physical capital rather than raising the return on money and thus allow more capital to be held in household portfolios. Even to raise such an alternative creates problems and assumes that the real world is, in actuality, bounded by the constraints of Tobin's model and that the amount of net investment is governed solely by the savings and portfolio decisions of households.

B. CAPITAL INTENSITY AND EQUILIBRIUM GROWTH

The analysis of an equilibrium capital intensity and equilibrium growth paths are essential to an understanding of Tobin's approach. Tobin (claiming Harrod's terminology) introduces a warranted rate of growth, which is defined for the Tobin system as the rate of increase of the capital stock that would satisfy the *ex ante* rate of savings in the system. There is only superficial similarity to Harrod's warranted rate which has been defined as 'that addition to capital goods in any period which producers regard as ideally suited to the output that they are undertaking in that period'.[2] Nevertheless, since Tobin does not permit an

---

[1] Harry Johnson, in a favourable reviewing of this model of Tobin's, looks only at the introduction of money as an asset competing with real capital in portfolios, although a page earlier, when speaking of the optimal level of real balances, he states: 'The proposition also abstracts from the practical point that the payment of interest on currency holdings is infeasible'. See H. G. Johnson, 'Recent Developments in Monetary Theory: A Commentary', in H. Croome and H. G. Johnson (eds), *Money in Britain* (Oxford: Oxford University Press, 1970) 106–7, 108–9.

[2] R. F. Harrod, *Economic Essays* (London: Macmillan, 1952) 260.

independent investment function it is hard for him to approach
Harrod's warranted growth concept from the point of view of
the entrepreneur. Harrod's warranted rate is not a full-
employment rate but may be greater or less. If, on the other
hand, Tobin's savings function is to set the warranted rate in
the system, then full employment and full utilisation of the
capital stock must be realised. If this were not the case the
consumption and savings of the system would be of different
value. In the formal analysis of the paper Tobin implicitly
assumes that the warranted rate is at full employment and full
utilisation of capacity.[1] Thus Harrod's basic problem of the divergence of the warranted rate from the natural rate is solved *ex
hypothesi*.[2] A natural rate of growth is also introduced by Tobin as
the rate consistent with a constant rate of increase of the labour
force. Technical progress is not explicitly dealt with except for
labour-augmenting progress which is implicitly included in the
capital intensity measurement (capital per effective man-hour).

Tobin then proceeds to trace the possible effects of an
inequality between the warranted rate and the natural rate. In
the absence of changes in technique this appears to be an
inherent paradox as, under normal definition, the two should, in
Tobin's model, always be equal. In the case where the rate
warranted by the full-employment level of savings is greater
than the natural rate of growth of the labour force, capital
deepening is assumed to occur. This, of course, implies either
some change in technique, in underlying conditions, or the
possibility of the familiar movement along the production
function with smooth factor substitution. Tobin mentions none
of these possible explanations. During these deepening movements, however, the productivity (yield) of physical capital
assets is falling. This decline in the marginal productivity of
capital causes reactions in portfolio balance. It is at this point
that what one might call 'Yale money' is introduced into the
picture to help determine the correct capital intensity which will
equate savers' required return on savings to the portfolio
managers' asset yield at the point of equivalence between the
warranted and the natural rate of growth. This is achieved by a

[1] Tobin, op. cit., 674.
[2] Cf. Chapter 8 below.

government deficit creating a 'Yale money' with a positive
yield that will compete with physical assets in portfolios such
that the yield with a given quantity of capital growing over
time at the natural rate is ruled by the rate of return on money.
The excess of *ex ante* demand for capital assets by savers is
deflated to the actual natural rate by satisfying the demand
with money of a sufficiently high positive yield. Thus Tobin
arrives at his equilibrium stock of money growing through time
at the same rate as the capital stock with both equal to the
natural rate. The rate paid on 'Yale money' is then the controlling variable in the system.

While this approach may hold for a Say's Law economy, it
still does not guarantee that equilibrium will be reached in a
real-world economy, for non-consumption is non-consumption
whether it takes the form of owning punch presses or the debt of
government. Unless the government is either willing to consume
or invest the portion offset by its deficit plus interest, Tobin's
ex ante relations will not emerge *ex post* and deficient effective
demand will cause changes in the rate of investment, profit,
wages and employment. Tobin avoids these possibilities by
positing neoclassical full employment and complete capital
utilisation *ab initio*. These assumptions eliminate any possibility
of a discrepancy occurring in the equilibrium and intensity
relations. The problems of effective demand are, with these
unrealistic restrictions, adequately taken care of by Say's
Law adjustments.

C. THE PRICE LEVEL

In a model dealing explicitly with money, as Tobin's does, it
might be expected that changes in the price level along with
concomitant effects on the system might be explicitly introduced. Tobin does deal with price changes but only in terms of
the effect of price level change on the value of the money asset.
He posits the strange case of both substituting for and increasing
the government deficit by the issue of money as deflation is
occurring so that the existing money assets will become more
valuable and thus cut the amount of new money creation that
the government need undertake to preserve equilibrium in

capital intensity. There is nowhere in the analysis any mention of the pattern of prices ruling in the system or of the effect of capital intensity on price or any other occurrence that might disturb the system of relative prices. Wages are likewise completely ignored in Tobin's system. There is no attempt to answer questions on the effect of changes in distribution of income on the pattern of prices or capital intensity. Factor shares are presumably determined in the same manner as they are in Meade's system – by the marginal contribution of factors.

D. SUMMARY AND CONCLUSIONS

Tobin's model remains an analysis in real terms, devoid of any monetary effects except in the limited sense of money serving, in a world of perfect certainty, as a substitute asset to be held in portfolios in place of physical capital hard objects. This does, however, help explain Tobin's approach to the marginal efficiency of capital as the 'weighted average of future marginal products',[1] and his utilisation of this so-defined concept as the 'true' rate of return on capital. There are no prices in the system and no rate of profit on the finance committed to capital for the production process. Tobin's capital is measured in terms of output and the return is also output. Therefore his measure can only be constant if there is no change in technique, composition of output, distribution and (if they existed) pattern of prices. These conditions, in the absence of prices, are difficult to determine. If the model does adjust by means of substitution then there are discrepancies as the rate of profits in different lines of production are being adjusted to equality. This of course implies price differentials that are changing over time.

The Tobin model then does not handle the question of the effect of distribution on growth, the essential question of the introduction of money, or an analysis of choice of techniques. The analysis collapses to an attempt to show how the system can be forced to the natural rate of growth and correct capital intensity through excessively unrealistic assumptions about the properties of money and the decisions concerning portfolio balance. In his conclusions, Tobin acknowledges that he might

[1] Tobin, op. cit., 674.

have better approached the problem by considering the composition of output as between the production of consumption and capital goods under assumptions of rigid wages and non-fluid downward price changes. This might have made an improvement in the applicability of the model, for as the analysis now stands it provides no direction as to the control of the money supply or the underlying determinants of growth. In the real world the former rarely, if ever, carries a positive yield and the latter is normally connected in some sense with entrepreneurial decision-making in the face of uncertainty. These real-world possibilities are not considered. All the model can do is show how one might introduce the concept of portfolio balance between physical capital and a money asset into a neoclassical, Say's Law model. It is doubtful that the neoclassicists were much worried about this problem, or that if they indeed allowed only for fixed capital to serve as assets, they would have considered it a great error. In a model where the rate of savings sets the rate of investment and full employment is always achieved, the assets are always held regardless of how balanced portfolios may be. In order for any of Tobin's so-called 'Keynesian difficulties' to occur, the investment sector *must* be treated independently and firms given the freedom to make their decisions on investment isolated from any limits as to how much savings the community will voluntarily provide. These latter Keynesian considerations Tobin has ignored in his attempt to graft portfolio balance into a strict neoclassical model.[1]

As for the rate of profits, Tobin, like Meade, has failed to provide the essential concepts necessary to determine it. This results just as much from Tobin's strange monetisation of the model as it does from the use of marginal concepts and the utilisation of jelly capital that comes from smooth moves along a production function. For Tobin the yield on capital

---

[1] Tobin's first model on growth was 'A Dynamic Aggregative Model', *Journal of Political Economy*, LXIII (Apr. 1955). His most recent writing, 'A General Equilibrium Approach to Monetary Theory', *Journal of Money, Credit and Banking*, I (Feb. 1969), suggests that he has not revised his views on money in respect to models of long-run growth. Likewise, his unpublished book, *The Theory of Money*, does not go beyond the use of marginal analysis.

is output quantity over input quantity. There is no attempt made to place a value on the quantities and neither quantity is insulated from value changes. A Marxian approach cannot help Tobin since there is no wage (and hardly any mention at all of labour) in the system. Using physical yield as a measure of the rate of profits is circular unless capital in the model is single valued such as the system provided by von Neumann. Sraffa has shown how this type of system can be expanded to meet different types of variations. In neither of the systems that could be applied to Tobin's problems, however, is the production function necessary or is there any use of marginal productivities to determine the rate of profits.

5 R. M. SOLOW:
RATE OF PROFIT AND RETURN ON INVESTMENT

In his recent work[1] Robert Solow has not produced what could be called a full-blown model of economic growth. The models that Solow (occasionally in collaboration with Samuelson) has put forward have been primarily generalisations of earlier work by Ramsey, von Neumann and Harrod, incorporating linear, homogeneous production functions, usually of the Cobb–Douglas variety, into the original models.[2] Solow's justification for this approach is that 'One usually thinks of the long run as the domain of neoclassical analysis, the land of the margin'.[3]

Following Solow's debate with Mrs. Robinson,[4] his use of marginal theory has, however, become more guarded and, in his 'Technical Change and the Aggregate Production Function',[5] he acknowledges some of the problems involved in utilising the production function and marginalist principles in an analysis of growth. Consequently, it is not possible to analyse a complete model of economic growth which can be attributed to Solow.[6] In the absence of such a complete model

[1] Up to mid-1969 the published work is unchanged in method (see p. 79, n. 2). However, during his sabbatical year at Oxford (academic year 1968–9), Solow has shown increasing doubt in some of his marginalist views and has stated that he is at work on what will be his last attempt at measuring technical progress via the production function.

[2] See 'A Contribution to the Theory of Economic Growth', *Quarterly Journal of Economics*, LXX (Feb. 1956), 'On the Structure of Linear Models', *Econometrica*, XX (Jan. 1952), and with Samuelson, 'A Complete Capital Model Involving Heterogeneous Capital Goods', *Quarterly Journal of Economics*, LXX (Nov. 1956), and 'Balanced Growth under Constant Returns to Scale', *Econometrica*, XXI (July 1953).

[3] 'A Contribution to the Theory of Economic Growth', op. cit., 66.

[4] See 'The Production Function and the Theory of Capital', *Review of Economic Studies*, XXVIII (1955–6).

[5] *Review of Economics and Statistics*, XXXIX (Aug. 1957).

[6] This is probably not surprising in view of Solow's previous emphasis on

the 1963 De Vries Lectures entitled *Capital Theory and the Rate of Return*[1] can be considered as most representative of Solow's published views, for two reasons. First, Solow is, in the Lectures, trying to formulate a neoclassical theory that is undamaged by attacks on neoclassical capital theory levelled by Mrs Robinson. The Lectures then present both a reasoned attempt to define and justify the use of the production function and any major modification of his earlier work. Secondly, Solow specifically indicates that the approach adopted in the Lectures 'has the advantages of linking up with contemporary efforts to refine the descriptive theory of asset preferences and monetary macrodynamics',[2] particularly the work of Tobin. In these Lectures, then, the refinements of neoclassical theory as it relates to growth, and as it fits in with other authors already treated in this work, are developed by Solow.

A. CAPITAL THEORY AND MARGINAL THEORY

Solow begins the first of the three Lectures by reviewing controversies in capital theory. He notes that the problem of capital measurement, as far as he is concerned, is not too important. He agrees that in the short run the measurement of the quantity of a 'thing' called capital may indeed be very difficult, and that the marginal productivity of this 'thing' may thus be of little relevance.[3] Although admitting this, Solow is not impressed with the consequences or with the possible relevance of the whole question. In an attempt to avoid these complications completely, Solow concentrates his analysis on planning efficient investment programmes and

---

attempts to isolate empirically different types of technical progress in the process of growth, rather than focusing on a complete model. Cf. Solow's introduction to 'Technical Progress, Capital Formation and Economic Growth', *American Economic Association Papers and Proceedings*, LII (May 1962).

[1] *Capital Theory and the Rate of Return* (Amsterdam: North-Holland Publishing Co., 1964).

[2] Op. cit., 28. See Chapter 4 above.

[3] Ibid., 10, 13.

determining the rate of return on investment in a planned socialist economic system.[1]

Initially Solow relinquishes the possibility of explaining distribution with this approach and instead he emphasises the consequences of investment decisions. Problems of uncertainty are summarily dismissed as unmanageable in the model. Solow sets out his new approach to capital theory through the method of planning as follows: 'Thinking about saving and investment from this technocratic point of view has convinced me that the central concept of capital theory should be the rate of return on investment. In short, we really want a theory of interest rates, not a theory of capital'.[2] This is quite a different approach from that previously put forward by Solow or any of the neoclassicists. This view denies that the marginal productivity of capital is relevant to the discussion or that the defined rate of return on investment has any relation to either the rate of profit *or* the observed market rate of interest that may be ruling at any point in time.[3]

The rate of return on investment must be defined and its role in neoclassical theory, and in Solow's model, must be developed. Solow takes an economy producing a single consumption good (or a fixed-proportions goods basket) with an infinite variety of factors of production and production processes as the starting point. A planning authority determines the allocation of resources in the economy subject only to the constraint that the allocation programme considered be efficient. Efficiency in this context implies that the planned production could not be produced by any other alternative allocation of factors such that an excess of factors remained, and moreover, that all factors are fully utilised in any chosen plan. Given a chosen allocation plan, the authority has to consider the amount of extra consumption that could take place in period $t+1$ by choosing an alternative allocation for period t that would involve more investment and less consumption but leave the system on the same level of growth in period $t+2$ as it would have been if the initial plan had been followed in period t. If h is the differential in consumption units resulting from choosing the alternative rather than the initial plan in time t, and k is the additional consumption that this choice will make possible in $t+1$, then the planning authority will choose from all efficient alternative allocations of a given value of h the one yielding the largest value of k subject to the required conditions for growth in period $t+2$. 'Thus by sacrificing h units of consumption in the present, society can earn an extra consumption of k units next period and suffer no ill effects thereafter.'[1] Thus the one-period rate of return from choosing an alternative plan with extra investment in the current period is

$$(k_{t+1} - h_t)/h_t = (k_{t+1}/h_t) - 1. \qquad (5.1)$$

This formulation is a rate of return over one period only. It assumes that the planning authority will revise its plans every period, consuming its extra investment goods at the end of the period. This hardly seems to be the type of behaviour to be expected of a planning board, but Solow, ever conscious of the necessity of short-run substitution in the theory that he has abandoned, supports the contention that investment projects 'come up for reconsideration every period and can be easily changed or even undone . . . .'.[2]

There can, of course, be no objection to the conception of the model world one chooses, but its implications may be crucial if further use is to be made of a concept in the context of growth in the real world. In discussing a growing economy, investment is usually viewed as *increasing* productive capacity (and as a generant of technical progress). Whatever view one takes of the elasticity of revision of investment programmes, the use of a single-period rate has little realistic application to the problem of planning investment in fixed capital structures (which may have life expectancies in excess of the planner himself).

This criticism does not imply that the concept of the return to society of additional investment, which can be defined as the relation of increased consumption in the future in relation to diminished consumption in the present by means of investment,

---

[1] Ibid., 19.

[2] See J. K. Galbraith, *The New Industrial State* (Boston: Houghton-Mifflin, 1967) 86–108, for an alternative view of what the world of production planning is like in even an unplanned economy.

is invalid.[1] Rather the criticism is aimed at applying the concept in a single-period context. The only step beyond this single-period rate of return that Solow makes is to construct an average rate of return by averaging periodic rates over different time profiles of investment and consumption–disinvestment.

The presentation of this concept causes Solow to exclaim that 'the whole process can be described without even once mentioning the word capital'.[2] Thus it appears that Solow is free from having to measure the quantity of capital. Moreover, Solow asserts that this approach is free of the normal attack on the neoclassical malleability assumption, and he suggests that 'Extreme assumptions like malleability and smooth substitutability make neo-classical theory easier . . .; but they are not essential to it'.[3]

---

[1] A concept first introduced by Mrs Robinson.

[2] *Lectures*, op. cit., 25. Solow does, however, in a later paper go beyond single periods and deal with 'the ratio of the perpetual consumption gain to the initial one time sacrifice'. In this paper Solow attempts to take Sraffa's work into account and still prove that 'the interest rate is an accurate measure of the social rate of return to saving'. His proof, however, still remains as an assertion that the rate of interest (or profits) is equal to the social rate of return via Samuelson's Surrogate. No formal proof is given. See R. M. Solow, 'The Interest Rate and Transition between Techniques', in C. H. Feinstein (ed.), *Socialism, Capitalism and Economic Growth: Essays Presented to Maurice Dobb* (Cambridge, England: Cambridge University Press, 1967) 30–9. Since the body of this present work was completed a valuable article by L. L. Pasinetti has appeared, which criticises this paper of Solow's along the same general lines as the criticisms of Solow's *Lectures* in the present chapter. See L. L. Pasinetti, 'Switches of Technique and the "Rate of Return" in Capital Theory', *Economic Journal*, LXXIX (Sep. 1969) 508–31. Pasinetti relates Solow's work to a more complete analysis of Irving Fisher's use of rate of return concepts. Solow's reply and Pasinetti's rejoinder appear in the following number. See R. M. Solow, 'On the Rate of Return: Reply to Pasinetti', and L. L. Pasinetti, 'Again on Capital Theory and Solow's "Rate of Return" ', *Economic Journal*, LXXX (June 1970) 423–8, 428–31. Solow appears not to have grasped Pasinetti's point. Solow has also published a book since the foregoing was completed, but his approach has not significantly changed. See *Growth Theory: An Exposition* (Oxford: Oxford University Press, 1970) and also a review of the book by John L. Eatwell in *Economic Journal*, LXXX (Dec. 1970).

[3] *Lectures*, op. cit., 25.

B. SIMPLE MODELS AND THE RATE OF RETURN

In concluding the first lecture Solow presents some examples of his new approach. The first model produces 'one all-purpose commodity which can be consumed or else used as a capital good and combined with labour in continuously variable proportions to produce more of itself'.[1] This model is, therefore, similar to those developed by Samuelson in constructing his Surrogate Production Function and the complete models of Meade and Tobin which have been examined in detail in the preceding chapters. Solow then proceeds to introduce a production function into the model. The production function that Solow introduces to determine the increase in output from an increase in investment is

$$Q_0 = F(S_0, L_0) \qquad (5.2)$$

'where $F(S_0, L_0)$ is the standard smooth textbook production function', and, in addition, '$F_1(S_1, L_1)$ is of course the marginal gross productivity of capital . . .'.[2] Solow claims that he is justified, within the confines of a simplified model, in 'speaking without embarrassment of the marginal productivity of capital'.[3] This despite Solow's disclaimer that it is unnecessary for a neoclassical model to either mention or measure a quantity of something called capital. This 'thing' is now introduced into the Solow analysis in the simplest form of jelly input–output variety that has already been described in the section on Samuelson's Surrogate Production Function.

Solow presents a second model[4] which is based on stricter fixed coefficients of production. In this latter model there is a capital sector and a consumption sector. There is one technique known for producing the single capital good produced in the system. This capital-producing technique requires no capital in its inputs. The consumption good can be produced by either machines or labour, or, in a handicraft sector, by labour alone. Under these assumptions there are no input coefficients for

[1] Ibid., 29.   [2] Ibid.   [3] Ibid., 30.
[4] This model stems from G. D. N. Worswick, 'Mrs Robinson on Simple Accumulation', *Oxford Economic Papers*, xi, n.s. (June 1959).

capital in the capital sector, while labour is freely substitutable in either the capital or handicraft consumption sector. The existence of the handicraft consumption-good sector in this model permits labour to be freely transferred to the capital sector. This permits a measure of the forgone consumption in any one period of the transfer of consumption-good producing handicraft labourers to the handicraft production of additional capital goods which will produce higher consumption the next period.

Solow claims that these handicraft producers are not necessary to his general argument. It is true that he could have dispensed with them if he had assumed perfect factor substitution and malleable output, but Solow has denied that he needs these assumptions for his neoclassical theory of capital. The second Solow model, however, 'permits no *direct* substitution between labour and capital'.[1] The case would be different, of course, if *both* capital and labour were required for production in both sectors and in fixed coefficient processes. With these restrictions it would still be possible to calculate the rate of return on investment in terms of the cost of investment in relation to consumption forgone. The presence of capital- and consumption-good handicraft sectors is simply a method to avoid explicitly postulating that there *is indeed free substitution* between labour in the capital sector (where no capital is needed) and the labour component in the handicraft and industrial sectors of the consumption sector. Unless the two components of the consumption sector are fixed in terms of the proportion of each in the total production of consumption goods, the model cannot claim to utilise fixed coefficients. Thus the simplified models, and their less than simplifying assumptions, have not aided Solow in the calculation that he says he is interested in making concerning the rate of return to society. The handicraft format of the second model is, however, necessary for the conclusions that Solow wishes to draw from it in relation to the first model in the context of the relationship between marginal analysis and the rate of return on capital. 'In this second model precisely the same thing is true: in competitive equilibrium, the rate of interest must equal the rate of return on investment.'[2]

[1] *Lectures*, op. cit., 30.   [2] Ibid., 33.

This startling result comes, however, without any explanations as to how the conclusions were reached save that in model one the marginal productivity of capital was purported to equal the rate of return. In the second model it is merely asserted that the rate of interest is equal to the marginal product of capital. Thus, apparently from the rule that two quantities equal to the same quantity are themselves equal, the relation is achieved. It is difficult to understand why Solow believes he has delivered on his initial promise to demonstrate the superfluous role of the quantity of capital and marginal productivities in neoclassical analysis. Solow initially wanted to determine a rate of interest (or a rate of discount of future to present consumption). In the end he derives the rate of interest from the marginal product of a quantity that he initially deemed unnecessary.[1]

C. TECHNICAL PROGRESS AND MARGINAL ANALYSIS

In the last two lectures, Solow turns to the problems of the measurement and effects of technical progress. The differences between embodied and disembodied technical change are discussed and models for measurement of the different types of technological change are introduced. The production function is again presented and there is a stock of capital and a net marginal product of capital, where the latter is 'Just as before

---

[1] Also, the introduction of the subsistence wage as the marginal opportunity cost of one more handicraft worker in the capital sector (in model two) does not demonstrate that, even at subsistence, the wage is equal to the marginal product of labour. Once the labourer leaves the handicraft sector he can no longer be assumed a self-sufficient peasant, and even if he continues to be paid in kind, his marginal cost to his employer is his subsistence output plus interest on the goods advanced to him for his subsistence standard of living. Thus the cost to the employer must be in excess of the wage which has been set (by definition) at subsistence. Thus the marginal cost of hiring an additional worker is greater than the wage that the labourer receives. It is reasonable to state that the opportunity cost of a consumption handicraft worker is equal to subsistence when transferred between handicraft sectors. This, however, has nought to do with the marginal cost to an industrial sector or marginal productivity. See 'A Digression', ibid., 52–3.

the one-period rate of return $r, \ldots$ '.[1] The quantity of capital which enters as an input in the production function must be measured somehow, but Solow does not indicate why capital, which in lecture 1 was not needful of mention, is suddenly admissible irrespective of measurement. It is true, of course, that a quantity of capital is not necessary to determine the one-period rate of return on investment as defined by Solow in the first lecture. Given this one-period rate of return, it is not logically correct to work backwards from this rate to create a value for the capital stock. While admitting that the rate of return on investment cannot be used to determine distribution, Solow continues to use it to determine the rate of return on capital. If the latter relation is logically feasible, then so should be the former. However, as has been shown, Solow continues to use unmeasured capital quantities and the production function to determine the rate of return on capital which he then equates with the rate of return of investment to society. When this equality is true the production function approach is no longer necessary. Unfortunately Solow provides no more logical proof than mere inference that the equality holds.

The inferred relation Solow maintains between the rate of return and the rate of interest in the neoclassical formulation does bring forward some revealing statements. Unwilling to give up the contention that more capital means lower rates of interest (rates of profits), Solow states that 'the return on investment will be lower and real wages higher in the high saving economy than in the low saving economy'.[2] In speaking of the rate of return, Solow is most probably referring to the neoclassical rate of interest on capital. First, there is no *a priori* reason why the rate of return *to society* from increased consumption realised by increased investment should be any different in a high or a low growth economy. In terms of the rate of return *on capital*, as explained in Chapter 2, it is impossible to say anything conclusive about capital or the rate of interest given the conditions Solow cites concerning high and low saving. Indeed, when it is realised that it is impossible to consider capital independent of the rate of profit, Solow's 'vague but plausible notion'[3] that capital intensity decreases interest rates

----

[1] Ibid., 33.   [2] Ibid., 36.   [3] Ibid.

(the rate of profit) is no longer vague, but truly implausible. It is most likely that a high saving economy will be a high investing economy, and that due to the larger capital sector in the high saving economy the amount of real consumption goods available will be less and thus the rate of profit higher than in the low saving economy. If both systems are facing the same technological conditions, the extra consumption gained from an additional increment of investment should not, in abstract terms, be different in the two systems.

D. SUMMARY

There are two branches to Solow's argument. Neither one gives him a determinate rate of profit on capital. In the first instance the rate of return is not, in any sense, a rate of profit, nor a rate or interest, nor the marginal product of anything. The social rate of return over any single period of time is quite independent of the historical investment decisions that have created the existing stock of capital and the profit that is being generated by the flow of goods from that stock.

Similarly, the rate of interest or marginal product of capital does not escape the challenges to determine the value of capital and the rate of profit that the one-period rate of return concept escapes. Solow vacillates between the two concepts, never actually obtaining a rate of profit to close the system and determine distribution. Solow freely admits that the rate of return concept will not determine distribution. Nevertheless, without a rate of profit the production function approach is also incapable of determining distribution.

Solow's emphasis on the savings–investment decision in a technocratic sense, and his dismissal of the problem of distribution in this context, can be judged to be quite realistic. Having denied himself, initially, the use of capital and marginal products, the marginal theory of distribution is unavailable to him. By trying to force the rate of return concept into the neo-classical mould of the rate of interest, he leaves himself without a rate of profit. Moreover, there is no determination of the wage and no pattern of prices without a rate of profits. Under these restrictions, the rate of return on investment is the only

approach open to Solow. When Solow moves to consider any
other problem beside the rate of return he instantly reverts to the
Cobb–Douglas production function in capital and labour,
refusing to measure capital or give up jelly, but unable to get
along without it or its marginal product. When Solow does,
in the second Lecture, move to cases of steady growth with a
constant rate of profit there is no reason why capital cannot be
valued, just as there is no reason to retain the remnants of the
production function. That Solow has not moved beyond the
original neoclassical tenets he originally disavowed is evidenced
by his attempts to retain the structure of marginal analysis while
trying, albeit unsuccessfully, to stay clear of the attacks that
have been launched against this type of approach.

Finally, it must be pointed out that Solow relies basically on
Samuelson's Surrogate Production Function for his treatment
of technological change, and his proof that the rate of interest
equals the social return of capital, and that labour is paid a
wage equal to its marginal productivity in production.[1] These
items have already been treated in the text above and in Chapter
2, section 3.[2]

The criticism of the Solow method is not based on the faulti-
ness of the concept of a rate of return on investment to society.
Nor is the method of analysing a planned economy faulty under
the conditions that Solow has set out. The only deficiency in
Solow's method is that these concepts bear no relation to the
rate of profits, for the former concepts can be determined
irrespective of past accumulation and the value of the capital
stock in existence, while the rate of profit cannot. The Solow
approach cannot be related, via marginal analysis, to the rate
of interest or any productivity concept of an unmeasured
capital stock. The two problems, determination of the rate of
profits and distribution, and the rate of return to an investment
project in terms of increased future consumption, are essentially
independent. For the planned economy this, of course, makes
no difference, for the rate of profits can be whatever it is

[1] Ibid., 52–6.
[2] See J. Robinson, 'Solow on the Rate of Return', *Economic Journal*,
LXXIV (June 1964) and L. L. Pasinetti, op. cit., for further criticisms of
Solow's approach.

D

desired to be, and distribution is set quite outside the normal methods of a capitalist system. For the socialist planners, the productivity of investment is the crucial variable of concern. They are interested in getting the maximum output from their limited resources which they can keep fully employed. The rate of profit, as such, is quite irrelevant in the socialist case while the most efficient, earliest-yielding investment programmes are the goal. It would be reassuring to think that these same items were relevant to the capitalist economy in the guise of the rate of profits. In fact, they are not.

6 SAMUELSON AND MODIGLIANI: THE UNSEEMLY PARADOX

The last system to be analysed in this section of neoclassical models of growth will be the *tour de force* prepared by Paul Samuelson and Franco Modigliani[1] in reaction to a limited growth model put forward by Luigi Pasinetti.[2] The paper's more technical treatment of the Pasinetti model will be dealt with only briefly at this stage as the formal presentation of Pasinetti's system will not appear until Chapter 10. More important than the criticism, however, is the neoclassical model that Samuelson and Modigliani formulate in their paper. It will be outlined and its claims analysed on its own merit as a neoclassical model of economic growth.

The two articles in question represent the most recent flowering of the so-called 'Two Cambridges Controversy', to which this present study is partially directed. No clarity will be lost in this study in avoiding this individual confrontation between the two pieces of analysis, while retaining the place of each in the more general context chosen in terms of the determinancy of the rate of profits in models of long-run growth.[3]

A. SCOPE OF THE MODEL

Samuelson and Modigliani (hereafter referred to as S–M) start by conceding a limited acceptance of the Pasinetti results.

[1] 'The Pasinetti Paradox in Neoclassical and More General Models', *Review of Economic Studies*, xxxiii (Oct. 1966) 269–301.

[2] L. L. Pasinetti, 'Rate of Profit and Income Distribution in Relation to Economic Growth', *Review of Economic Studies*, xxix (Oct. 1962) 267–79.

[3] It may be helpful to the unacquainted reader, however, first to review Chapter 10 below before starting the present chapter, as it will place the Samuelson–Modigliani model in context as a neoclassical attempt to formulate a model that is both consistent with marginal theory and the results achieved by Pasinetti.

Nevertheless, they claim that the same results can be obtained by a neoclassical formulation, and that such a formulation will show the limits to the Pasinetti model by presenting a more general case. The 'dual' growth theorem presented by S–M shows that the average product of capital depends on the ratio of the rate of growth to the savings propensities of *workers* and that all other variables in the system depend on that ratio, and the form of the production function chosen for the analysis.

S–M set out the basis for their model as follows: 'Our own analysis shall deal primarily with a neo-classical production function capable of smooth factor substitution and with the case of perfectly competitive markets'.[1] The S–M[2] model is set in real terms, with output produced by two factors of production: labour and homogeneous capital. Capital ownership is separated into two classes: those who receive only income from capital, and those who, in addition, receive income from their own labour. Total output is composed of consumption output and net capital formation. *All output, no matter which sector, is assumed to have the same proportion of capital to labour in its production,* i.e. there is only one production technique for all output. Prices are therefore proportional to labour values. Moreover, 'We shall posit neo-classical smoothness and substitutability and perfect markets under which conditions competition will enforce at all times equality of factor prices to factor marginal productivities . . .'.[3] The authors, however, maintain that 'for most of our results it is not necessary that r and w be equal to the marginal product of capital and labour'.[4]

It is on these statements that the S–M model, in the context of this study, must be judged. After a bare outline of the basic relationships of the model and its claim for generalisation, these

[1] 'The Pasinetti Paradox in Neoclassical and More General Models', op. cit., 270.

[2] The outline of the model will be of a very limited fashion, culling out the crucial features only, for the S–M paper is very long and highly mathematical. In essence, a critique would have to go no further than analysis of the assumptions to derive the conclusions finally reached after consideration of the actual model.

[3] 'The Pasinetti Paradox, etc.', op. cit., 271.

[4] Ibid., n. 3.

statements will be analysed to see if the S–M claim, that it is possible to relinquish the marginal approach, is plausible.

B. THE BASIC RELATIONS

The S–M model can be set out symbolically:

L = labour
K = capital
K_c = capital owned by capitalists
K_w = capital owned by labourers
$\dot{K} = dK/dt$ = net capital growth over time
C = consumption sector output
Y = total real output
$\dot{K} = \dot{K}_c + \dot{K}_w$.

Thus, $Y = C + \dot{K}$.
Putting the factors into production relations yields

$$Y = F(K_c + K_w, L) \qquad (6.1)$$

which is the production function, with constant returns, that S–M use in their analysis. Using lower-case letters to represent the variables per unit of labour, e.g. $y = Y/L$, etc., the production function for the system can be rewritten as

$$y = F(k,) = f(k\,1), \quad \frac{\partial F(k, 1)}{\partial k} = f'(k) > 0. \qquad (6.2)$$

The conditions governing distribution of total output in the model as derived from equation (6.2), the production function, are then:

$$r = \text{rate of interest} = \frac{\text{Total profits}}{\text{Total capital}} = \frac{P}{K} = \frac{P_c + P_w}{K}. \qquad (6.3)$$

By assumption the rate of interest is equal to the marginal product of capital, e.g.

$$r = MP_k = \frac{\partial F(K, L)}{\partial K} = f'(k). \qquad (6.4)$$

For labour income

$$w = \text{real wage} = \frac{\text{Total wages}}{\text{Total labour}} = \frac{W}{L} = \frac{Y - rK}{L} \quad (6.5)$$

which is, by assumptions equal to the marginal product of labour:

$$w = MP_l = f(k) - kf'(k). \quad (6.6)$$

Given these basic relations for the determination of the rate of profits and distribution, the savings–investment identities for the two classes of capital owners can be written:

$$\dot{K}_c = s_p P_c = s_p(rK_c) = s_p K_c \frac{\partial F(K_c + K_w, L)}{\partial K} \quad (6.7)$$

for the capitalists, and

$$\dot{K}_w = s_w(W + P_w) = s_w(w + rK_w) = s_w(Y - rK + rK_w)$$

$$= s_w(Y - rK_c) = s_w\left(F(K_c + K_w, L) - K_c \frac{\partial F(K_c + K_w, L)}{\partial K}\right) \quad (6.8)$$

for the workers, where s_p and s_w are the average propensities to save by capitalists and workers respectively. Stating the savings–investment behaviour in this manner, and assuming full employment, implies that all savings of households are automatically invested in physical capital. Thus the savings of the capitalists, s_p, multiplied by their profits, $r(K_c)$ (where r is shown in equation (6.4) as the marginal product of capital), is equal to the growth of their capital, $\dot{K}_c$, when all their savings are invested. Similarly, the wages saved by labourers, shown as the output residual after profit on total capital $(Y - rK)$ plus the earnings saved from capital owned by labour $(s_w rK_w)$, is equal to the growth of capital owned by labour: $\dot{K}_w$. More simply, capitalists earn $P = rK_c$ and labour earns $W = (Y - C)$ or everything that is left over when $Y = P + W$, $S_w + S_p = S(Y)$, and $\dot{K}_w + \dot{K}_c = \dot{K} = sY$.

Using the above relations in terms of the aggregate values per head of the effective labour force (i.e. in lower-case notation), and writing $\dot{L}/L = n$, S–M derive the steady-state equilibrium values of the variables k, k_w and k_c. Given the exponential growth of the labour force, the natural rate of growth in the system is n.

Thus from equations (6.3), (6.4) and (6.7):

$$\dot{k}_c = s_p f'(k) - n \tag{6.9}$$

and from equations (6.5), (6.6) and (6.8):

$$\dot{k}_w = s_w(f(k) - rk) + (s_w r - n)k_w. \tag{6.10}$$

Setting the last two equations equal to zero, the steady-state value of k: k^*, is solved as

$$f'(k^*) = r^* = n/s_p. \tag{6.11}$$

That is, the marginal product of capital is equal to the rate of interest and both are determined by the rate of growth of the labour force and the savings of capitalists.

The relation is, however, as indicated by S–M, dependent on the form of the production function that enters into the steady-state solution. This is the general result for k^* when $s_p > s_w$. If $s_w = 0$, then $k^* = k_c^*$, i.e. when workers own no capital.

S–M demonstrate that if s_w becomes positive there will be some critical value, depending on the rate of growth of labour and the production function, at which the rate of growth of workers' capital will exceed that of capital owned by capitalists, so that over time k_w^* will approach k^*. At positions past this critical point it is the value of n and s_w that determines, along with the production function, the equilibrium rate of growth of the system. These two possible solutions are the dual relations presented in the S–M paper and are both based on the same initial relations given in equations (6.1)–(6.8).[1]

C. ANALYSIS OF PREMISES AND CONCLUSIONS

Ignoring questions of stability of the system, concentration will be given to the premises of the model, for these premises will determine its applicability. The S–M system is based on the

[1] These relations bear a resemblance to the equations of the other systems that are treated above and below. The feature of interest is the determination of the variables that enter into these relations.

distribution scheme of marginal productivity. The authors, however, claim that neither marginal productivity conditions nor the assumption of competition are necessary for its formulation. Instead they state that 'All we need is that r should be a determinant function of K/L . . . provided only that the profit rate is a declining function of the ratio of capital to labour – call it $r = \phi(K/L)$ –'.[1] Thus the idea that the rate of profit is the marginal product of capital can be abandoned and competition is not needed to support the marginality conditions as long as there is a monotonically declining relationship between the rate of profit and the ratio of capital to labour. The S–M system, however, still leaves two problems, namely (1) the measurement of the stock of capital, and (2) the proposition that a monotonic relationship of the form $r = \phi(K/L)$ exists.

The problem of the measurement of capital is completely ignored by S–M. Disregarding the problem of the necessity of having a quantity from which a marginal product can be derived, a measure of capital in value terms is still necessary to determine the ratio of profits to capital in equation (6.3) above.

For proof of the second proposition, the relationship $r = \phi(K/L)$, S–M merely refer to the Surrogate Production Function approach that has been treated in Chapter 2, section 3, above. Using this construction S–M claim a completely general model in terms of the values assigned to the inequality postulated between the savings propensities of capitalists and workers. Nevertheless, their whole analysis is indeed restricted to the special case where $r = \phi(K/L)$ holds, that is, when the capital–labour ratios are identical for all output that is produced in the system, be it capital or consumption output. Only if the capital–labour ratios are identical for all output processes will the Surrogate be valid. Hence it will be applicable in the present model, for a single-valued capital–labour ratio was initially assumed.

The general case presented by Samuelson and Modigliani thus collapses to one in which there is one and only one production process, or, as stated in Chapter 2, to a case of jelly output. Under this assumption only forward switching can occur, while changes in distribution will have no effect on the

[1] 'The Pasinetti Paradox, etc.', op. cit., 287.

output of the system or the values of the system. Under this regime *r must* be a monotonically declining function of K/L. It is the only case, however, where the relation is true. The S–M model is therefore just as restricted, just as isolated, and just as devoid of meaningful content as the Surrogate was shown to be. There is no need for a theory of income distribution, for in this special case the value of capital is completely independent of the real wage and the rate of profits. No matter what distribution is, there is no effect on the values of the system, non-forward switches[1] can never occur and therefore the relation postulated between r and K/L is assured.

There is no difference, therefore, between utilising the present S–M approach and the full-bodied neoclassical production function. Thus, the S–M model can ignore the value of capital (problem 1), but it is in mid-air determining the rate of profits and distribution. Sraffa has shown conclusively that the rate of profit is not necessarily a single-valued monotonically declining function of the ratio of capital to labour. Only in the very limited case of single capital-goods technologies with uniform capital–labour ratios and all forward switches (i.e. in Samuelson's 'Special sub-class of realistic cases') does the S–M model have any real significance. Accordingly, the S–M model does not represent any advance over the previous neoclassical models in generating a determinate rate of profits and thus a theory of distribution upon which to base a model of economic growth. Neither does it provide an analysis of the other two possible keys to the rate of profits and distribution: the determination of the real wage or the rate of exploitation.[2]

[1] Non-forward switches (or backward switches or re-switches) in technique simply refer to the Sraffa result that there is no universal law that can be derived for the relation between the rate of profit and production intensity. A forward switch, as seen in the Surrogate, follows the S–M relation $r = \phi(K/L)$. Sraffa showed that once a technique was superseded by another technique of different intensity, it was possible for it to reappear, at a different rate of profit, as again superior (or as a backward switch).

[2] The only hint of any possible restrictions on their model comes in a long footnote where the authors consider the possibilities of a model with fixed production coefficients to qualify the statement that '. . . if smooth marginal productivities were well defined one would have no need for a genuinely alternative theory of distribution'. It is true that no alternative is needed for the fixed coefficient model if it is single valued in the capital–

S–M do present the possibility that the Pasinetti theorem has a limit if taken outside its assumptions. If the workers save a sufficient amount from both wages and profits and if all household savings take the form of physical capital, there will be some point at which the ownership of capital by labourers will outweigh that of the profit-earners, and over the millennium they will eventually own all the capital in existence. It must then be assumed that capitalists hire themselves out for a wage to keep themselves from starvation, or they take the honourable way out. There seems, however, to be little point in preserving the nomenclature of a capitalistic system after it has long ceased.[1]

D. GENERAL CONCLUSIONS: NEOCLASSICAL MODELS

The analysis of this section's neoclassical representations shows that the neoclassical models in general exhibit the following characteristic features:

(1) The wage bargain is made in real terms.

(2) The use of homogeneous jelly capital or its corollary, jelly output.

(3) Automatic investment of all savings to obtain full employment.

(4) The use of a production function and the corresponding marginal principles to obtain a theory of distribution

---

labour ratio. But this is where Ricardo started his research and the same position that caused Marx so much trouble and academic scorn. It does not seem to be any more tenable as an assumption today than it was a hundred years ago. See 'The Pasinetti Paradox, etc.', op. cit., 290–1 and n. 1.

[1] The whole question at this point becomes one of semantics. The savings propensities of the wage group will indeed become crucial in the dual case presented by S–M. It should be seen, however, that this in no way damage the Pasinetti results if the wage-earners are now carrying out exactly the same functions that the capitalists originally undertook. The crucial thing is the point at which the change occurs, not in what one chooses to call the group that exercises the controlling function.

There is also another large social and political question raised by the transfer of power, which has been seen up to the present time in history as only achievable by force. This significance, however, is of a more controversial nature than should be the contentions of this study.

with the marginal product of capital equal to the rate of profit.

(5) Perfect competition in all markets.

The chief criticisms have focused on points (2) and (4), which are in essence the same proposition, utilising the argument of switching and the impossibility of determining marginal values without identifying the value of the quantity from which the derivative is taken. The production function has further been criticised as a circular method for determining the rate of profits and thus the value of capital, since both must be known before either can be derived from the function.

These criticisms have attempted to show that the neoclassical models presented are indeterminate in providing an explanation of the rate of profits and therefore contain no theory of distribution. It is the contention of this study that both are critically necessary for the analysis of economic growth in a realistically defined mature capitalistic system. Furthermore, points (1) and (3) have been sufficiently criticised by Keynes in his *General Theory of Employment, Interest and Money*. The relevance of Keynes's critique is not damaged by the move into the long period.

Thus, when the underlying marginal analysis is thoroughly studied, it can be shown that a rate of profits does not exist in the neoclassical models. This deficiency is enough to question the validity of models of growth based on these neoclassical concepts. Modern neoclassicists have not developed the theory significantly from the time of Walras, despite their attempts to answer the attacks that have been made on their method of approach.

In the next five chapters the work of the Keynesian tradition will be presented in terms of its attempt to deal with the problems of growth in line with the concepts outlined in Keynes's *General Theory*. The emphasis will, of course, remain on the treatment of the rate of profits in these models. The criticisms will quite naturally be of a much different nature from those made in reference to the neoclassical tradition.

7 KEYNES AND KALECKI: THE FORERUNNERS

Having completed a limited coverage of the propositions of writers on growth showing a distinct neoclassical bias, models of the Keynesian persuasion will be discussed in the next four chapters. The purer Keynesian models that will be reviewed here owe, as their nominal title suggests, substantial debt to the reorganisation of economic thinking perpetrated by the writings and actions of J. M. Keynes. Although, during the period of his work, Keynes's influence was unique, subsequent writers have had convenience to the strikingly similar, and often more direct, work of the Polish economist, Michal Kalecki.[1] Thus this chapter, showing the theoretical foundations for the work presented in subsequent chapters, will deal with the insights provided by both writers whose work appeared almost simultaneously in their respective spheres of influence. Particular writers' utilisation of these seminal ideas will not be spelled out explicitly, for they should in most cases be obvious, with some relying merely on the work of Keynes and others on both (and with a good deal of Karl Marx included in Kalecki's influence). Neither will an attempt be made to distinguish all the major points of difference between Keynes and Kalecki or between the two and the received body of economic theory as it existed at the time of their work. The emphasis will then be on the ideas put forward

[1] There is not, unfortunately, complete accord with the present view of Kalecki's contributions. Bronfenbrenner says 'Kalecki's claims rest on . . . (1) an anticipation of Keynes' *General Theory*, marred by brevity and unreadability . . .' in a review of *Essays in Honor of Michal Kalecki* (in *Journal of Economic Literature*, VII (Mar. 1969) 73). Bronfenbrenner devotes a majority of his review to downgrading Kalecki's work and influence. It is not the purpose of this chapter to analyse Kalecki's work as such, but to point out the highly original and seminal ideas that it expressed from a Marxist view of the capitalist system. The present author cannot disagree more vehemently with Bronfenbrenner's position.

by the two writers which served as building blocks for later growth theories that have been awarded the appellation 'Keynesian'.

A. J. M. KEYNES

It is indeed odd that, although the economic writings of Keynes have been embraced by all the writers treated thus far as they apply to problems of the short period, when the discussion is moved to the analysis of long-period growth the modern neo-classicists reclaim the many classical[1] myths that were exploded by Keynes's writings.[2]

Keynes's views about growth can be most perspicuously discerned in *A Treatise on Money* and *The General Theory of Employment, Interest and Money*. The *General Theory* provides Keynes's reactions to his conception of the received classical[3] theory at the time of his writings. In this latter work, Keynes explicitly rejects the proposition that the wage bargain is made in real terms, and that the concept of time is meaningless in the formulation of theory. It is at this stage that Keynes provided an integration of Kahn's multiplier into a theory of income and output determination which yielded a redefined view of the savings–investment equality and the explicit denial of Say's Law.[4] Unfortunately, classical propositions, which Keynes rejected and disproved, have survived to modern times in the guise of Walrasian general equilibrium analysis and the fluid capital which that system requires if growth is to be considered within its context.[5]

[1] The term 'classical' is here used in the sense employed by Keynes. For Keynes all economics of the type he was attacking, whether of the classical or neoclassical mode, was labelled as 'classical' economics. The two main references of Keynes's work are *A Treatise on Money* (London: Macmillan, 1930) 2 vols, and *The General Theory of Employment, Interest and Money* (London: Macmillan, 1936).

[2] See especially Solow's statement on 'the land of the margin', quoted above, Chapter 5.

[3] See above, n. 1.

[4] For a highly sophisticated and refined proof of Keynes's rejection of Say's Law, see P. Davidson, 'A Keynesian View of the Relationship between Accumulation, Money and the Money Wage Rate', *Economic Journal*, LXXIX (June 1969) 300–23.

[5] For an explicit treatment of the problems of accumulation and the

In addition, the revision of the classification of economic variables, initiated in the *Treatise*, is probably Keynes's most important contribution to the analysis of growth. Keynes radically changed the way economists view the relevant economic quantities and variables in the system. This is clearly shown in his Fundamental Equations and his fables of the widow's cruse and the Daniad jar.[1] The analysis of the flow of income and classification method employed in the *Treatise* is indeed the base upon which most modern neo-Keynesian growth theory rests and provides at the same time a base for an underlying theory of distribution.

In this Keynesian scheme, output is divided into available (consumption) and unavailable (capital goods) output. Wage costs are the primary costs of production for both types of outputs. Thus, in very simple terms, the sum of the wages paid to labour producing both types of output is exercised as purchasing power over only the available (consumption goods) output. The prices that will then clear the market of the available output are higher than the total labour costs of their production by the excess of the wages bill in both sectors used for consumption purchase (plus profit-earners' expenditure on available output) over the labour cost of production of the available output (the wage bill of the consumption sector). This gives rise to a margin of prices over prime costs that is dependent on the utilisation of available labour between the production of available and unavailable output, i.e. directly related to the rate of investment.

In order for the price level to be constant over time,[2] wage-earners in the two production sectors and the profit recipients must save enough of their income (non-consume) to equal the value of non-available output produced. That is, non-consumption must balance non-available output, or: savings must equal investment. If this condition is not met and the value of un-

---

Walrasian system see Joan Robinson, 'Stationary States', 'Interest and Profits' and 'Non-Monetary Models', in *Economic Heresies* (New York: Basic Books, Inc., 1970; London: Macmillan, 1971) 3–15, 25–51, and 64–76.

[1] This is one of the respects in which Keynes corresponds closely to Kalecki. See *A Treatise on Money*, op. cit., I, chap. 9.

[2] Price stability was a main preoccupation of the *Treatise*.

available output exceeds the non-consumption (savings) in the system, market clearing prices will change. The new set of market clearing prices will create windfalls (profits in excess of normal profits, i.e. those ruling at the old level of investment and saving) which will keep the balance between savings and investment. With a given level of wage and profits expenditure the real consumption from money wages will fall as prices rise while savings out of profits rise, thus raising the amount of total savings sufficiently to equal the value of investment.

The question of distribution in the Keynesian analysis is primarily concerned with which of the two groups, profit recipients or wage-earners, does the necessary savings, *and* the manner in which the real income of each is affected by changes in prices related to the burden of non-consumption. It should be recognised that this approach to the savings–investment relation is not precisely similar to that related to the concept of the multiplier where the two are always equal, and changes occur in output and employment producing changes in income rather than prices at less than full employment. The *Treatise* emphasises disequilibrium changes in prices while largely neglecting possible short-run changes in output, employment and total income. This analysis of price equilibration is somewhat similar to a *General Theory* situation at full employment and full capacity. In both works the decision to invest is placed with entrepreneurs and is independent of the balances of the system. The decision of investing in unavailable output is thus primary and the consumption sector must accommodate itself to it. The prices for the system are, however, set in the consumption sector. This type of income flow classification is the foundation for further extension into long-period analysis and is used in some form or other by all the writers in the following chapters.

B. M. KALECKI

Kalecki's contributions, while essentially similar, are generally more concise and compact then Keynes's. Kalecki has the same views as Keynes concerning (1) the wage bargain, (2) the futility of effecting employment through reduction of the money wage, (3) the emphasis on time, and (4) the concern with effective demand, output, etc. In addition Kalecki[1] also derived a very similar classificatory system and analysis of income flows. He simplified his system extremely by initially explicitly assuming that wage-earners do not save. Thus Kalecki divided the gross national product of the economy into the following categories:

Gross Profits + Wages and Salaries = G.N.P., and
Gross Investment + Capitalists' Consumption
+ Workers' Consumption = G.N.P.

Assuming workers' wages and salaries are automatically equal to workers' consumption, then it follows that Gross Profits are equal to Gross Investment + Capitalists' Consumption or:

$$P = I + C. \qquad (7.1)[2]$$

This relationship is a reversal of the equation Kalecki presented in earlier writings, where

$$I/K = P/K. \qquad (7.2)[3]$$

The revised equation, where P = gross profits, K = capital and I = gross investment, with the classical savings assumptions, shows the reversed causality

$$P/K = I/K \qquad (7.3)$$

and will soon be recognised as the same basic formula derived by Kaldor and as a representation of the base of the system developed by Joan Robinson.

Thus Kalecki presents a more stylised formulation than emerged from Keynes's work, although both men started with essentially the same views on the flow of national income and classification of economic variables. The savings–investment equality is also an essential element in the Kalecki approach but savings are seen as specifically accruing to profits as a result of

[1] Kalecki learned his economics from the writing of Marx.

[2] 'A Macrodynamic Theory of Business Cycles', *Econometrica*, III (July 1935), 'A Theory of the Business Cycle', *Review of Economic Studies*, IV (Feb. 1937), and *Theory of Economic Dynamics* (London: Allen & Unwin, 1954) are but a few of the relevant references.

[3] See *Studies in the Theory of Business Cycles, 1933–39* (New York: A. Kelley, 1966) chap. 1.

changes in the rate of investment. Thus as profits increase as more resources are utilised in the investment sector,[1] the reduction of real wages is transferred to the capitalists as profits which, given the latter's propensity to save, results in increased total savings which equals the new level of investment. Whether this increased savings is called savings by workers (forced savings through price changes), savings by profits recipients, induced lacking, or windfalls as in Keynes is immaterial.[2] The basic result is that, as well as providing a theory of profits and investment, the view provides a theory of distribution upon which a theory of growth may be constructed.

Keynes was dubious about the possibility of measuring capital[3] and as such his rate of profit in the pure sense is not explicit. Kalecki, on the other hand, does not handle the problem of measurement, but does spell out explicitly a theory of the determination of total profits and the rate of profits. By reversing the causality in the profits equation, and given the savings assumptions, Kalecki emerges with a defined theory of distribution. This view is modified somewhat by Kalecki's pricing system which rejects competitive pricing and substitutes a mechanism involving cost of production plus monopoly mark-up to determine prices. This pricing approach may come closer to reality, although it permits a certain indeterminacy in distribution in the sense that the resultant degree of monopoly is not systematically determined in the system. Thus Kalecki formally presented a theory of profits and distribution that was independent of the received neoclassical theorems.

Although both economists treated the problem of capital measurement in an unsatisfactory manner, which mars the fullness of their approaches, the groundwork that Keynes and Kalecki laid out for the generalisation of the *General Theory* must be fully recognised. There is little doubt that had English writers had earlier reference to Kalecki's work their task of

[1] Based on Marx, Kalecki recognises a capital-good, a wage-good and a luxury-good producing sector, much similar to Departments I and II of *Capital*.

[2] The same mechanism works in the *Treatise*, but the explanation is not so concise.

[3] *General Theory*, op. cit., 38–9.

applying Keynes's theories to long-run growth would have been greatly eased. The point of emphasis here is that modern Keynesian growth theory is in no sense an original creation of modern writers. The basic relations that underlie the systems of modern Keynesian theorists are traceable directly to the work of both Keynes and Kalecki.

Kalecki's contributions to growth theory have by no means ceased and he is a regular contributor on the subject. His most recent views[1] are that modern growth theories fail truly to represent the types of economic systems they attempt to analyse. Kalecki cites Russian interest in Keynesian models and Western interest in Kantorovich linear programming-type models as examples. Moreover, Kalecki is explicitly hesitant about the possibility of adequate long-run price adjustments to changes in investment. To meet these deficiencies Kalecki has devised a formula that he believes to be applicable to all types of economic system:

$$\Delta Y = I_g/m - \alpha Y + \mu Y \qquad (7.4)$$

where Y is output, I_g is gross investment, $m =$ the capital–output ratio, $\alpha =$ the loss of equipment, and $\mu =$ disembodied technical progress (embodied technical progress is incorporated in m). Dividing by Y, the equation gives the rate of growth of output:

$$r = 1/m \; I/Y - \alpha + \mu. \qquad (7.5)$$

The parameters α and μ may be affected by deficient effective demand over time. Thus, in a capitalist economy where full employment and utilisation of resources is not guaranteed, the values of the parameters will differ from the values that would be applicable in a planned economy. By applying different values of α and μ and m, as they fit different systems, Kalecki reaches what he considers more realistic results for differing systems.

The equation, while providing more variables for relation to particular systems, is seen, however, to be closely related to

[1] Presented in a lecture, 15 May 1969, at Cambridge, England. The same general structure is elaborated more fully in a subsequently published book. See M. Kalecki, *Introduction to the Theory of Growth in a Socialist Economy* (Oxford: Basil Blackwell, 1969).

Kalecki's previous formulations. Given the savings–investment equilibrium of steady growth and Kalecki's savings assumptions, the equation can be fitted to his former relation. Thus, write m as K/Y. Then

$$\Delta Y/Y = \frac{1}{K/Y} I/Y - \alpha + \mu$$
$$= Y/K \, I/Y - \alpha + \mu \tag{7.6}$$
$$= I/K - \alpha + \mu.$$

If savings equal investment then $S/K = I/K$; and if all savings come from profits, $S/K = P/K$. The formula can then be re-written, with $G = \Delta Y/Y$, as

$$G = P/K - \alpha + \mu. \tag{7.7}$$

This relation, given Kalecki's theory of profits, where $P/K = I/K$, says that the rate of investment will set the rate of profit which, given the classical savings assumptions, will be equal to the rate of growth of output. Thus the basic mechanisms in the new growth equation are unchanged from Kalecki's previous views, but he has introduced the parameters α and μ to take account of differing performances of different economic systems.[1]

[1] He also does this in a slightly different manner in 'Observations on the Theory of Growth', *Economic Journal*, LXXII (Mar. 1962), and 'Trends and Business Cycles Reconsidered', *Economic Journal*, LXXVIII (June 1968). It should be pointed out that the manipulation of Kalecki's formula is quite outside the spirit in which it is viewed by its author. The final derivation (7.7) requires the assumption that savings equal investment. This is one of the assumptions that Kalecki is trying to get around with the introduction of the parameters.

8 R. F. HARROD: METHODOLOGY AND DYNAMIC GROWTH

A. DYNAMIC METHODOLOGY

Sir Roy Harrod is, without much dispute, the first economist to consider the analysis of economic growth as requiring dynamic concepts of a very unique nature. The Harrod conception of dynamism was initially formulated in a 1934 paper, 'The Expansion of Credit in an Advancing Economy', where Harrod states that 'It is an enquiry into the relation between the rates of increase in a regularly advancing society . . .'.[1]

Sir Dennis Robertson's criticism of the paper elicited a 'Rejoinder' from Harrod which shows even more clearly Harrod's approach to dynamics. In discussing the difference between analysing a move from a stationary to an advancing state and the conditions in an already advancing system, Harrod explains that

> The difference between the two sets of problems is analagous to the difference between the dynamics of getting a train to move and the dynamics of a train in motion at a constant velocity. I was concerned to investigate the latter problem . . . and to find out what assumptions with regard to the increase and mutual relations of the factors concerned are self-consistent and consistent with normal economic motives.[2]

Although the substance of Harrod's analysis has changed markedly over time, it is clear that the methodology was determined in the early 1930s and it is consistently adhered to in all Harrod's subsequent work in economic growth.[3]

[1] 'The Expansion of Credit in an Advancing Economy', *Economica*, I, n.s. (Aug. 1934) 287.

[2] 'A Rejoinder to Mr D. H. Robertson', *Economica*, I, n.s. (Nov. 1934) 478.

[3] Cf. especially 'Themes in Dynamic Theory', *Economic Journal*, LXXIII

The dynamic method, in Harrod's view of analysis, lies in developing explicit relations of economic variables which are expressed as rates of change per unit of time. Moreover, the Harrod conception of dynamics explicitly excludes either the dynamising of a static model by the mere addition of time lags – a method often utilised in econometric models[1] – or by merely looking at a system at two different points of time in its development. In this respect Harrod states: 'I hold that all the values in a regular advance should be referred to at one date only, being governed by determinants operating at that date'.[2]

Harrod thus poses a very precisely outlined dynamic methodology to be used for the analysis of the growing economy. This approach involves the study of the possible equilibrium values of the rates of change of the system's variables (which may imply, but does not depend upon, lags) and their determinants at one point in their movement through time. The type of macroeconomic system that Harrod chose to manipulate under this methodology is (in all work after the 1934 paper) that developed by Keynes in *A Treatise on Money* and *The General Theory*. It was Harrod's express intention to dynamise this Keynesian approach.[3]

The foundation of Harrod's analysis is best understood via his 'Fundamental Relation'. It is unfortunate, however, that Harrod's contribution to growth theory has been viewed solely in terms of this three-variable equation with little attention given to his effort to bring economic analysis on to the broad field of dynamics and the varied problems this effort opened to

---

(Sep. 1963), 'Regular Advance'; 'An Essay in Dynamic Theory', *Economic Journal*, XLIX (Mar. 1939) paras. 1–2; 'Second Essay in Dynamic Theory', *Economic Journal*, LXX (June 1960) para. 3; 'Domar and Dynamic Economics', *Economic Journal*, LXIX (Sep. 1959); and *Towards a Dynamic Economics* (London: Macmillan, 1948) Essay 1.

[1] See 'Domar and Dynamic Economics', op. cit., para. 11, for a reasoned explanation, or *Towards a Dynamic Economics*, op. cit., 12–13, or 'An Essay in Dynamic Theory', op. cit., para. 2.

[2] 'Themes in Dynamic Theory', op. cit., 403.

[3] This Harrod supports in 'Are Monetary and Fiscal Policies Enough?', *Economic Journal*, LXXIV (Dec. 1964) 14, and 'An Essay in Dynamic Theory', op. cit., para. 1, in relation to the incorporation of Kahn's multiplier with the accelerator principle.

investigation. The fundamental relation is often viewed *in vacuo*, without consideration of the methodological and analytical bases of its development. In addition to methodology, Harrod's contribution involves four areas: (1) the relation itself; (2) the definition and determinants of the variables; (3) the instability proposition; and (4) the knife-edge conundrum.

B. THE FUNDAMENTAL RELATION

Growth in the system is in terms of income or output, Y. The rate of increase is then $\Delta Y/Y = G$. The production of an increased level of output requires new net investment, I. The investment in new capital equipment that is necessary to raise output by one unit is then $I/\Delta Y = C$ or the marginal capital-output ratio.[1] Given the average propensity to save of the community, a given level of output will be associated with a magnitude of total savings such that $s = S/Y$. It is thus possible to construct the truistic relation $GC = s$ or $\Delta Y/Y \, I/\Delta Y = S/Y$, which collapses on manipulation to $I/Y = S/Y$ or $I = S$ (the Keynesian savings–investment relation) which, as stated above, is the theoretical basis of the approach. In a causal form the relation may be rewritten as $G = s/C$, which Harrod calls the 'Fundamental Equation'.[2]

C. THE VARIABLES

The capital implied in Harrod's C is not separated into producer's or consumer's sectors and includes not only capital goods but output of all kinds produced in the system. The rate of growth, G, also has no distinction as to sectors of production. The remaining term, s, is simply the fraction of total income saved, in the period chosen, for all income recipients.

[1] Along any path of steady growth the marginal and average values are equal. Along G_a the marginal and average values will most probably not be equal, similar cases occurring with variations around G_w or G_n. The definitions of the various possible values of G are given below.

[2] Harrod has never been explicit as to the problem of aggregation and units of measurement for the variables.

Within the concept of G there are three distinct rates of growth that Harrod analyses. G_a is the actual observed rate of growth being undertaken by an economy. It is not necessarily either an equilibrium or a full-employment rate. The natural rate of growth, G_n, is the highest rate of sustainable increase in output attainable. It is thus limited by the growth of the labour force and the advance of technical progress, which is assumed to be neutral and occurring at a steady rate. This is, of course, a full-employment (or constant per cent of unemployment) equilibrium rate. The third, the warranted rate of growth, G_w, is more complex. This may also be a sustainable equilibrium rate. It is described as that rate of increase 'in which producers will be content with what they are doing'.[1] Or 'it represents the one level of output at which producers will feel in the upshot that they have done the right thing, and which will induce them to continue in the same line of advance'.[2] 'My warranted rate is simply the dynamised version of Keynes's excess or deficiency of aggregate effective demand in relation to what is required for full employment.'[3] Thus, the warranted rate of growth may be defined as the rate of growth generated by a rate of investment by entrepreneurs that is *compatible in the sense of maintaining a level of effective demand which is consistent with entrepreneurial expectations and with the exogenously given savings of the community.* If this rate of investment is continued by entrepreneurs they will find that their expectations of sales from new capital utilisation are satisfied and thus should be willing to continue with the same rate of increase in the following periods.

Important and fundamental differences exist between the three rates and it is through these differences that Harrod approaches the possible movements of a dynamic system. G_a is dependent upon the actual behaviour of investment and output in the system. It need not agree with, but can be limited by, the determinants of G_w and G_n. G_n is a maximum attainable equilibrium rate given by the exogenously determined growth of the labour force and technical progress. G_w, on the other hand,

---

[1] 'Are Monetary and Fiscal Policies Enough?', op. cit., 81.
[2] 'An Essay in Dynamic Theory', op. cit., 22.
[3] 'Domar and Dynamic Economics', op. cit., 456.

is the rate that is compatible[1] with the exogenously determined rates of community savings to income.

With the three rates determined by different factors there is little reason to believe that they will coincide at any point in time, although they may be interdependent. Thus Harrod's fundamental equation has three equational forms:

$$G_a = s/C \tag{8.1}$$

is the actual rate of growth. The warranted rate can be written as

$$G_w = s/C_r \tag{8.2}$$

and the natural rate with its required savings ratio, s_r, is

$$s_r = G_n C_r \tag{8.3}$$

where $G_n = \phi(\Delta N/N, \Delta C_r/C_r)$; that is, N is the effective labour force and $\Delta C_r/C_r$ is an expression for technical progress which is assumed to be neutral. Both expressions are assumed to grow at a steady rate, with s_r the savings required to allow G_n to attain its exogenously determined value. The technical relation given in the capital–output relation, C, is the new capital actually introduced to produce new output, while C_r is an optimal relation 'valued on the basis that the new investment is no more nor no less than that required to produce a growth of output'.[2] Thus, when the existing capital stock is capable of producing the existing level of output, C_r is the marginal capital requirement necessary to produce output to meet the marginal increase in income per period in the growing system. Thus while C is an *ex post* concept, C_r must be equal *ex ante* and *ex post* for either G_w or G_n to be achieved. In the case of steady advance both marginal and average C_r are equal.

Viewing C, alternatively called the capital coefficient, merely as physical capital requirements is not strictly correct, for Harrod includes a much broader range of output than producer's goods in the concept. It is simpler, however, to view C in more restrictive terms when the nature of technical progress

[1] Given the value of C required to produce the rate of change of new output implied in G_w.

[2] 'Domar and Dynamic Economics', op. cit., 452.

is incorporated in the capital coefficient. In the equation for G_w, it is obvious that if the G_w rate is to be a constant and an equilibrium rate with a given fraction of income saved, then the changes in technology should be such as to leave the capital–output ratio unchanged. To assure this constancy Harrod explicitly assumes both a constant rate of interest and neutral technological change. The latter 'implies ... that the productivity of labour embodied in machines is raised in equal measure with that of those engaged on minding machines'.[1] Thus, on balance, new inventions will be neutral in terms of their effect on C_r. This is, of course, a necessary requirement if G_w is to remain steady in the face of unchanging s. If, on the other hand, the average propensity to save, s, could be varied, then C_r could be free to move as long as s could be adapted to it subject to the constraint of a constant G_w over time.[2] In addition Harrod holds the rate of interest constant to prevent changes in the rate of interest affecting either C or s.[3]

Concerning the relation between the capital coefficient and the rate of interest, Harrod has been forced to reiterate constantly:

'The value of C depends on the state of technology and the nature of the goods constituting the increment of output. It may be expected to vary as income grows and in different phases of the trade cycle; it may be somewhat dependent on the rate of interest'.[4]

Harrod, while being criticised for his failure to make the neoclassical relation between capital intensity and the rate of interest, has consistently dealt with these criticisms by never

[1] *Towards a Dynamic Economics*, op. cit., 23.

[2] This, however, subverts the whole definition upon which G_w is based, i.e. on the given value of s. See, however, p. 112, n. 1, below, and R. F. Harrod, *Money* (London: Macmillan, 1969) 191–201.

[3] Harrod deals at some length with the latter (s) relationship in *Towards a Dynamic Economics*, op. cit., Essay 2, and 'Themes in Dynamic Theory', op. cit., 404 ff.; 'Second Essay in Dynamic Theory', op. cit.; 'Are Monetary and Fiscal Policies Enough?', op. cit. These discussions lead to an equation for the rate of interest that will be omitted as an idiosyncrasy. The relation between the rates of interest and investment decisions will, however, be dealt with below.

[4] 'An Essay in Dynamic Theory', op. cit., 17.

committing himself, in essence, to more than this afore-mentioned guarded statement.[1]

Thus, in relation to the three forms of the fundamental equation, none of the three need be equal at any point in time. Likewise any two may be equal but not equal to the third ($G_w = G_n \neq G_a$ or $G_n = G_a \neq G_w$). Similarly s will not necessarily equal s_r nor C equal C_r. This is due to the independent determination of each of the three possible values of G. These relations will be discussed more fully when instability and the knife-edge are discussed.

The final feature of Harrod's fundamental relation is the incorporation of the multiplier and accelerator concepts. The value of s is, of course, the reciprocal of the multiplier. While the multiplier is usually given in terms of the marginal value of the savings propensity, in steady growth the average propensity is sufficient since average and marginal values are equal.

The accelerator comes into the picture when the representative entrepreneur bases his investment decisions on the rate of change of current activity or the actual realisation of his investment and sales expectations in setting his future capital outlay. To dampen this relation a portmanteau term, k,[2] is added such that $GC = s - k$. The reduction of k from s indicates the possibility of purely autonomous or non-output-increasing investment in the short period. Over time k must disappear as the investment in k yields returns. It will only maintain a positive value if the investment yields zero contribution to output, i.e. if truly non-productive investments persist in the long period.

D. INSTABILITY

Two main areas of incompatibility are potentially present in the Harrod system. These are (a) the possible inequality between the actual and warranted rates, and (b) the possible inequality between the warranted and natural rates of growth. There is no

---

[1] See, for example, 'Themes in Dynamic Theory', op. cit., 404–7, and 'Second Essay in Dynamic Theory', op. cit., 282–3.

[2] See 'Domar and Dynamic Economics', op. cit., 461; 'An Essay in Dynamic Theory', op. cit., paras. 12 and 13; and 'Are Monetary and Fiscal Policies Enough?', op. cit., 79.

force inherent in the system that will guarantee that these rates will be equal or that they will ever be achieved.

Suppose that the warranted rate is being achieved by entrepreneurs, but that they decide on net to increase their rate of investment per period and raise their planned capital outlays, i.e. G_a rises above G_w. Initially the demand for new capital will be greater than that which is actually being produced. Even though the new G_a is unsustainable and incompatible with the existing value of s, there will be an immediate impact as inventories are drawn down to meet the additional demands. Consequently, entrepreneurs will try to rebuild their inventories and thus the accelerator will push the system even further from G_w as producers try to meet increased demand and retain inventories. In a similar manner a chance drop in the actual rate below G_w will lead to an unwanted expansion of inventories and result in further cut-backs in orders. Thus the system will, unless entrepreneurs have very damped expectations, tend to be *inherently* unstable at any rate other than that warranted by the existing savings ratio and technological requirements.

Similar problems will occur when the warranted rate is in conflict with the natural rate. This is possible since the two rates of growth are determined by different forces. Thus there is no reason why s and s_r should be equal at any point in time. The value of s will (with C_r) determine G_w while G_n will require a value of s, s_r, that will allow a rate of investment that fully utilises the growing labour force and technical developments. If s is greater than s_r, then G_w will exceed G_n. However, if G_w is actually realised, it cannot over time exist, for it is limited by the value of G_n. Thus when a warranted rate that exceeds the natural rate is carried out, the system will be plagued by Keynesian depressions as expectations are disappointed and plant is under-utilised. On the other hand if $G_w < G_n$ the warranted rate is sustainable over time but at the cost of forgone possible output and Marxian unemployment as the potential labour force is not fully employed. It is only with the proper technological relations and $s = s_r$ that $G_w = G_n$ (but even this does not guarantee that the G_a undertaken by entrepreneurs will be equal to G_w!). Thus Harrod's basic conclusion that even if an equilibrium rate of growth is attained there will be no tendency towards long-run stability at that rate in a closed capitalist system. Thus the instability problem deals with the maintenance of stability on a given path. This leads to the possibility of the existence of such a path and the problem of the knife-edge.

E. THE KNIFE-EDGE

The so-called problem of the knife-edge is perhaps much less crucial as well as being simpler than that of instability. The concept involves the uniqueness of a sustainable equilibrium rate of growth.[1] It is quite plain that, given the independent nature assigned to s and the assumptions made to assure the stability of C_r, there can exist only one possible value of G_w.[2] With a stable G_w, a changing value for C_r is incompatible with a constant and independent value of s. Thus with s and C_r given, there exists one and only one warranted rate between zero and infinity. In the sense of unique existence at any point or period in time rather than stable maintenance, the knife-edge is a proposition distinct from instability. In the case of a given G_n, on the other hand, there is a required s_r. To be on the knife-edge s must equal s_r. Instability deals with the problem of falling off the edge. The knife-edge deals with the notion that there is only one value of $s = s_r$ that allows it to exist at all. With G_w the problem is not with s, but with G. There is only one value of increasing output, given s, that will allow G_w to occur. The two problems are related, however, in the respect that stability is meaningless if either there are no attainable rates or if all attainable rates are steady rates. In any case, Harrod's primary purpose was to show that there is nothing inherent in

[1] Harrod himself is not clear on this point. For example, compare his original essay 'An Essay in Dynamic Theory', op. cit., 17–18, where G_n is solved for given s and C, with 30 where 'Indeed, there is no unique warranted rate, the value of the warranted rate depends upon the phase of the trade cycle and the level of activity'. This appears contradictory unless Harrod is referring to possible changes in the variables that determine G_n over the cycle and with the level of activity. In this case, then, Harrod is moving from his claim of looking at 'only one point in time', which is, however, done often throughout his works.

[2] See p. 109 above.

the system to guarantee that it will indeed reach any stable growth path (much less the natural rate of growth), and that if by chance or good guidance it did reach such a path that there is nothing inherent in that (or any) path to make it persist.

F. SUMMARY AND CRITIQUE

The four points covered above provide a basic representation of the propositions included in Harrod's dynamic literature.[1] It is now possible to proceed to the analysis of the amalgam of Harrod's work in terms of the basic criteria necessary for the treatment of growth as set out in Chapter 1.

Harrod has correctly claimed that, in introducing a new methodology and fundamental relation, he has purposely ignored certain complications in his development of a growth system in order to highlight the essentials. Further, Harrod hesitates to even call his work a model;[2] rather he views it as a presentation of causes ('the basic antimony') at work in the process of stable growth.[3]

(i) *The rate of interest*

Harrod's view of the interest rate is of initial importance. He has escaped criticism in this study by his continual refusal[4] to yield to neoclassical critics and specify a relation between the rate of interest and the capital–output ratio. For Harrod the rate of interest is a monetary phenomenon and he makes no attempt either to introduce the concept of a production

[1] Obvious by absence is Harrod's interest rate formulation and the 'model' he has presented (see 'Themes in Dynamic Theory', op. cit., 404–7; 'Second Essay in Dynamic Theory', op. cit.; and 'What is a Model?', in J. N. Wolfe (ed.), *Value, Capital and Growth: Papers in Honour of Sir John Hicks* (Edinburgh: Edinburgh University Press, 1968) 173–91), these aspects having been judged of less relevance and seminal value than the rest of Harrod's work.

[2] See 'Notes on Trade Cycle Theory', *Economic Journal*, LXI (June 1951), and 'What is a Model?', op. cit.

[3] Although see 'soluble systems' in 'Themes in Dynamic Theory', op. cit., and 'Are Monetary and Fiscal Policies Enough?', op. cit.

[4] See p. 109 above.

function[1] explicitly into the relation or equate the rate of interest with the rate of profits.

Harrod's greatest concern is the relation between the savings ratio and the rate of interest on the one hand, and the manipulation of the rate of interest so that changes in investment might occur which would make steady growth possible on the other.[2]

The most striking deviation of the 'fundamental relation' from Keynesian analysis is the apparent primal nature of saving. Many economists have interpreted Harrod's system as requiring that the other variables in the system must accommodate themselves to the rate of savings if steady growth is to be achieved. This is partially a result of an implicit belief by Harrod that the post-war problems of developed capitalistic economies would be deficiency of capital requirements and investment opportunities in relation to the full-employment level of savings; i.e. the steady rate of investment required to yield full employment at given thriftiness conditions would be greater than the natural rate. If this proved correct, the solution would involve the necessity of a falling interest rate and lessening savings propensities to close the gap (changes in induced biased technical progress aside). First of all this has not appeared to be the main problem; second, Harrod relies too heavily on the operation of the accelerator as an inducement to invest; and thirdly, Harrod's model is readily remedied by realising that the primary role of investment is restored by merely reversing some of the wording in Harrod's analysis subject to his post-war prognosis. Investment as the generator of both income and savings is still at the fore in Harrod's analysis; the emphasis in part merely depends on where one picks up the string in relation to the problem in view.

(ii) *The inducement to invest*

The second point of the previous paragraph deserves more elaboration. In Harrod's early formulations there was very little mention of why the entrepreneur chose any particular level of investment or why he chose to expand it outside of the personal reaction of contentment with satisfied expectations and a desire

---

[1] See 'Second Essay in Dynamic Theory', op. cit., 283–6, for his closest approach.

[2] See especially 'Are Monetary and Fiscal Policies Enough?', op. cit.

to maintain this contentment leading to a similar increase in the next period. The question of what constitutes contentment is never discussed.[1] When questioned on this point Harrod provided an alternative postulate.[2] His postulate 'B' involved the construction of a representative entrepreneur (similar to Marshall's representative firm) who stands at the mean of all entrepreneurs such that the investment actions of all greater or less than his own tend to cancel, leaving his actions representative of all. This average conceptualisation of all entrepreneurs is viewed to repeat his last period's absolute level of investment in the current period and either to increase or decrease this amount of investment for the current period by the amount last period's investment level was deficient or excessive in terms of actual events. This approach could be called either constant 'under-capacity of plant' or constant 'effort to reduce over-capacity utilisation to normal level' inducement to invest. In either view the entrepreneur is consistently wrong or discontent just as in Harrod's first explanation there was consistent contentment. In essence there is not much difference between the two postulates; reactions to conditions prevail in both cases. Neither approach can be said to provide an adequate appraisal of why an entrepreneur will maintain or move from a rate of steady increase once it appears sustainable and it is achieved. All it actually provides is a rationale for doing the same thing over each period.

(iii) *The rate of profit*

Harrod's view of entrepreneurial behaviour does, however, lead to a basic omission in the system. Harrod never considers the rate of profit.[3] The main thesis of this work, that the

[1] This must be seen as as reasonable as any explanation of the basis of induced investment – mere reaction to events.

[2] 'Notes on Trade Cycle Theory', op. cit., 273–5.

[3] Harrod does make a very vague reference in 'Themes in Dynamic Theory', op. cit., 409, when discussing capital markets and the 'operative rate of interest (or profit)' being insensitive to interest rates and thereby monetary policy.

For an explanation of his exclusion of profits, see *Towards a Dynamic Economics*, op. cit., 8: '– I conceive the theory of profit to lie within the field of Statics'.

determination of the rate of profit and the inclusion of a theory of distribution is necessary in the analysis of growth, makes this omission crucial. Harrod's neglect of the profit rate prevents him from presenting a theory of distribution which ultimately leads him first into the knife-edge and then into a basic indeterminacy. These shortcomings provide the major objections to Harrod's approach.

In Harrod's system, the savings ratio is an exogenous datum given for the system at any point in time. Nevertheless, one of the most important endogenous determinants of the rate of savings is the distribution of income across the members of society. While Harrod takes the savings decision as the sum of differing particular decisions by individuals, he ignores the effect that the distribution of income will have on this summation. Distributional effects require the determination of the rate of profit which will provide not only a method by which saving can be accommodated to any steady growth rate below the natural rate but will also shed light on the problem of the investment decision.

There is nothing in Harrod's approach that suggests what might determine the rate of profits. It might be said that part of entrepreneurial contentment is in a satisfactory rate of profit being achieved in each period, but that does not explain what that rate may be or how it is determined. Given the independently determined savings ratio, the necessary rate of profits required to generate the warranted rate of investment and thus the warranted rate of growth must be discovered. Given that $G_w = s/C_r$, then G_w bears a functional relation to C_r. It is often assumed that the rate of profit will influence capital intensity (or vice versa), but in Harrod's formulation C_r is either constant with neutral technical progress or the level of contentment sets investment choices and then C_r is determined. There is no possible determination of the rate of profits through a functional relationship with C_r. Indeed, it is difficult to discover what the correct value of the rate of profit may be when it is not explicitly treated in a model.

One thing is possible, however. The level of the rate of profits will affect the pattern of prices ruling in the system. By taking different combinations of the rate of profits and the investment–

output ratio (C_r) and the patterns of prices associated with each, there should be one combination that generates a value of G_w such that it satisfies the given s. Thus, for example, a rate of profits so high that real wages are at bare subsistence can be postulated. However, no matter the distribution of income implied by the rate of profits and prices, as long as the level of income is unchanged, the average propensity to save, s, is unchanged. Likewise, a zero rate of profit, implying prices proportional to labour values, would generate the same value of G_w to satisfy the same value of s. No matter the level of prices or the rate of profit, the savings ratio in Harrod's analysis is single valued. If this rate of investment provides 'contentment' at the value of C_r, then the growth path is stable and unique and this would still be so *no matter what value the rate of profits takes between zero and the subsistence level of real wages*. If, on the other hand, the rate of profits could affect C_r, then the acceptable rates of profit would be limited by the acceptable values of C_r or the rate of investment would be affected by the elasticity of change in C_r over time.[1]

Since it is impossible to pin down the value of the rate of profits in Harrod's system, there is no possible way of determining the effect of differing rates of profit and rates of growth on (1) the distribution of income, (2) the composition of output, (3) the inducement to invest, (4) the choice of technique, and most crucially (5) the value of the capital stock in existence. Nevertheless, the analysis of growth need not be so restrictive as set out by Harrod. Income recipients can be viewed (as suggested by Kalecki) in groups by their differing propensities to save. With this assumption, if distribution is allowed to vary the value of s (between the value of savings from profits and savings from wages) through a defined rate of profit, there is no reason to restrict the number of admissible substainable rates of growth to the unique knife-edge rate specified by an independent s. Any number of rates between the lowest acceptable

[1] See Joan Robinson, 'Harrod after Twenty-one Years', *Economic Journal*, LXXX (Sep. 1970), for an analysis of the problem of the level of prices and a possible solution. Harrod's comment to this paper is particularly revealing.

See also Chapter 12 below for a detailed analysis.

E

real wage (highest rate) and the minimum acceptable rate of profit are then possible. Specifying the rate of profits also allows for the analysis of differing techniques (capital requirements) and differing rates of growth and distributions of income. Linking the rate of profits to the inducement to invest also makes it possible to reduce the reliance of the Harrod analysis on a simple accelerator or over-capacity postulate; consequently such an extension limits the possible wild divergence possible from the warranted path (although it makes it no easier to reach it). It is indeed strange that Harrod has not dealt with distribution in his models, since he has recognised its importance at an early stage.[1]

Harrod has provided a much needed methodological approach and a valuable start towards placing the *General Theory* in a dynamic context. The idea that the warranted and natural rate are not necessarily the same or equal and the complications that arise when they are not ranks as a basic contribution to growth. The general approach, however, lacks the necessary variables to answer other important problems in growth.

[1] See *Towards a Dynamic Economics*, op. cit., 15–16.

9 N. KALDOR: GROWTH AND TECHNICAL PROGRESS

A. THE HARROD MODEL AND DISTRIBUTION

Nicholas Kaldor, like many other theorists in the Keynesian tradition, takes his initial starting point from Harrod's challenge to produce a dynamic growth theory.[1] Unlike Harrod, however, Kaldor recognises the possibility of incorporating the guides laid down by Keynes and Kalecki; consequently Kaldor achieves a very different conceptual result by using the same methodological framework. In addition, Kaldor recognises the necessity of distributional aspects, a perception which Kaldor derives from an appreciation of the early work of Ricardo and the extensions of Marx and von Neumann. This view involves explicit recognition of the importance of the rate of profits on capital.

Kaldor's recent work[2] begins with a Harrod model[3] in terms of physical capital growth, G_k ($=s/v$, where s is the average propensity to save of the community and v the ratio of capital stock to output; which approaches Harrod's required capital coefficient, C_r). With the addition of the Keynesian saving–investment equilibrium condition, $S=I$, then $s=I/Y=G_k v$. At this stage Kaldor departs from the Harrod formula by assuming that all savings are equal to aggregate profits in the community such that $s=P/Y$ (or the von Neumann savings conditions), which simply implies that workers do not save and profit recipients do

---

[1] See 'Economic Growth and the Problem of Inflation', *Economica*, XXVI, n.s. (Aug.–Nov. 1959) 213.

[2] That is, since 1950.

[3] As in 'Capital Accumulation and Economic Growth', in F. A. Lutz and D. C. Hague (eds.), *The Theory of Capital*, International Economic Association, Corfu Conference (London: Macmillan, 1961).

not consume. Consequently, Kaldor obtains the following equational results:

$$s = P/Y \tag{9.1}$$

$$P/Y = I/Y = G_k v. \tag{9.2}$$

$$P/Y = G_k \ K/Y, \tag{9.3}$$

but since

$$P/K \equiv P/Y \ Y/K \tag{9.4}$$

$$\therefore \ P/K = G_k. \tag{9.5}$$

Equation (9.5) is recognised as the von Neumann result with the explicit rate of profit on capital, P/K, equal to the rate of growth of capital. Thus Kaldor has performed an integration of the von Neumann–classical approach and the Harrod–Keynesian approach by using the simplifying assumption that $s = P/Y$, a provisional statement of distribution.

B. A KEYNESIAN DISTRIBUTION MECHANISM

Kaldor's approach to distribution is made more explicit in a paper on 'Alternative Theories of Distribution'.[1] A theory of distribution based on Keynes's *Treatise on Money* and the similar work of Kalecki is outlined in this paper. The approach provides a method of distribution and stability for a long-run, fully employed, steady growth path.[2]

At the foundation of Kaldor's scheme is the concept of the division of income into earned and unearned (or wage and profit) income, with the condition that savings out of the former share are a much smaller proportion of income than the latter. Thus, given the savings–investment relation and the

[1] 'Alternative Theories of Distribution', *Review of Economic Studies*, XXIII (1955–6). Part iv concerns Keynesian distribution.

[2] The assumption of full employment in this case may appear dubious, but it stems from a proposition, singular with Kaldor's work, which will be outlined fully below.

extreme case of classical thriftiness,[1] the relation between profits, P, and investment, $I(S=I)$, becomes

$$P = 1/s_p \ I. \tag{9.6}$$

With classical savings the propensity to save out of profits is unity, so

$$P = I. \tag{9.7}$$

This is seen as simply an equational statement of Keynes's 'widow's cruse'[2] or the distributional result of Kalecki's analysis[3] where the capitalists get what they spend and the workers spend what they get.

The essential requirement for this type of distributional system is the flexibility of prices relative to money wages (profit margins) over the long term such that profits will, at the expense of wage incomes, always provide the requisite savings to accommodate the value of the investment–output ratio at full employment. This approach is consistent with the Keynesian view that (*a*) investment decisions are independent of decisions to save, (*b*) investment will initiate the change in income from which saving will arise,[4] and (*c*) firms are the initiators of investment decisions based on their expectations of future profit streams.

---

[1] This is similar to the von Neumann conditions, i.e. capitalists do not consume and workers do not save. In the classical case the consumption of workers is not a technical production condition as in von Neumann but a behavioural statement of the conditions at work in the system.

[2] J. M. Keynes, *A Treatise on Money*, I (London: Macmillan, 1930) 137–40.

[3] Kalecki, as seen above, had stated this result in almost coincident equational form. Cf. Chapter 7, section B, above.

[4] The statement applies to both less than full-employment and full-employment equilibria. At less than full employment an increase in investment raises output, engages unemployed resources, and through the multiplier savings arise as the level of income rises. At full employment price changes alter income distribution *at the full-employment level of income*, thus increasing total savings (transferring income to those who save more out of income) and transferring resources from consumption to investment. This is, of course, the basis of the 'widow's cruse' and is a quite simple allocation through the price system. It has, however, not been properly studied or understood by many neo-neoclassicists.

The Keynesian assumption of the independence of I/Y from households' savings propensities is incorporated by Kaldor into Harrod's system, e.g. $I/Y = Gv$, where, given the assumption of full employment, growth is equal to Harrod's natural rate. The savings–investment relation thus becomes $I/Y = s_p P/Y$. The Harrod problem of the possibility of the inequality of G_w and G_n cannot occur as long as changes in the profit's share relative to the wage share will, given flexible profit margins, yield a value for the average propensity to save equal to s_r, the savings required for G_n.[1] Since s is no longer exogenous to the system, Kaldor seeks other causes for the possibility of smooth growth. The search leads Kaldor to a further inquiry into entrepreneurial inducement to invest and its relation to technical progress and growth. Before pursuing this line, however, Kaldor's contention that steady equilibrium growth implies the existence of full employment should be developed.

C. FULL EMPLOYMENT AND LONG-RUN EQUILIBRIUM

The justification for assuming full employment in long-run equilibrium analysis is dealt with in two of Kaldor's papers.[2] Kaldor uses the device of a completely integrated representative firm so that the prime costs of production equal labour costs. Up to the point of optimum capacity utilisation, constant average cost (implying constant marginal costs) is assumed. With an imperfect market structure, excess capacity can exist so that available labour is the primary constraint to the level of output achieved. Firms are assumed to defend a certain margin of profit over prime costs no matter what the state of demand in the market. Thus the supply curve of the firm is determined by (1) the minimum acceptable supply price, and (2) the full-employment output (or that level of output producible with all available labour in the economy fully employed). This is

[1] The conditional restrictions for the completion of this model will be omitted here as they will appear in a similar form in a more recent Kaldor model dealt with below.

[2] 'Economic Growth and the Problem of Inflation', op. cit., and 'Capital Accumulation and Economic Growth', op. cit.

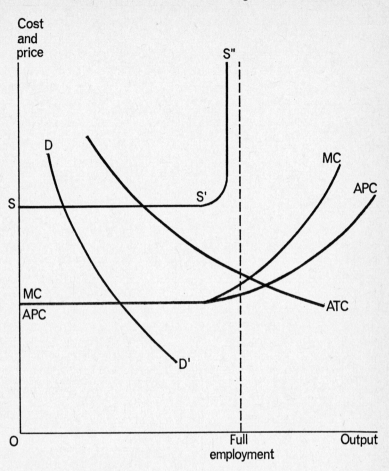

Fig. 9.1

graphically[1] shown in Fig. 9.1, where *OA* represents average unit labour costs (until full employment) and therefore *OS* is the minimum supply price set by the minimum acceptable margin of profits over unit labour costs, i.e. *OS–OMC*. *SS'* is the output limit set by labour availability at full employment and *SS'S''* is the short-run supply curve of the firm. Marginal and

[1] Figs. 9.1 and 9.2 are taken from 'Capital Accumulation and Economic Growth', op. cit.

average prime costs are constant up to optimum capacity and then rise. Average total costs, ATC, fall over the feasible range, as MC is constant as fixed costs fall.

The introduction of a schedule of 'effective' demand quantities at each alternative possible price is necessary to complete the diagram. If demand price meets the expected supply price along SS', normal profits will be earned over time on the existing plant. At that level of output where the demand price just covers total cost at that level of output (and employment) there will be no inducement to increase investment.

Given constant money wages, then each possible price suggests a different relative distribution of income so that the higher the price relative to prime costs, the greater the profits share and therefore aggregate savings out of full-employment income are greater. Hence the higher the price the smaller the quantity of consumption goods demanded from the representative firm for any level of investment. Consequently the demand curve can be expected to fall over its relevant range (i.e. as the margin of prices over prime costs declines, the share of wages in total output increases and, with $s_p > s_w$, the greater is effective demand). Thus in Fig. 9.1 the curve DD' represents the demand curve. If, however, increases in output are carried beyond $DD' = SS'$ (where, if output is being sold at the supply price, average total costs including normal profits are being more than covered), then additional investment will be induced as profits are above their expected normal level.

If this induced investment increases with employment past $DD' = SS'$ then for any given level of output past this point aggregate investment will increase. If the demand curve is to show points of effective demand, this requires higher savings ratios past this point, such that, given $s_p > s_w$, the share of wages in total output must decline. Hence profit margins (demand prices) must increase, causing the demand curve to incline upwards. This is shown in Fig. 9.2, which exhibits the equilibrium DD' curve. When output is carried beyond the point I, induced investment will take place and cause DD' to slope upwards after that point. At P_1 there exists an under-full employment equilibrium, but with nothing inherent in the position to cause induced investment. At P_2 effective demand

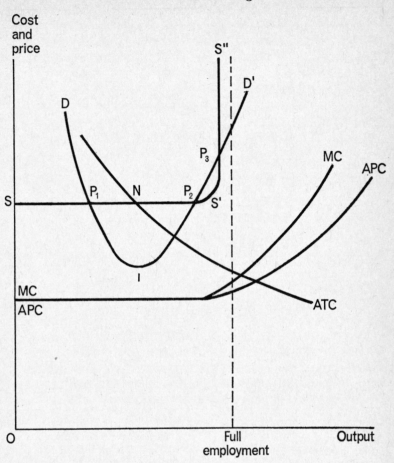

Fig. 9.2

balances supply price, but this is an unstable equilibrium position since a small displacement in either direction will set up forces to move further away from P_2. Thus P_3 is the only stable point compatible with investment and expansion of output and growth. This point, and only this point, is at full employment.

Consequently, the basis for Kaldor's continued use of the assumption of full employment in his growth models is that only P_3 provides a stable equilibrium growth solution; while the stable less than full-employment equilibrium (point P_1) is incompatible with long-run steady expansion of investment and output. Moreover, the steady rate of investment generated must produce a margin over prime costs equal to or in excess of the acceptable minimum as given by the SS' curve. If this were not so, DD' would not cut the $S'SS''$ range, full employment would not be attained and there would be no inducement to continue the rate of investment; the system would revert to the P_1 case, one of chronic Keynesian unemployment.

D. ENTREPRENEURIAL BEHAVIOUR AND TECHNICAL PROGRESS

Kaldor's analysis of the level of employment in steady growth ultimately hinges on the question of what makes an economy grow, or more precisely, what are the relations between entrepreneurial investment, growth, and the effects of technical progress. Kaldor stated his initial view as: 'Saving and Capital Accumulation therefore are in no different position from Technical Progress and Population Growth, as being one of the features that characterise progressive societies rather than as the ultimate stuff and substance which *makes* societies progressive'.[1] In this respect Kaldor emphasises what he calls the 'technical dynamism' of an economy, which involves the basic attitudes towards expansion held by entrepreneurs. Enough dynamism will, according to Kaldor, bump the natural rate and cause it to approach the warranted, if the latter is above the former. Kaldor's paper (with James Mirrlees), 'A New Model of Economic Growth',[2] can be taken as the most recent representation of his views on the subject.[3]

Entrepreneurial behaviour is viewed as subject to two conditions: (*a*) maintenance of the rate of profit, and (*b*) meeting a

[1] 'The Relation of Economic Growth and Cyclical Fluctuation', *Economic Journal*, LXIV (Mar. 1954) 67.

[2] *Review of Economic Studies*, XXIX (June 1962).

[3] Intermediate positions on the questions of inducement and technical progress are found in 'Economic Growth and the Problem of Inflation', op. cit.; 'Capital Accumulation and Economic Growth', op. cit.; and 'A Model of Economic Growth', *Economic Journal*, LXVII (Dec. 1957).

finite pay-off period on capital investment. For condition (*a*) it is assumed that firm's investment is subject to the constraint that the return earned on fixed investment should be equal to that earned in the rest of the economy such that at the end of the anticipated life of the investment it has earned a surplus in excess of depreciation that yields a rate of profit at least equal to the expected rate of profit of new investment in the rest of the system. 'In other words we assume that the firm is guided by the motive of maximising the rate of profit on shareholders' equity, which involves different decisions from the assumption of maximising the rate of profit on its fixed investment'.[1] Thus the rate of profit decision is not on the existing rate but the rate expected on competing lines of investment. The degree of difference in these views will be seen more clearly below.

Condition (*b*) brings in the effect of changing technical progress offsetting the expected useful life of investment. In terms of the possible changes in technology, demand or money wages, the near future is viewed with more confident expectations. Thus in a world where the future becomes more uncertain the longer the time horizon, long-term fixed capital investments must be viewed by the entrepreneur as being able to recoup initial cost in the first few years of operation (given the strength of entrepreneurial expectations concerning changes in technique, demand and wage rates). This necessity to recoup capital costs in a short period is termed the corporate pay-off period criterion. Risk and uncertainty are thus introduced into Kaldor's model via the concept of the pay-off period, a condition separate from the normal postulate of equality of rates of profit expected on capital employed in all lines of production.

The explicit introduction of technical progress completes Kaldor's analysis of entrepreneurial investment. Given the full-employment equilibrium analysis presented above, available labour will be a limiting factor in new investment decisions. The other factor will obviously be the amount of new investment necessary to equip new labourers entering the labour force as population grows. Kaldor suggests that, with available labour limited in any period, there will be a tendency towards over-capacity in the system, due to lack of hands, which entre-

---

[1] 'A New Model of Economic Growth', op. cit., 177, n. 2.

preneurs will want to hold below some specified maximum. Any given piece of capital equipment has a variable labour coefficient associated with it. Kaldor calls this a limitational relationship such that by reducing labour connected with a process of production (increase capital per head on existing plant) it is impossible to raise the productivity of remaining labour.[1] Thus labour can be applied in varying amounts in a certain range up to the optimum amount (or limit), but the average product of labour is constant over this range up to the limit and zero thereafter. This concept is virtually the same as fixed labour–capital coefficients, but is different in that it allows production of output at less than the rigid specifications of the required amount of labour. Thus, one of the determining factors of technical progress is the rate of change of investment per man, for productivity cannot be affected by changing the complement of labour to existing machines. If $i_t = I_t/n_t$, where i is investment per man and I is gross investment in fixed capital, n is labour and subscript t represents a given period of time, then $\Delta i/i$ is the formulation for the rate of change of investment per man. The productivity of existing fixed capital is assumed to be fixed over the life of the machine. Thus changes in productivity can only arise through gross investment, i.e. the actual introduction of new machines or replacement of existing machines with new machines.

(i) *The technical progress function*

Kaldor approaches technical progress through the necessity of gross investment. Thus, if P is a given level of productivity per worker, $\Delta P/P$ is the rate of change in productivity per worker related to a change in technical progress through gross investment. Given the assumption of a constraint via the amount of available labour, Kaldor's conception of a Technical Progress Function implies that the rate of growth of productivity caused by applying labour to new machines is a function of the rate of growth of investment per worker, $\Delta i/i$.[2] This latest conception of

[1] That is, the marginal and average product of labour are equal up to the boundaries of the flexible limitational range.

[2] For alternative expositions of the Technical Progress Function, see 'Economic Growth and the Problem of Inflation', op. cit., 220–4; 'Capital

the Technical Progress Function explicitly highlights Kaldor's belief that, given the available labour limitation, the rate of technical progress is dependent on the rate of gross investment (or

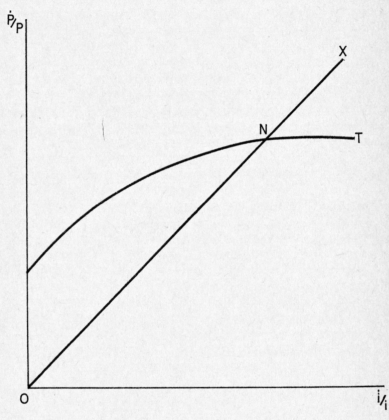

Fig. 9.3 The Technical Progress Function

the rate of expansion or technical dynamism) of the system. The function is presented graphically as in Fig. 9.3. The positive intercept of the y axis makes allowance for some technical

---

Accumulation and Economic Growth', op. cit., section viii; and 'A Model of Economic Growth', op. cit., 595–8.

progress when investment is zero, since there may be 'learning by doing' as replacements continue with old techniques. The introduction of new equipment per worker raises productivity per worker but at a decreasing rate (there are diminishing returns to investment). At point N, the two rates are perfectly balanced in the sense that the rate of change of investment and productivity are equal.

This diagram permits one to deduce different types of technical progress that can appear by comparing different values of the variables. To the left of point N, for example, productivity per worker is increasing faster than capital per worker and therefore the capital–output ratio is falling. The opposite result occurs for positions to the right of point N. Only at the point N where T is cut by the 45° line will progress be balanced, i.e. neutral. Thus the function shows through its height and slope (which may vary) that there can be no specified relation between growth and the type of technical progress.[1] It also shows that this point, at which balanced steady growth will occur (assuming T does not shift), is where the rate of increase in productivity and investment are constant, and therefore the capital–output and capital–labour ratios are constant with a constant rate of profit. This steady condition will of course yield a state of constant relative shares. If either there is a tendency for the system to seek point N, or if shifts in the curve cause only temporary disjunctures in the equivalence of the ratios which eventually return to a new N, then Kaldor, in addition to providing a new approach to technical progress, has linked technical progress into an explanation of the constancy of relative shares.

E. THE KALDOR SYSTEM IN BRIEF

There are many features of Kaldor's approach that are unique to him and represent shifts from the basic type of analysis presented in the previous chapter. A sketch of Kaldor's latest model can be used to illustrate how he fits the pieces in a comprehensive system.[2]

[1] Kaldor's personal explanation will be given below.
[2] 'A New Model of Economic Growth', op. cit.

From the outset, Kaldor presents a 'differentiated' model to achieve a steady growth equilibrium which he defines as:

> where the rate of growth of output per head is equal to the rate of growth of productivity of new equipment and both are equal to the rate of growth of (fixed) investment per worker, and to the rate of growth of wages . . . and where the share of investment in output I/Y, the share of profits in income π, and the period of obsolescence of equipment, T, remain constant. Finally we shall show that there is a unique rate of profit on investment in a steady growth equilibrium.[1]

The model involves a closed system with a constant exogenous rate of population increase and continuous technical innovation. The replacement of capital is determined by profitability and not by physical life, i.e. old plant becomes less profitable each time a technically superior plant is introduced until it can no longer earn sufficient profit over prime costs at the rising level of real wages. In addition some plant and equipment radio-actively disintegrates at a constant rate.[2]

Kaldor explicitly rejects the possibility of measuring the capital stock and thus relieves himself of the necessity of determining either the rate of capital accumulation or the rate of profit on existing capital. He chooses to work only with the value of *current* gross investment in fixed capital per unit of time and the rate of change of this variable. The inducement-to-invest conditions, as have already been indicated, involve the amount of new investment per worker as a function of the general rate of profit being earned on investment when the latter is the return after amortisation (considering the prospective rise in wages and any radioactive depreciation). In addition, the outlay of the investment must be recovered in a fixed pay-out period which reflects the entrepreneurial expectation of the investments becoming obsolete through the introduction of new machines. This view of investment is different

---

[1] Ibid., 180.

[2] This takes care of acts of God, but does not make him consistent. The assumption conveniently disposes of the valuation of a stock of capital of unbalanced age composition, a problem Kaldor dismisses as unmanageable in any case, balanced or not.

from usual Keynesian approaches which use only the differential between the rate of interest and the marginal efficiency of capital or the rate of profit on capital to determine the level of investment in any period.

The analysis of technical progress does not make use of either the capital stock or the rate of profit. It is quite clear that the burden of growth, in Kaldor's view, rests mainly on technical progress:

> The model shows technical progress – in the specific form of the rate of improvement of the design, etc., of newly produced capital equipment – as the main engine of economic growth, determining not only the rate of growth of productivity but – together with other parameters – also the rate of obsolescence, the average lifetime of equipment, the share of investment in income, the share of profits, and the relationship between investment and potential output (i.e. the 'capital/output ratio' on new capital).[1]

As in previous models, the Keynesian distribution system is kept intact and savings out of wages are assumed to be zero. The distributive relation is given as

$$\pi = P/Y = 1/s \; I/Y, \tag{9.8}$$

which is, as shown above, derived from both Keynes and Kalecki and stems from Kaldor's analysis in 'Alternative Theories of Distribution'.

Kaldor's system is subject to the conditions that the minimum real wage must be above subsistence and the rate of profits must be above a certain minimum.[2] Relations are also set down to determine the expected increase in money wages over time (at a rate equal to experienced rises). Population growth is at a constant rate and economic life of equipment is

---

[1] 'A New Model of Economic Growth', op. cit., 188. Cf. the quote given above, p.126. All this is implicit to some extent in the point N of the Technical Progress Function, and of increased importance when the function shifts or changes shape.

[2] Here the reliance on the marginal efficiency–profit rate gap comes through whether it is called degree of monopoly, mark-up or margin.

equationally defined as the point where profit fails to cover prime costs. For the oldest remaining machine the difference between profit and prime costs approaches zero. The share of wages then, given π and Y, is simply a residual.

The model gains its initial stability from the Technical Progress Function, for at point N, where $\dot{P}/P = \dot{i}/i$ there is equilibrium, in terms of neutral progress on balance, which guarantees that the capital–output and capital–labour ratios are constant. With the existence of this point, N, over time, the share in output of wages and profits will be constant. If this is the case, then wages will increase at the same rate as technical progress raises output per head; a condition which is necessary for effective demand to increase sufficiently to match increased output and satisfy producer's expectations. Thus, given the increase in population and labour force, with continual full employment, the increased output per head will attain the same rate when technical progress is constant and neutral.

Once the rate of increase of the wage is known, given the particular vintage of any capital good at the ruling rate of profit, the profitable life of capital also becomes a constant, for the margin of surplus return over prime costs falls at a constant rate and thus the total economic life of capital goods is fixed. Nevertheless this involves the rate of profits being predetermined, the last of the conditions that must be fulfilled to close Kaldor's model. A predetermined rate of profits becomes exceptionally difficult to discuss when it is remembered that Kaldor has explicitly ruled out the necessity of valuing the stock of capital.

Kaldor introduces the rate of profits in intuitive terms. If the economy is in a steady equilibrium, at the point on the technical progress function given by N, then expectations must be realised in order for the system to be in steady growth equilibrium at N. This is just another way of saying that the realised rate of profit that the system generates will, indeed must, be the same as the expected rate of profit. If the rate observed in the system is continually expected and realised over time, then it must be the steady-state equilibrium rate of profits. Thus Kaldor derives the rate of profits which enables him to value new capital investment, subject to the value of savings out of profits. If the rate of growth of output, given by the Technical Progress Function at point N, is γ and if σ is the proportion of net profits saved *for investment purposes*, then with λ equal to the rate of growth of the labour force the full-employment steady growth relation can be written

$$\sigma\rho = \gamma + \lambda \tag{9.9}$$

where ρ is the expected rate of profit on new capital investment.

The left-hand term of equation (9.9) is the proportion of net profits saved multiplied by the rate of profits (or the value of the increased stock of new capital) which must be increasing at the same rate as the right-hand term if steady growth is to be achieved with output steadily increasing over time and the labour force fully employed. With Kaldor's assumption of classical thriftiness, all profits are invested and $\sigma = 1$ such that the steady growth relation becomes

$$\rho = \gamma + \lambda \tag{9.10}$$

with the rate of profit equal to the rate of growth of output generated by employing the labour force. Accumulation of capital, in terms of output to come, will thus increase at the same rate as the equal, constant rate of profits. All the claims that Kaldor has made on the model are thus fulfilled, despite the initial disclaimer about the value of capital stock in existence. The solution to the model is concluded with the proviso: 'Outside a golden age equilibrium a rate of profit on investment does not exist in the sense of an *assumed* rate of profit, based on a mixture of convention and belief, which enables entrepreneurs to decide whether any particular project passes the test of adequate profitability'.[1] Kaldor is not maintaining that real-world entrepreneurs experience rate of profit illusion or that they are unable to make projections of the rate of profit. Without perfect expectation, supported by experience, Kaldor is claiming that it is impossible to make correct future projections from the current rate of observed (or assumed) profit as this rate may not be consistent with the value of existing capital or the flow of revenue from newly installed capital.

[1] 'A New Model of Economic Growth', op. cit., 186.

F. DETERMINATION OF THE RATE OF PROFIT AND TECHNICAL PROGRESS: COMMENT

The essential novelties of Kaldor's system may be summarised as (*a*) the development of the concept of the Technical Progress Function, (*b*) the rejection of long-run under-employment equilibrium, (*c*) the view that the inducement to invest does not depend on a marginal efficiency of capital–interest rate comparison, (*d*) the belief that technical progress is the engine of growth, (*e*) the introduction of a distribution mechanism into the Harrod model, and (*f*) the rejection of the need of an explicit valuation of existing capital stock to provide the solution of the value of the rate of profits.

These points can now be analysed in the overall context of their uniqueness and consistence with the rate of profits and distribution criteria. There is little question that Kaldor has satisfied the necessity of introducing a system of distribution into his model of growth. Kaldor utilises the flexible profit margin as the mechanism that provides the redistribution of income which affects the savings ratio. As he has shown, this removes many of the rigidities of the Harrod system. The model presented is not, however, completely free from criticism,[1]

[1] For some different contemporary critiques from those that will be presented, see A. M. Moore, 'A Reformulation of the Kaldor Effect', *Economic Journal*, LXXVII (Mar. 1967); B. T. McCallum, 'The Instability of Kaldorian Models', *Oxford Economic Papers*, XXI (Mar. 1967) 56–65; and especially D. M. Nuti, 'The Degree of Monopoly in the Kaldor–Mirrlees Growth Model', *Review of Economic Studies*, XXXVI (Apr. 1969) 257–9.

Moore attempts to determine the *modus operandi* of the Kaldor price–profit adjustment mechanism, but uses a downward adjustment mechanism which in essence violates Kaldor's full-employment proof and is thus inapplicable until Moore disproves the full-employment analysis. McCallum attempts to show that the models are locally unstable, but reaches the same conclusion when the Technical Progress Function is replaced with a proper production function, thus drawing the wholly unwarranted assumption that the instability must come from the adjustment mechanism. It is interesting to note that when the neoclassical necessity for instantaneous price–profit and expectation adjustment is removed from the model (it never existed in Kaldor's formulation), local stability becomes plausible. Nuti's objection is more serious, calling consistency to question. If the model assumes under-capacity plant utilisation to take advantage of market imperfections, this for two reasons: (1) the treatment of the capital stock–rate of profit problem, and (2) the Technical Progress Function.

(i) *Capital and the rate of profit*

The problem of capital is initially the most crucial. Kaldor starts by claiming he can work his model using only the value of new investment and not be concerned with the existing capital stock. This, however, implies that the model can be developed without an explicitly defined rate of profit, i.e. net profit on the value of capital in existence. Nevertheless, constancy of the expected rate of profit on new investment is one of the conditions that must be satisfied in Kaldor's model. If the rate of profits expected on new capital results from Kaldor's assertion that it is the rate that has been experienced in the past, then this profit rate must be applicable for the entire capital stock in existence.[1] Nevertheless this does not aid in discovering what the rate of profit is. Kaldor simply maintains that if equilibrium is attained and the expected profit rate is always realised, then that is what the rate of profit is. Whether this rate is then used to value new investment in fixed capital or existing capital, the solution for determining what the rate is, is far from satisfying.

---

clashes with the obsolescence criterion, e.g. when prime costs are equal to price, profit per machine is zero and it is scrapped, implying competitive price set at marginal cost. Nuti suggests the addition of a degree of monopoly variable to the equations, but makes no attempt to analyse the consequences.

In 'A Further Note', *Review of Economic Studies*, xxxvi (Apr. 1969) 260–2, to Nuti's comment, Joan Robinson suggests a further conundrum. If there is under-capacity plant utilisation it must arise either from labour shortage or lack of effective demand. Kaldor assumes the first but does not consistently distinguish between the two, i.e. market imperfection is consistent with under-full employment. She does not view Nuti's revelation as a defect that is of damaging nature and presents a possible interpretation of a solution to the problem.

[1] Kaldor, however, maintains (in personal conversation) that there is a methodological difference between applying the expected rate to new capital and projecting forward and applying the rate to value the capital in existence. Kaldor merely maintains that they are different and it is on account of this difference that he can derive the rate of profits without reference to the existing stock, only to experience of the realisation of expectations on the existing stock. It is hard to see the rationale behind such a view. For a possible explanation, see Appendix B, pp. 203–7 below.

Kaldor seems to be saying that if the system is in equilibrium at its natural rate, one need not be concerned with the value of the existing stock or the value of the rate. This is, of course, valid unless one wants to determine how the system came to be in equilibrium and the effects that the rate of profits has on the system before or after it is in equilibrium. Most of these questions are solved by Kaldor with the concept of the Technical Progress Function. A further complication[1] results when it is realised that the rate of obsolescence depends primarily on the value of the rate of profits. The question that remains is how the system happened to fall into a particular equilibrium rate of growth and profit.[2]

(ii) *The Technical Progress Function again*

It is for the resolution of these questions that Kaldor brings the Technical Progress Function into play. Initially the function does too much. At the neutral technical progress point N, as seen above, almost all the requisites for steady equilibrium growth at the natural rate are satisfied by the very definition of that position. If N is maintained over time the rate of investment is constant, the growth of output per head is constant and the capital–output and capital–labour ratios will become constant, with a constant rate of growth and rate of profit subject to the real wage rising with output per head. Thus, if the function does not shift, it provides not only the possibility of steady paths without biased technical progress, but appears to vortex itself towards the point N, due to changing capital–output and capital–labour ratios meeting limits of labour or finance availability.

There are a number of ways in which the Technical Progress Function can be analysed. These will be dealt with later,[3] taking only Kaldor's current explanations[4] of the concept.

[1] Among others. See Nuti, op. cit.

[2] This in no way invalidates the distribution mechanism and flexibility of margins – just the fact that in Kaldor's equilibrium analysis it is never necessary to use it, thus the lack of its importance in determining a defined rate of profit and growth for the system.

[3] See Appendix B below.

[4] Conversations between the author and Professor Nicholas Kaldor, Cambridge, spring 1969.

Kaldor's most revealing published statement is that *accepting* the function 'shows the futility of regarding the movements in the . . . character of the stream of inventions – according as they are predominantly "labour-saving" or "capital-saving" in character'.[1] Indeed, this is precisely the interpretation that Kaldor places on the function. It is not to be used over time or even to interpret bias in techniques. The whole concept of technological bias is 'neo-classical' and 'so much bilge' in his view. The function is viewed by its creator in a completely macroeconomic sense and he feels that discussions on the nature of technical development are inherently useless.

Given the mony sum that is slated for investment in new capital, in any period the economy is faced with a range of new technical innovations. Those new techniques which increase output per head by the greatest amount over expenditure per head to put them into operation are the most profitable techniques to employ from the point of view of the investor. These new innovations are ranged according to their profit-ability (output per head less cost of introduction per head) in a schedule (much akin to the marginal efficiency of capital schedule) which is the Technical Progress Function. The greater the amount invested per head in new machines in any period, the further to the right the system will push along the Technical Progress Function and the less profitable will be the last technique chosen. At some point on the schedule, given no limit to investment, an innovation will be reached which does not yield enough increased output per head to meet the minimum requirement of profitability because of its high cost per head. This point will, in some sense, approximate the point of balanced return or neutral effective technical progress on balance. The idea that there is a certain type of progress that is unique and that its special property is that of neutrality is meaningless in Kaldor's opinion.

Kaldor takes a high hand with any form of classification of inventions. For him classification is illusory and at best a micro problem. In each period the system is faced with a new schedule of innovations and will always take the most profitable first no matter what the bias may be. Each new schedule faced may

[1] 'A Model of Economic Growth', op. cit., 597.

have as its most profitable technique one that requires more capital cost per increased output per head. Thus, in relation to last period it appears capital-using, but in relation to all others available in the period it is capital-saving. Hence Kaldor's contention that it is illusory and unimportant to view any stage in technical knowledge as to its bias, for it is unnecessary to think that the variety of techniques have, on net, a bias in one direction or the other. Thus Kaldor dismisses the problem of choice of technique as micro and neoclassical. It is not a question of which technique but how much or how many.

This explanation of the function is more comprehensible than Kaldor's published views, but it still raises problems. If techniques are viewed individually the approach is certainly microeconomic. The method by which the questions of how much or how many of the new techniques will be chosen is, however, still to be answered. It is possible that the first technique will be available to more than one productive unit or industry. If all investment in a particular period goes into just one innovation, there will be no move along the curve to point N. If this is viewed in a macroeconomic sense it is possible for a low investment per head technique (which could, but need not, be capital-saving in comparison with both existing and new innovations) to be consistent with a high rate of investment and rate of growth. For Kaldor's constant point to be reached, the whole range of techniques up to point N must be either adopted or passed over.

Indeed it is possible for the curve to shift up or down, yielding successive intersections at N that will generate a changing capital–labour ratio and thus changing relative shares. The solution of Kaldor's model ultimately depends on a constant value at N, over time, for the determination of the other variables (and income shares) as constants. It is theoretically possible to obtain such a case with an adequate rate of investment per period even with a shifting Technical Progress Function, but Kaldor provides no economic justification of why this possible manipulation should be a 'stylised fact' of any system. With equilibrium and N assumed, the system loses much operational significance except as a study of possible equilibrium states. Indeed the schedule concept for technical

progress is inventive, but it is not as macro as Kaldor would like
to believe and suffers from a lack of both theoretical analysis of
its operation and an adequate behavioural justification for its
foundation.[1]

In summary, although Kaldor does provide a distribution
mechanism, he does not adequately provide a determination of
the rate of profit in his most recent work. This is due, on the one
hand, to the basic equilibrium nature of his models which
allows him to ignore the problem, and on the other hand to too
great a reliance on the not fully thought-out concept of the
Technical Progress Function.

[1] Some of these questions will be taken up in more detail in Appendix B
below.

10 L. L. PASINETTI:
WHEN WORKERS SAVE

A. AN OMISSION

Kaldor's basic distributional formulae, upon which his distribution theory rests, were corrected for certain omissions in a 1962 paper[1] by Luigi Pasinetti. Pasinetti pointed out that, although Kaldor had made allowance for workers' savings in his equations, he had not extended to them the possibility of purchasing capital with their savings, nor analysed the effects of the income the workers might receive from owning assets. After making the appropriate alterations, Pasinetti concluded that Kaldor's results were valid, irrespective of the savings of workers.

B. THE KALDOR FORMULATION

Kaldor had divided total net income into wages, W, and profits, P, such that

$$Y \equiv W + P. \tag{10.1}$$

Given the savings by these two income groups, total saving in the system is

$$S = S_w + S_p. \tag{10.2}$$

If proportional savings propensities are assumed for each group so that $S_w = s_w W$ and $S_p = s_p P$, (10.2) becomes

$$S = s_w W + s_p P \tag{10.2A}$$

with the restriction that $s_w \neq s_p$ and both propensities are positive

---

[1] 'Rate of Profit and Income Distribution in Relation to the Rate of Economic Growth', *Review of Economic Studies*, XXIX (Oct. 1962) 267–79.

and less than one. The dynamic equilibrium condition is then

$$I \equiv S \tag{10.3}$$

which can be rewritten as

$$I = s_w W + s_p P = s_w Y + (s_p - s_w)P. \tag{10.4}$$

Dividing (10.4) by Y yields

$$P/Y = 1/(s_p - s_w) \, I/Y - (s_w/s_p - s_w). \tag{10.5}$$

If the savings of workers are nil, then (10.5) becomes

$$P/Y = 1/s_p \, I/Y \tag{10.6}$$

and with full classical thriftiness $(s_p = 1)$

$$P/Y = I/Y. \tag{10.7}$$

Hence Kaldor's result that the share of investment in output determines the share of profits in output subject to the thriftiness conditions.

C. THE CORRECTED SYSTEM

Pasinetti first expands (10.5), (10.6) and (10.7) to deal also with the rate of profits on capital. Dividing by K instead of Y yields

$$P/K = 1/(s_p - s_w) \, I/K - (s_w/s_p - s_w) \, Y/K, \tag{10.5A}$$

$$P/K = 1/s_p \, I/K \tag{10.6A}$$

and

$$P/K = I/K. \tag{10.7A}$$

The system is restricted to the rate of profits being constant at some positive level $(s_w < I/Y$, i.e. savings out of wages is less than the share of investment in output such that profits are positive) and a positive level of the real wage rate $(s_p > I/Y)$ subject to some acceptable lower limit of subsistence wages. The system functions through changes in prices and profit margins as demand prices exceed supply prices and cause real income to be transferred from wages to profits such that equation (10.3) is maintained at full employment.

It is at this point that Pasinetti makes his correction and raises a most interesting distributional distinction. If workers are allowed to save they must be able to purchase physical capital (or titles to physical capital). If workers save *and* own capital they will have, in addition to their wages income, income from their savings, or profits income. It is at this point that the distributional distinction between types of income (wages and profits) and income classes (workers and capitalists) must be noticed, for they are no longer identical. To analyse the problem in the class sense it is necessary to define profits as

$$P = P_c + P_w, \tag{10.8}$$

which requires that the savings relations be rewritten as $S_w = s_w(W + P_w)$ and $S_c = s_c(P_c)$, so that (10.4) now becomes

$$I = s_w(W + P_w) + s_c(P_c) = s_w Y + (s_c - s_w)P_c. \tag{10.9}$$

Thus (10.5) and (10.5A) must be rewritten as

$$P_c/Y = 1/(s_c - s_w) \ I/Y - (s_w/s_c - s_w) \tag{10.10}$$

and

$$P_c/K = 1/(s_c - s_w) \ I/K - (s_w/s_c - s_w)Y/K. \tag{10.11}$$

Equation (10.10) now becomes the relation for social distribution. The two equations (10.10) and (10.11) do not relate to total profits, P, but only capitalists' profits, P_c. Equation (10.10), as stated, does show what will be called the social distribution between workers and capitalists, but equation (10.11) has no operational meaning as it does not refer to total profits. Thus the workers' profits P_w/K must be added to the relations and $P/K = P_c/K + P_w/K$ must be determined.

If workers' savings are loaned to capitalists and a rate of return, r, is paid on these loans, then K_w is workers' capital and their earnings from capital is $r(K_w/K)$. Adding P_w/K to both sides of (10.11) yields

$$P/K = 1/(s_c - s_w) \ I/K - (s_w/s_c - s_w)Y/K + r(K_w/K). \tag{10.12}$$

If all workers' savings are given to capitalists to be invested, then in equilibrium $S_w = K_w$ and

$$S_w/S = K_w/K = s_w(Y - P_c)/I = (s_w s_c/s_c - s_w)\,Y/I - (s_w/s_c - s_w) \tag{10.13}$$

where $(Y - P_c) = (W + P_w)$. Correcting both (10.12) and (10.10) to deal with profits subject to (10.13), (10.12) becomes

$$P/K = 1/(s_c - s_w)I/K - (s_w/s_c - s_w)\,Y/K + r\left(\frac{s_w s_c}{s_c - s_w}\;Y/I - (s_w/s_c - s_w)\right) \tag{10.14}$$

and (10.10) becomes

$$P/Y = 1/(s_c - s_w)\;I/Y - (s_w/s_c - s_w)$$
$$+ r(s_w s_c/s_c - s_w)\,K/I - (s_w/s_c - s_w)K/Y. \tag{10.15}$$

These two equations ((10.14) and (10.15)) remedy the deficiencies noted above for (10.10) and (10.11) and now include workers' profits. Equation (10.14) now gives the rate of profits (replacing Kaldor's (10.5A) and equation (10.5) is now represented by (10.10), the social distribution relation, *and* (10.15), the distribution of income between total wages and total profits. The last two equations ((10.10) and (10.15)) must be recognised as two distinct types of distributional phenomena.

Equations (10.14) and (10.15) are unfortunately rather unwieldy and complex. Pasinetti is able to simplify the two equations by assuming that workers receive the ruling rate of profit on their invested savings. Thus when $r = P/K$, workers' return on savings is $(P/K)K_w = (P/K)S_w$. If r is set equal to the rate of profit, then equation (10.14) yields:

$$\frac{P}{K}\left(1 - \frac{s_w s_c}{s_c - s_w}\;\frac{Y}{I} + \frac{s_w}{s_c - s_w}\right) = \frac{1}{s_c - s_w}\frac{I}{K} - \frac{s_w}{s_c - s_w}\;\frac{Y}{K}$$

and

$$\frac{P}{K}\,s_c\,\frac{(I - s_w Y)}{I} = \frac{I - s_w Y}{K}. \tag{10.16}$$

Under the conditions postulated, that workers' savings do not constitute the entire savings invested in the whole economy, so that

$$I - s_w Y \neq 0, \tag{10.17}$$

and dividing both sides of equation (10.16) by $(I - s_w Y)$ and rearranging terms yields

$$P/K = 1/s_c \, I/K. \tag{10.18}$$

Similar manipulation on (10.15) produces

$$P/Y = 1/s_c \, I/Y. \tag{10.19}$$

If it is assumed that capitalists do not consume, i.e. $s_p = 1$, even though $s_w > 0$, equations (10.18) and (10.19) become respectively

$$P/K = I/K \tag{10.20}$$

and

$$P/Y = I/Y. \tag{10.21}$$

Thus the same results that were reached via Kaldor's scheme in (10.7) and (10.7A), that both the share and the rate of profits are determined by the share and rate of investment, have been achieved without the assumption that workers do not save. These two relations are seen to be independent of savings out of wages and totally dependent on the savings out of profits and the level of investment. Pasinetti's startling result shows that as long as $I - s_w Y \neq 0$ the savings propensity of workers has absolutely no effect on the distribution between wages and profits or on the rate of profits that the system generates.

D. BENEATH THE EQUATIONS

It must be noted, however, that the savings propensity of workers will have a very definite effect on the social distribution between workers and capitalists. Pasinetti's result is indeed startling, but the economic causes that produced his equational results must be determined. Pasinetti notes the fact that his model is predicated on an institutional principle such that wages are paid in proportion to the amount of labour provided and similarly profits are received in proportion to the amount of capital owned in the system. Thus when all savings are invested in physical capital, each group receives profits in proportion so its savings and the relation

$$P_w/S_w = P_c/S_c \tag{10.22}$$

must hold in the long run. Thus, when the workers' propensity to save is undifferentiated as to wages or profits income the source of this income will have no effect on their total consumption. The effects can be seen most clearly by looking at the difference in total savings when part of total profits is redistributed from capitalists and paid to workers as a result of the latter's saving. When workers initially save, the system's total saving is greater by $s_w W$, but the income that they receive from this saving is saved and consumed in the same proportion $(s_w P_w)$. This saving is less than the capitalists would have saved out of the same profits $(s_w P_w < s_c P_c)$ and thus total savings from profits is lower. The excess consumption from profits (in excess of what capitalists would have consumed from P_w) is offset by workers' savings out of *wages alone* in the same proportion so as to leave the total level of savings unchanged as a result of workers saving in the same proportion from *both* wages *and* profits. That is, the lower savings from profits, P_w, is offset by the savings from wages and the total saving from $P_w + W$ is unchanged. Thus the difference in consumption of profits $(1 - s_w) - (1 - s_c)P_w$ is offset by $S_w W$ which can on manipulation be written

$$\frac{P_w}{s_w(W + P_w)} = \frac{P_c}{s_c(P_c)} \qquad (10.23)$$

which is simply (10.22) with the addition of savings propensities. In general, then, when workers save and receive profits income, the income received from profits is proportional to their savings such that the system's increased consumption out of profits is offset by workers' savings out of wages such as to leave their proportion of total savings no greater than before and the total savings in the system unchanged. Thus the existence of workers' savings can have no effect on the rate of profits or the total wages–profits distribution as the capitalists still set the rate of investment and the share of investment in total output. The level of workers' savings does, however, have an effect on social distribution through its effects on the level of effective demand and pattern of prices associated with any rate of investment.

It must be stated very explicitly that Pasinetti's result depends on the same workers' propensity to save out of both wages and profits income. The relation becomes much more complex if the restriction is dropped.[1] As long as the restriction remains, the capitalists, retaining total power over the investment decision, will determine the rate of profits and therefore the profits income going to workers. The workers' propensity to save can, in Pasinetti's model, only affect the split of profits income between them and the capitalists; it cannot affect the distribution between total wages and total profits.

It should further be pointed out that the basic relation is not dependent on any assumptions about permanent social classes or permanent savers. It does strictly depend on the relation $I - s_w Y \neq 0$, that is, that workers' savings are not the whole of, or greater than, total investment carried out in the system. Moreover, the stability condition $s_c > 0$ must hold, that is, the capitalists must do some saving or the system will become explosive.

E. THE NEO-NEOCLASSICAL REACTION

At this point it is necessary to recall the criticisms that were raised by Samuelson and Modigliani[2] in relation and reaction to Pasinetti's conclusions. They claimed that Pasinetti's model was not truly general and demonstrated that there existed a point at which, if saving from wages incomes $(P_w + W)$ became high enough so as no longer to satisfy (10.17), the workers' propensity to save becomes crucial and a dual regime takes over and is a mirror of that in which the capitalists had control. This is all very true, but it is ruled out as a possible realistic case by Pasinetti, and is therefore inconsequential to the Pasinetti results. By trying to place the contentions made for the income (wages–profits) determination relation into the social (workers–

---

[1] If, due to retained earnings, wage-earners have a higher savings propensity out of their unearned income, it only serves to make the problem of balance so much the easier. It is still the case that the real value of wage incomes must accommodate itself to the available goods; when some of their potential income is saved for them it increases their income in real terms as the excess of demand over supply of consumption goods is lessened. It still does not give them a crucial role in determining the rate of profits, only the value of the total income they receive.

[2] See Chapter 6, pp. 87–95 above.

capitalists) relation, Samuelson and Modigliani hoped to disprove the wages–profits relation by making wholly acceptable if inconsequential, assertions about the social distribution relation. As was pointed out above, they are not identical relations and must be dealt with individually. The point is that the Pasinetti mechanism works, and the results hold, no matter what social class distinctions one might like to choose. The model works, not because the savings propensities are attached to different classes or income sources, but because it has its roots in the Keynesian postulate of the independency of the investment decision from decisions to save.[1]

Samuelson and Modigliani do, however, raise one question of logical consistency in the model. In order for total savings to be unchanged when workers receive profits income, workers must spend in excess of their *received* profits income if some of it is withheld by corporations as retentions.[2] This is a direct result of the single savings propensity for *both* wages and profits income on the part of the workers which was pointed out above. Again, this does not change the essential mechanism or conclusion, only the direct simplicity of the relation.[3]

In general the neo-neoclassical critics have not been mindful of the distinction drawn between the social distribution and the wage–profits relation and the determination of the rate of profits. By missing this distinction they have missed the whole point of the article: to point out that it is not the savings assumptions as such which make the model consistent, but the Keynesian basis. As Pasinetti comments:

[1] If this is not already clear, the reader will be re-exposed to this proposition in Chapter 12. Thus Samuelson and Modigliani do not seem to be directing their criticism to the main point (see section F). Even Pasinetti, who tries to make this point in his original paper, seems forced to admit in section 7 of his reply that permanent classes of income receivers are necessary. (See 'New Results in an Old Framework: Comment on Samuelson and Modigliani', *Review of Economic Studies*, XXXIII (Oct. 1966) 306.) This of course is not the case. See N. Kaldor's reply to Samuelson and Modigliani, 'Marginal Productivity and the Macro-economic Theories of Distribution: Comment on Samuelson and Modigliani', *Review of Economic Studies*, XXXIII (Oct. 1966) 310–11.

[2] Unless the retention ratio is below the workers' propensity to save.

[3] See N. Kaldor, ibid., appendix, 'A Neo-Pasinetti Theorem', 316–19.

When Mr Kaldor presented his theory of income distribution, he pointed out that the interpretative value of the
theory depends on the Keynesian hypothesis on which it is
built. In particular it depends on the crucial hypothesis . . .
that investment can be treated as an independent variable
governed by technical progress and population growth.[1]

While not all Keynesians agree on what governs the independent variable (Pasinetti included), they do all agree on its
crucial nature. *This is a basic underlying premise of all the models in
this section.*

F. PASINETTI'S PARADOXICAL
CONTRIBUTION

Pasinetti has then provided three things. He has opened the
way to the substructure of the Keynesian models and their
internal mechanisms. In doing this he has further elaborated
the dependence of these models on the assumptions with which
they work. Thirdly, and not least importantly, he has made the
very sharp distinction between two approaches to distribution,
both of which are of importance to economists. The first deals
with the functional income separation between wages and
profits and the effect of the rate of profit. It is here that the
savings propensities out of wages (and by workers), under
Pasinetti's assumptions, are irrelevant. He also deals with
social distribution in terms of social groups. In this case the
savings propensity of workers does not determine, although it
definitely can affect, the distribution of total income between
classes. It may be that the latter type of distribution is the most
important consideration in the modern context.

    Pasinetti's model is less than general on two points in particu-
lar. First, no attempt is made to deal with the problem of the
valuation of capital stock. While the rate of profits is determinate, given the stock of capital, it is of little value for predictive purposes or the analysis of technological change.
Secondly, Pasinetti does not deal with the implications of the
rate of profits on the level of the real wage. This has more effect

---

[1] 'Rate of Profit, etc.', op. cit., 279.

F

on social distribution than on the wages–profits relation and the determination of the rate of profits, as the former is concerned directly with social class income shares. Since the latter was the restricted subject of the paper, it was not unreasonable for Pasinetti to omit these points in such a short piece. Both problems could have been handled in the context of the model, but were outside the scope chosen by Pasinetti to highlight the striking results concerning the effect of saving out of wages on the wages–profits distribution and the possibility of equilibrium and profit rate determination in a system where workers save *and* own capital.

One unfortunate result of the paper (and this is no fault of Pasinetti's) is that it tended to focus discussion and criticism of the Keynesian models on the assumptions about propensities to save and the historical existence of income classes. This unfortunate reading has tended to mask the real contribution of the paper in terms of its exposing the real emphasis that the models place on investment and their Keynesian basis.

11 JOAN ROBINSON: THE RATE OF PROFIT, DISTRIBUTION AND ACCUMULATION

A. THE LONG-PERIOD AND THE GENERAL THEORY

As one of the Cambridge economists working closely with Keynes during the development of the *General Theory*, it is not surprising to find Joan Robinson among the main contributors to the extension of the Keynesian framework into the long period. In fact, Professor Robinson had developed, as early as 1936, an extension of the theory of employment to long-run considerations.[1] It was not, however, until Harrod's later work that Mrs Robinson concerned herself primarily with long-period growth, and even then she chose not only to look to an extension of the Harrod model in the context of Keynes and Kalecki, but also to delve into existing classical and neoclassical theory in search of a generalised theory of growth.[2] Her cognisance of the propositions and deficiencies of both previous approaches has led her to a thorough and broad-based analysis of the problem.

B. EASY QUESTIONS AND DIFFICULT ANSWERS

Mrs Robinson's first concerted challenge to existing theory came in a paper entitled 'The Production Function and the

[1] See especially 'The Long-Period Theory of Employment', republished in *Essays in the Theory of Employment* (London: Macmillan, 1937) 105–38. 'Unfortunately', says Mrs Robinson of the essay, 'I analysed the problem from a stationary state where net savings are zero. A very daft way to look at it'. The essay does, however, show definite seeds of her later work. All of the essays in the book provide a useful insight into the broad range of ideas brought forward by the *General Theory*, some of which took many years to bring to fruition.

[2] Again, her dissatisfaction with neoclassical theory is not new; cf. 'Indeterminacy', in *Essays in the Theory of Employment*, op. cit., 231–5.

Theory of Capital',[1] when she openly challenged the neo-classical economists to define the value of the capital term used in the production function to determine distribution via marginal productivity. By 1955 she had completed her own analysis of the problem in *The Accumulation of Capital*.[2] The book contained not only the method of analysis used later by Kaldor and Pasinetti, but also a preliminary analysis of the problem of switching of techniques and an extended treatment of the effects of technical progress. Analysis of land, rent, marginal productivity doctrine, monetary factors and an extension of the theory to international trade are also included. These latter aspects of the work have been largely overlooked. Professor Robinson's other writings on these subjects appear primarily in Parts I and II of *Collected Papers*, Volume II,[3] and her most recent views on accumulation in *Essays in the Theory of Economic Growth*.[4]

The presentation of Professor Robinson's work will come in the main from the two books and will be very basic in nature, her work being so wide-ranging and precise as to make it impossible, for the task undertaken in this study, to present more than a mere sketch of the more prominent conceptions.

The system is generically based on Keynes and Kalecki[5] and presents an analysis of long-run accumulation starting with a simple model and progressing to models of increasing complexity. The basic formulations that will be dealt with here concern (i) the income flow system, (ii) the determination of the rate of profit, (iii) the requirements for steady growth, (iv) the degree of mechanisation, (v) the measurement of capital, (vi) technical progress, (vii) technical progress, mechanisation,

[1] *Review of Economic Studies*, XXI (1953–4).

[2] *The Accumulation of Capital* (London: Macmillan, 1956).

[3] *Collected Economic Papers*, volume II (Oxford: Basil Blackwell, 1960) 59–221.

[4] *Essays in the Theory of Economic Growth* (London: Macmillan, 1962). See also 'Harrod after Twenty Years', *Economic Journal*, forthcoming, and for an additional view on switching (with K. A. Naqvi), 'The Badly Behaved Production Function', *Quarterly Journal of Economics*, LXXXI (Nov. 1967) 581–91.

[5] Although Marshall, Marx and Wicksell among others are acknowledged. There is little doubt that Rosa Luxemburg should also be included.

and relative shares, (viii) growth with neutral technical progress, (ix) transition states with biased technical progress, (x) the golden age, (xi) the effect of rentier consumption on accumulation, (xii) rent, and (xiii) the marginal product of capital and the marginal product of investment.

C. ASSUMPTIONS AND METHOD OF ANALYSIS

The basic assumptions of the simple model can be conveniently listed at this stage, noting at each stage of the analysis which have been removed or varied. The assumptions of the simple system include (1) homogeneous labour, (2) fixed composition of commodity (consumption) output, (3) blueprint (fixed coefficient) technologies, (4) tranquillity, e.g. entrepreneurs confidently expect that present rates and prices will continue in the future, (5) a closed economy with no government, and (6) long-run costs of production which are independent of the rate of output.

The economic agents in the system are workers who consume all their income, entrepreneurs who have no life or function outside the firm, and rentiers who live, save and consume from dividends, rent and fixed interest obligations. The analysis is, when possible, carried out in terms of movement within one economy.

Mrs Robinson makes it clear that it is highly misleading to draw any theoretical or policy conclusions from this approach. Thus a majority of the analysis deals with comparisons between two economic systems, each with its own historical past and its own expectations of the future. In this way the effects of actions that accumulate through time can be kept consistently in mind and analysed.[1] This aids in isolating the effects of different variables in the system and is one of Mrs Robinson's major concerns throughout her work. Mrs Robinson justifies this approach by noting: 'Our chief concern is with the relation between wages and profits, and the argument is conducted in

---

[1] 'Time is a device to prevent everything from happening at once' (Bergson). Quoted on the title page on *Essays in the Theory of Economic Growth*, op. cit.

terms of (1) the relations of the stock of capital to the available labour force, (2) the influence of competition, and (3) the techniques of production'.[1]

D. THE ROBINSON APPROACH TO ACCUMULATION

(i) *The income flow system*

The economic system is divided into two sectors. One sector produces capital goods for replacement and expansion of its own capital goods and for replacement and expansion of the other sector which produces goods solely for consumption by labour. The sales value of the output of the consumption sector[2] will be equal to the wage bill paid in the consumption sector (cost of production of consumable output) plus the wage bill paid in the investment sector, since all wages paid to labour will be exercised as effective demand over the available consumption output. The money prime costs of production for the output of the consumption sector are equal to the wage bill paid for its production. The excess of sales value of output over prime costs of output in the consumption sector (quasi-rents) is then equal to the wages bill in the capital sector. The ratio of the wages bill (or employment when the money wage rates are the same in both sectors) in the capital sector to the wages bill in the consumption sector sets the ratio of quasi-rents to wages bill (or quasi-rents per man) in the consumption sector.[3] Accordingly, profit margins and prices are determined for consumption output and are seen to depend on the level of activity in the investment sector (the ratio of investment to total resources available in the system given the technique of

[1] *The Accumulation of Capital*, op. cit., 10.

[2] Ignoring rentiers. The model is initially worked through with the assumption that workers do not save, and ignoring rentiers prohibits any consumption out of profits. The effects of lifting this assumption will be dealt with below.

[3] It is of course not possible to make a precise distinction between the two sectors or simply to equate investment with the capital sector; investment in working capital, etc., in the consumption sector will cause crossover problems. However, if these variables are constant the analysis can be carried through with the broad groupings outlined.

production). To purchase the output of the capital sector, on the other hand, a purchaser will have to pay the wages cost of the item plus a notional profit-margin on the finance committed to its production from its inception to the time of sale. This notional profit margin provides quasi-rent which must be equal to that which could be earned by applying the finance in any other line of production, including the production of consumption goods.

The quasi-rents in the consumption sector are thus available to purchase replacement and new capital goods from the investment sector. Total profits in the sector less depreciation are then equal to the increment of new capital goods in the consumption sector or net profits. In the capital sector net profits are equal to the output of new capital less replacements in that sector. Then total profit in the system exceeds the profits in the consumption sector by the value of the increment of new capital produced less purchases of capital goods by the consumption sector and the capital sector's own replacement. The ratio of total profits to the value of existing capital used in production is the rate of profits for the system and for each sector.[1]

(ii) *The determination of the rate of profit*

The income flow system can be used to demonstrate the determination of the level of the rate of profits and its effect on distribution. Given the money wage, the available labour force and a single technique of production, if entrepreneurs had chosen a higher level of investment then a greater proportion of the labour force would have to have been employed to produce non-consumable output. The ratio of the wages bill in the capital sector to the wages bill in the consumption sector would have been higher and thus consumption sector quasi-rents would have been higher. The total profits would

---

[1] For an equational representation of the model, see P. Davidson, *Theories of Aggregate Income Distribution* (New Brunswick, N.J.: Rutgers University Press, 1960) 71–82. Note that equation (3), 73, should read $Q_c = W_I$, not $Q_c = Q_I$ as printed. See also G. Gandolfo, 'Some Critical Remarks on J. Robinson's Growth Model', *Revista di Politica Economica*, LVII (Feb. 1967).

then be greater and the increase in capital larger. At the same time, with a given money wage rate, real wages would have been lower as profits (and prices and margins) were higher.

This very simple comparison illustrates the effects of investment on the level of profits and the distribution of income between wages and profits. If the comparison had been viewed as a comparison between two systems, one with the higher and the other the lower ratio of investment to total output for a given level of resources, then it could also be unequivocally stated that the rate of profit would be higher in the former system. The main initial difference in the comparison was the rate of investment. The rate of investment, in Mrs Robinson's view, will determine the rate of profits, prices, margins, real wages, and thus distribution.

This is a very simplistic explanation of the system. There are upper and lower limits to the values of real wages and the rate of profits. If the rate of investment becomes too high, so as to force the level of real wages below the level at which labour is willing to work, the system becomes untenable. Either production stops entirely or labour demands a higher money wage which sets off a wages–profits inflationary spiral. This results in the lower limit to real wages which Mrs Robinson calls the inflation barrier. Technical progress which increases output per head, or an increase in the available labour force, will affect the rate of investment and accumulation at which the inflation barrier becomes operative. When technical progress raises the real wage by raising output per head, it will offset the decrease in the real wage from a higher rate of investment thus allowing a higher investment rate inside the inflation barrier. Likewise, an increase in the growth of the available labour force, if fully employed, will allow a higher rate of accumulation with a given level of real wages.

The other limit to the rate of accumulation, in Mrs Robinson's system, is the rate of profits. The return that results from a given rate of investment must at least meet some required minimum rate of profits. If the expected rate of profits is too low, or if the expected increase in the rate of profits from increasing the rate of investment is not enough to offset increased risk, investment will not be expanded. The investment relation is double-edged. The rate of profits must be sufficient to justify increasing investment, but unless there is investment the rate of profits will be insufficient to justify investment. Technical progress and increasing size of the labour force will also affect this condition, as will become apparent below.

The analysis thus far has not included rentiers and thus the system resembles von Neumann's in that all profits have been automatically invested by entrepreneurs. Under these assumptions it is only necessary for workers in the consumption sector to be productive enough to produce a surplus over their own needs to meet the consumption needs of investment workers. Since the entrepreneurs have no life capacity, the rate of profit, when total profits are fully invested, is equal to the rate of capital accumulation or the rate of growth at the given technique.

Once consumption out of profits is introduced, however, an additional money demand is placed on the amount of available consumable output. Consumption goods must now be shared out among workers in the consumption sector, workers in the investment sector *and rentiers*. Accordingly, the higher the level of consumption spending out of profits income, the higher will be the pattern of prices and margins relative to the money wage rate. If the overall rate of profits is to be kept equal with the higher profits of the consumption sector, then margins in the investment sector must increase so that the rate of profits is equal and higher in both sectors. Margins are now determined by the ratio of the investment wage bill plus consumption spending out of profits to the wage bill in the consumption sector. The existence of rentier consumption, therefore, breaks down the simple equality between the rate of profits and the rate of growth of the system. The rate of profits remains unchanged when some profits are spent on consumption, but the rate of growth falls because a smaller proportion of total profits are now being invested. The existence of consumption expenditure out of profits also affects income distribution by lowering the real wage attainable for any given rate of investment and hence brings the inflation barrier so much the closer. Thus the distributional system will serve to accommodate any rate of investment and spending from profits within the inflation barrier by transferring real income from wages to profits, such that savings from profits will balance investment.

In sum, the determinants that have come into play in the Robinsonian system thus far are (1) the technique of production, (2) thriftiness of profit recipients, (3) growth of the labour force, (4) investment expenditure, (5) money wage relations, (6) the existing stock of capital and entrepreneurial expectations, and (7) competitive conditions.

(iii) *The requirements for steady growth*

If there is only one technique of production available to the system, as has been assumed thus far, then steady growth of the economy will require that the production of machines is geared to the availability of labour to man them. Thus the rate of accumulation of capital cannot exceed the rate of growth of the labour force. Moreover, if there is no spending out of profits in the system, then the rate of profits must be equal to the rate of growth of capital, which is in turn equal to the rate of growth of the labour force; and the relative size of the capital sector and consumption sector is dependent on the technique of production. When spending out of profits by rentiers is present in the system, the rate of profit and the rate of growth are no longer equal as the rate of investment is reduced when the total of profits is no longer used for investment but consumed. Nevertheless, this will not affect the level of the rate of profits.

(iv) *Technical change: the degree of mechanisation*

The existence of technical progress will cause changes in techniques of production that will alter the output per head of a constant labour force employed. This will affect the attainable rate of growth and the proximity of the inflation barrier. While the introduction of technical progress greatly increases the scope of the pattern of growth, it also adds much to its complexity.

Mrs Robinson views technical change as occurring in two possible ways: (*a*) changes in the state of technology or the spectra of techniques available, and (*b*) changes in the technique employed from those available within any spectrum of technology existing at a point in time. Different techniques within a spectrum are chosen in relation to their profitability at different levels of the real wage (or in connection with the scarcity or abundance of labour or finance). It is possible to speak of the nature of technical progress in relation to (*a*), but this distinction must be carefully analysed with respect to (*b*), where there may be differences in the capital–labour ratio which are also associated with differences in the rate of profits and real wages.

(*a*) *Technical progress – changing spectra.* Technical progress can be viewed as an increase in output per head over *all* available processes of production, whether or not they are chosen for use. Hence, equipping a constant labour force with a more productive technique from a new spectrum of available techniques has the same effect on total output as equipping an expanding labour force with machines of unchanged technique. In both cases, however, the rate of investment must match the common rate of increase in output. In the constant labour supply case, real wages must rise in step with productivity to provide the purchasing power required to purchase the increased output. With a growing labour force a constant real wage will match the increase in output to the growing total purchasing power of total wages. If this stability between increasing output per head and purchasing power is to be maintained, technical progress must occur simultaneously in all sectors, the rate of investment cannot be allowed to lag, the increase in real wages for the constant labour force case must be unimpeded, and there cannot be inordinately large increases in output per head. All these factors relate to securing both the necessary investment and increase in real wages to assure that the increase in output from technical progress will be sold, and that a smooth absorption of technical progress is possible.

(*b*) *Change in technique – within a spectrum.* It is also possible for shifts to occur in the technique chosen from the list of available techniques that make up a spectrum of technical knowledge. At any point in time an entrepreneur is faced with a choice among a number of possible techniques of production within the spectrum of techniques with which to replace old plant or to be embodied in new plant to expand output. His object will be to choose the technique which will yield the highest surplus over cost, given the price of output, money wage and the cost of capital. Each technique available requires different amounts of labour, work in progress, and cost of physical machinery. Given the price of output and the money wage per man, techniques that produce higher output per man will yield higher profits per man employed. When techniques have predetermined ratios of labour to machinery, then, in general, higher output per head is associated with more capital per man, at given prices for capital, labour and output. Techniques which require greater capital per man will be viewed as having a higher degree of mechanisation. Thus techniques of a higher degree of mechanisation will give higher profit per man but only at an increased cost of capital per man. The entrepreneur must decide which degree of mechanisation to choose. This decision will depend on the money wage he must pay and the rate of profits ruling. With a given amount of funds available for investment, a technique of a higher degree of mechanisation will require less labour and produce a smaller total output.[1] The decision will thus depend on the difference between the reduced wages bill and the reduced total revenue from decreased output. If the technique with a higher degree of mechanisation reduces wages cost by more than the reduction in total proceeds from the lower total output, it is preferable, at that wage and price level, to techniques of a lower degree of mechanisation. The profit per man working on the more mechanised technique is higher when a given amount of funds is available for investment. A technique of higher mechanisation is no longer more profitable when the loss in total revenue exceeds the savings on the wages bill.

As the wage–profits distribution changes, a higher wage per man will require a higher increase in output per man to offset it in order to make higher degrees of mechanisation more

[1] Given two feasible, competing techniques of differing levels of mechanisation, if the same money sum were available for investment the technique of higher mechanisation will employ less labour, but produce a higher output per head. Total output for the more mechanised technique must be less, for if the less mechanised technique, requiring more labour and thus a larger wages bill, produced a smaller output it would not be a feasible technique in the first place.

profitable. In general, over different phases of technical development, 'On each spectrum a lower rate of profit is associated with a higher degree of mechanisation (ruling out perverse cases)'.[1]

(*c*) *Perverse cases: the problem of switching.* Within the analysis of changes in the degree of mechanisation of technique, exceptions to the relations between the rate of profits and the degree of mechanisation must be noted. What are the 'perverse' cases that must be ruled out for the general relation to hold? Up to this point the problem of valuation of plant at different levels of mechanisation has been ignored. It is necessary for the cost of plant for each technique to be calculated, if profitability is to be determined. So far, however, only the difference between output per man and wage per man at different levels of mechanisation has been discussed. Nevertheless the overall rate of profit must enter into the valuation of plant and equipment needed for differing levels of mechanisation. The cost of an outfit of capital goods will depend, not only on the wages cost of its construction, but also on the commitment of finance to the project in terms of materials and wage payments from the inception of the project to the time it starts producing saleable output. Thus both the rate of profits and the real wage rate will affect the cost of the capital necessary for any given technique by changing the relative weights of the wage component and the return to committed finance.

By applying his capital to the production of a machine, the entrepreneur will require the ruling rate of profit on the total funds he commits, for this is the return he could get by investing them in some alternative line. Thus the higher the rate of profit the higher will be this component of construction cost. Likewise with a higher profit the real cost of the labour component will be lower with lower real wages. Thus, in order for a choice of technique decision to be taken, the rate of profit must be known and confidently expected to continue in the future. In addition to the finance committed over the construction period, account must be taken of the speed of recovery of this finance. Some amount of finance will be locked into the machine until it is

---

[1] *The Accumulation of Capital*, op. cit., 133.

fully amortised. The total sum committed at any point in time will fall, however, as quasi-rents are earned and the amortisation fund increases. Thus, in estimating cost of production, a notional rate of return must be calculated on the amount of finance committed less amortisation over each time unit of productive life until the principal sum is recovered.

If the amortisation fund can be invested and earn the ruling rate of profit, then the amortisation fund will increase at an increasing rate over time until obsolescence. The difference between the portion of finance committed (total construction cost) over the life of the capital good plus its compound interest (at the ruling rate of profit), and the amortisation fund plus interest (at the same rate), will be the required notional return that must be added to the cost of capital. Since the initial commitment of finance (construction cost) falls slowly and the amortisation fund only becomes large late in plant life, the process of compounding interest on both sums will cause the total on the former to exceed the latter.[1] Thus the average commitment of finance to any capital good is something over half its initial construction cost, becoming greater the longer the life of the plant, the higher the rate of profit, and if there is a difference between the ruling rate of profit and the interest received from the investment of the amortisation fund.[2] Thus the elements of cost of a new technique will include (a) labour time, (b) the rate of return of the total finance committed over the construction period, and (c) the rate of return on the commitment over the operating life of the machine. Differing rates of profits and real wages will thus affect all the components of the total cost of a technique of a given degree of mechanisation.

---

[1] Thus the proportion of total finance committed starts from unity and falls to zero at the scrap date. Conversely the amortisation fund starts from zero and rises to unity. When the ruling rate of profit is applied to both streams, the total value of the former will exceed the latter, for the rate of interest on the initially large finance terms is $(1+r)^n$ whereas the larger amortisation figures have only a few years' compounding. The difference between the two streams is then the notional finance commitment.

[2] For a mathematical statement of this proposition, see R. F. Kahn and D. G. Champernowne, 'The Value of Invested Capital', in an appendix to *The Accumulation of Capital*, op. cit., 429–35.

Recalling the general relation that a higher wage rate would be associated with a higher degree of mechanisation, it is possible that if the technique of lower mechanisation has a longer life or a longer construction period, its reaction to a changed rate of profit will be greater. In such a case it may be possible that the reduced wages cost from a more mechanised technique will be more than offset by the reduction in cost (from the reduced rate of profit) of the less mechanised technique such that its cost per head is lower in a greater proportion than its profit per head is less. Normally the more mechanised technique will be chosen at lower rates of profit, but when a lower rate of profit reduces the cost per head of a lower mechanised technique by more than the technique of higher mechanisation increases profit per head, it is the lower and not the higher degree of mechanisation that is most profitable. Hence the perverse cases and the exception to the normal relation.

This relation Mrs Robinson credits to Miss Ruth Cohen[1] and calls 'A Curiosum'. This perverse possibility, the denial of the 'rate of profits being a monotonically declining function of the capital–labour ratio', is simply the same relation as exposed by Sraffa, and its relation to the double-switching controversy is apparent. It is also apparent that Mrs Robinson did not attach, in 1955, the importance to this perverse case that it has lately achieved.[2] It can also be recognised as one of the chief arguments used above[3] to dispute the results obtained from neo-classical production function analysis.

---

[1] This, says Mrs Robinson, is a private joke. See 'Capital Theory up to Date', *Canadian Journal of Economics*, III (July 1970) 309. Miss Cohen is University Lecturer in Economics and Principal of Newnham College, Cambridge.

[2] See *The Accumulation of Capital*, op. cit., 109, n. 1. For her most recent view, see 'Capital Theory up to Date', op. cit., and 'The Measurement of Capital: The End of the Controversy', paper presented to the Second World Congress of the Econometric Society, Cambridge, 11 Sep. 1970, mimeo.

For a view of these relations by a learned practitioner of production functions, see Murray Brown, 'Substitution-Composition Effects, Capital Intensity Uniqueness and Growth', *Economic Journal*, LXXIX (June 1969) 334–47.

[3] See Chapter 2, sections 2 and 3, esp. pp. 18–47, and Chapters 3–6.

(v) *The measurement of capital*

The problem of changing degrees of mechanisation raises
another problem that has thus far been avoided, namely the
valuation of the existing capital stock. One of the initial
questions Mrs Robinson asked of the neoclassical theory was
how the term 'capital' was measured in the production function.
She argues that the quantity of capital has no meaning until the
rate of profits has been determined. Thus using the quantity of
capital to determine the rate of profits is to argue in a circle.
The analysis of section (iv), on the other hand, has shown that
the value of the rate of profits will have an effect in determining
the cost of any particular outfit of capital goods. Thus, if there
are capital goods in existence that have been produced under
differing rates of profit, they will have different values, even
though they may have the same physical characteristics. Thus
it is not possible to make comparisons of different points of time
within a single economy or compare different economies when
they have differing levels of real wages and rates of profits.
Concerning this problem Mrs Robinson comments:

> Indeed, in reality it is insoluble in principle, for the compo-
> sition of output, the characteristics of men employed and
> techniques in use are all different in any two positions, and
> in any position the stock of capital goods in existence is not
> that which is appropriate to the conditions obtaining in that
> position, but is made up of fossils representing the phases of
> development through which the economy has been passing.
> The historic cost of existing equipment is out of gear with its
> value based on expected future earnings, and that value is
> clouded by the uncertainty that hangs over the future. Only
> the roughest kind of measurement can be made in actual
> cases.[1]

The entire problem of valuing output then boils down to,
given the assumption of the constant goods basket of consumption commodities, the measurement of the capital stock and its
accretion when profit rates, wages, and thus techniques, differ.
Mrs Robinson puts forward four possible methods of measure-

----

[1] *The Accumulation of Capital*, op. cit., 117.

ment for capital: (1) in terms of physical quantities of capital goods; (2) in terms of physical productive capacity; (3) value in terms of commodities (or in money with a given purchasing power); and (4) in terms of labour time embodied in production. Methods (1) and (2) are limited by their physical nature. The first is consistent only if capital goods are similar item by item. If techniques are different, capital will not be near enough similar, and if rates of accumulation are different the age composition of the capital stock will not be the same. For the second method to be utilised, a balanced composition of the capital stock is also necessary for comparison. Different techniques ruling in different economies will show a consistent difference in productive capacity even if both economies are growing at the same rate. This comparison, however, requires a precise difference in rentier consumption such that different rates of profits can exist at similar rates of growth. Even if this condition is fulfilled the composition of output may be different and exact comparison can only be made in the unlikely case of zero accumulation.

The last two measures of capital have more promise. There are three possible ways to approach the measurement in terms of commodities: (*a*) selling price of a productive unit, (*b*) the future profit stream of the productive unit discounted at the rate of profits, and (*c*) the costs incurred in constructing the productive unit, accumulated over its life less any profit up to the time of measurement. In steady, equilibrium growth at the natural rate all three come to the same thing, for in such a case (i) prices are constant over time, (ii) the rate of profits is constant over time, and (iii) real wages are constant over time. Thus in two systems satisfying these conditions capital per man can be compared as the value of capital within each system is comparable. Such a comparison will show the relative utilisation of capital and labour as between the two economies, but it does not give realistic comparisons of relative productive capacity. If the two economies are in a position where their techniques of production are similar but they are at a transitional wage rate (i.e. at a level of the real wage where two different techniques are equally profitable and a movement of the wage markedly up or down is required for one or the other technique to become absolutely the most profitable), then even with physically similar machines the wage costs and notional interest costs on their finance may be different even though they may be of equal value in terms of commodities.

Going one step further, by dividing the value of capital in terms of commodities by the commodity wage rate will yield a measure of value in terms of labour time. This ratio provides the fourth measure of capital which Mrs Robinson considers the most significant, for she considers the expenditure and application over time of labour effort as the essence of the production process. This measure, however, runs into the same problems as Sraffa's reduction to dated labour.[1] In both cases it is impossible to value capital completely in terms of labour without having some means of production left to work with labour. In the simple case this is the wage fund. Thus two machines requiring exactly the same amount of labour time, irrespective of differences in the wage rate, with the same time pattern of production, will have different values as the notional rate of profits on the wages fund is different.

Consequently none of the four measures is ideal and Mrs Robinson concludes that it is impossible to measure capital consistently apart from the rate of profits. Only if the rate of profits is constant within a system or equal across systems can realistic comparisons of capital stocks be made. For situations when these conditions are not met Mrs Robinson chooses to use an amalgam measure: the real-capital ratio. This is defined as: 'The ratio of capital reckoned in terms of labour time to the amount of labour currently employed when it is working at normal capacity we call the *real-capital ratio*, for this corresponds most closely to the conception of capital as a technical factor of production'.[2]

When an economy is growing in full-employment equilibrium with productive capacity increasing in line with the increase in the labour force, capital per man in terms of commodities rises as the real wage rises with increasing output per head; capital (in terms of commodities) per unit of output remains constant; and the real-capital ratio (the commodity

---

[1] See Chapter 2, section 2, pp. 18–31.
[2] *The Accumulation of Capital*, op. cit., 123.

value of capital per the commodity wage rate all divided by
the current employment of labour) will thus be constant.

Taking two economies in steady, equilibrium growth, this
measure will then provide a means of comparison when
different wage rates or different degrees of mechanisation are
ruling in the two systems, where the latter implies differences in
both the rate of profits and the real wage. It will also allow the
problem of differing shares in total output to be analysed when
differences occur in rates, techniques and technical progress.
The real-capital ratio is thus an aid in measuring and comparing
existing stocks of capital, but it is not a cure-all.

(vi) *Technical progress: changing spectra*

The concepts of neutral and biased technical progress in Mrs
Robinson's scheme can only be applied to shifts in the state of
the arts or in the spectrum of available degrees of mechanisation
associated with a given spectrum. A new technique from a new
phase of innovations (a new spectrum) is neutral, as compared
to the old technique, if its real-capital ratio is unchanged but
output is greater with the same expected physical life. Looking
at the problem in terms of the two sectors of production, an
improvement is neutral if it raises output per head in both the
capital and consumption sectors equally. That is, the increase in
productive capacity produced per head in the capital sector is
equal to the increase in output of commodities per head in the
consumption sector producing with the new equipment.

Capital-saving improvements are then defined as improvements which lower the real-capital ratio or raise output per head
in the capital sector more than in the consumption sector.
Capital-using bias, on the other hand, increases the real-capital
ratio and raises the labour time per unit of capacity in the
capital sector by a greater amount than in the consumption
sector.

An improvement in technique is said to be superior when it
increases output per head both per man and per unit in terms
of labour time. Neutral improvements will always satisfy this
criterion, but biased changes, if of large enough degree, can
offer changes in output per plant and per man in opposite
directions. Thus if savings in capital cost reduce output per

head the technique will only be used if the savings in cost of plant more than offset the reduced revenue. With these classifications in hand it is possible to make comparisons between growing systems to analyse the effect of different states of the arts (spectra of techniques), degrees of mechanisation, and rates of profit on the system's growth paths and relative shares.

(vii) *Progress, mechanisation and relative shares*

All the major concepts and variables used by Mrs Robinson in the analysis of economic growth have now been presented. Mrs Robinson applies these concepts to investigate systems exhibiting differences and similarities in their make-up and to analyse the effects of the differences in internal values of these variables.

For example, take two economies on differing spectra of techniques but where both techniques used are of neutral bias. The real-capital ratios of the two systems will be the same and the rates of profit will be equal when both are at the same degree of mechanisation within their respective spectra. In this case the real wage will be higher in the economy with the more advanced technology by the same proportion as output her head is higher from using the advanced technique. This is a necessary condition, for if the additional output per head is to be purchased the real wage must rise with productivity to keep demand sufficient to maintain the rate of profit. The value, in terms of output, of the more productive capital in the advanced technique economy is also higher in the same proportion as real wages are higher and thus the shares of capital and labour in both systems are the same, but the labour force in the advanced system benefits from the technically advanced conditions.

Similar conclusions cannot be drawn, however, if the two economies are at different levels of mechanisation across neutral spectra of technique. In such a case profit rates will be different and will influence the notional rate of return in the value of capital. Thus it would not be possible to compare real-capital ratios or make statements about relative shares. Nevertheless, it will be true that wages in the advanced system must be higher because (*a*) the spectrum that it faces is superior and neutral, and (*b*) since the rate of profit will be lower if the level of mechanisation is higher in the advanced system. Thus wages will be higher by more than in proportion to the differing output per head from a superior neutral spectrum by reason of the higher degree of mechanisation. This higher level of mechanisation in the advanced system will also cause the amount of labour per unit of output to be less, so the labour share cannot be said to be higher. Neither can the real-capital ratio be defined, for at a lower rate of profit (unless it is known how much lower) there is a lower rate of profit compounded over the cost of labour time. This particular case exposes the crucial nature of the rate of profits in growth through its effects on the level of mechanisation chosen and the statements that can be made about systems when profit rates differ. From the viewpoint of analysis, differences in the degree of mechanisation caused by differing rates of profit cause much more difficulty than bias across spectra of techniques.

As an alternate example, if two systems are viewed with equal rates of profit and each facing a different spectrum, but it is also assumed that the system with the more advanced technology has a lower real-capital ratio, there is a case of capital-saving bias between spectra.[1] If the bias is truly superior, then output per head is higher while the wage is higher than in proportion to the less advanced technique, because (*a*) the superior technique raises output her head and thus necessitates that the wage is at least raised in proportion to the productivity, and (*b*) the real-capital ratio is lower due to the bias and thus capital per unit of output is lower. With an unchanged rate of profit and higher real wages, the share of wages in the value of output will be higher and the value of capital lower. Again, it should be noted that these comparisons can only be made when the rates of profits are equal and therefore both economies exist on the same degree of mechanisation within the respective spectra they face.

(viii) *Growth with neutral progress*
Having looked at the possibilities for comparing different systems at different stages in technical knowledge, it is necessary

---

[1] This case is simpler, but essentially the mirror of capital-using bias.

to determine the effects of technical progress within a growing equilibrium system. If the existence of technical progress tends to cause disequilibrium it will throw doubt on the validity of the comparisons that have been made between growing systems. For a system to exist in equilibrium conditions of expansion, with a constant rate of profits, it must be able to absorb technical progress. If technical progress is neutral the shift from one spectrum of techniques to another will leave the real-capital ratio constant, raise output per head in both sectors equally and thus leave their relative proportions and relative shares in output unchanged with the rate of profits constant and real wages rising in step with increasing output per head due to the new techniques. Thus it is technically possible for a system to undergo neutral technical progress over time without dislodging its equilibrium relationships. The actual process of the introduction of plants of a higher level of technique is, however, quite intricate and requires a substantial movement through time and co-ordination between the capital and consumption sectors to achieve the full changeover from a lower to a higher technique stock of plant. Expectations will also be of a precise nature. The more detailed movements in such a change are spelled out in the first section of Appendix C which deals with problems of transition in general when there is a change in the spectrum of techniques faced by an economic system.

(ix) *Biased technical progress and growth*
In the case of neutral technical progress there was no tendency for the introduction of more advanced techniques to dislodge the equilibrium relations of the system. This occurred because neutral progress does not affect the value of the real-capital ratio, leaving shares in output and the rate of profits unchanged. With biased technical progress, on the other hand, the value of capital and productive capacity in the two sectors changes at unequal rates and thus neither the real-capital ratio nor the rate of profits will remain constant in the face of capital-saving or capital-using bias. The relative shares in output then may also change. It is possible, however, to have semi-equilibrium conditions (rate of profit constant but shares changing, etc.) with non-neutral changes in techniques. Transition mechanisms

between spectra become more complex than those involved
with neutral progress and thus this too is dealt with in Appendix
C.

(x) *The concept of a golden age*

For any growing economic system the maximum attainable
rate of accumulation is limited by the rate of increase of the
labour force and the rate at which technical progress is increasing productivity per man. An economy that is growing at this
maximum attainable rate with a constant rate of profit is said
to be, in Mrs Robinson's terminology, in a *golden age*. A true
golden age additionally requires that relative shares of capital
and labour in output are constant (technical progress is not
biased) and the existing capital stock is compatible with the
division of output between the two sectors. A system satisfying
these conditions is then achieving the golden age rate of
accumulation. If the rate of profit in a system is constant but
bias in technical progress causes changing relative shares,[1]
the system is said to be in a quasi-golden age.[2] When the rate of
investment is not constant or technical progress is biased but not
consistently so, a golden age is impossible to attain. Prices,
profit margins and the rate of profits will all be changing and
the precise valuation of the capital stock becomes impossible as
equipment which was built under a given rate of profit and
expectations will exist in a time when these conditions no
longer prevail. In such cases even the rate of profit becomes
non-determinate. Income shares cease to have precise meaning
and the reactions of labour and entrepreneurial 'animal spirits'
may be disappointed by unfulfilled expectation of prediction.
It is thus easy to see why Mrs Robinson emphasises that a
golden age 'represents a mythical state of affairs not likely to
obtain in any actual economy'.[3]

The analysis up to this point has been based on the assumptions that there is no spending out of profits income or savings
from wages. The labour force has been held constant through-

---

[1] See Appendix C, section 2.
[2] For a review of the possible different types of quasi-golden ages, see
Essays in the Theory of Economic Growth, op. cit., 52–9.
[3] *The Accumulation of Capital*, op. cit., 99.

out the simple presentation of the effects of technical progress. This has been done to isolate changes in output per head rather than combining it with the analysis of growth through an increasing labour force. In addition, to simplify the valuation of output and the capital stock the composition of the consumption basket has been held constant. The rudimentary exposition of Mrs Robinson's system, giving the initial assumptions, is now complete. The following sections will deal with the relaxation of some of the more crucial assumptions.

(xi) *The effect of rentier consumption on accumulation*

The introduction of rentiers will bring some, though not crucial, changes into Mrs Robinson's system. The life functions of the entrepreneur are seen in his role as rentier, the recipient of interest, rents, dividends or profits from individually owned firms. The effects of spending out of profits on the level of margins, prices and the rate of profits has already been noted. It is because of spending out of profits that the relationship between the rate of growth and the rate of profits is no longer one of equality. The effect of rentier spending comes at the expense of the real wage of employed labour, for the available consumption output must be shared with rentiers as well as among the labour force.

In terms of a golden age, rentier consumption also must be of a very precise nature to preserve tranquillity. Thus the proportion of the constant relative share of profit in a golden age that is consumed must be constant to preserve the constant rate of profits. Rentier consumption will then grow at the same rate as total output. For this to occur, the dividend pay-outs by firms must be a more or less constant proportion of net profits and the proportion of these dividends used for consumption must be stable. As will be pointed out in more detail in the next chapter, the value of savings out of dividends plus retained earnings plus any workers' savings must be equal to the value of investment. In addition the borrowings from rentiers by firms to finance investment purchases must be a constant proportion of total investment so that interest payments to rentiers rise by a constant per cent per unit of time. This is achieved with a constant rate of interest. Thus as long as rentier consumption is a constant portion of the share of profits, which is itself a constant proportion of total output, the amount of purchasing power exercised over consumption goods will increase at the same rate as the output of consumption goods is increasing, and hence the rate of profits will remain constant.

The nature of payment of rentier income will tend to complicate the process of transition associated with technical progress. The fact that dividends are seldom paid out and spent until well after they accrue to the firm will put a lag into the growth of rentier incomes. Fixed interest and other contractual payments will not immediately alter with price changes and thus cause changes in rentier real income. These aspects will temper and complicate transitions, as rentier income and thus consumption spending out of non-wage income may be out of phase with the actual conditions of the economy.

(xii) *Land, rent and marginal productivity*

Mrs Robinson's study also covers the effects of the inclusion of land as a scarce factor of production earning rent. When land is considered, a trade-off arises between techniques which are either land or labour-intensive. The existence of rent will effect the level of real wages by giving an additional income to rentiers and thus additional purchasing power over commodities. In so far as this will affect the proximity of the inflation barrier it will also affect the attainable rate of accumulation. As far as entrepreneurs are concerned, payment of rent has little effect on aggregate profits, for if the majority of rent out-payments are used for consumption then profit margins and prices are increased (having the same effect as non-wage consumption) and the entrepreneurs get back in higher prices much of what they pay out as rent. Thus, when the existence of rent affects the rate of profits, the main burden is upon wage recipients. The level of rents, then, has an effect on real wages and thus may affect the choice of technique. Rent payments, in Mrs Robinson's view,[1] are seen as a charge on the economic system that is not in the least related to increasing productivity, but will, through the effect on the inflation barrier, limit the rate at which society may accumulate.

[1] Much like Ricardo's view of rents in this case.

An outgrowth of Professor Robinson's analysis of the role of land is the relation of marginal products to income shares. Mrs Robinson rejects the neoclassical direct relation between factor marginal productivities and distribution although maintaining the concept in the slightly different sense of factor utilisation. The marginal product of labour, however, is not equal to the real wage when the wage fund is considered. Entrepreneurs will require a rate of return equal to the ruling rate of profit on finance used to pay labour wages in advance of the sale of output that they are being paid to produce. When this charge on the wage fund is recognised,[1] the marginal products cannot fall short of the wage *plus* interest on the wage and it is thus not possible for labour to be paid a wage equal to its marginal addition to product.

As for the return to capital, Mrs Robinson has demonstrated that the value of capital has no meaning apart from knowing the rate of profits. Thus it is logically inconsistent to argue that the rate of profits is determined by the marginal product of capital when the rate of profit must be known to determine the capital value initially.

(xiii) *The marginal product of capital and investment*

The only precise use that Mrs Robinson can find in marginal analysis is the concept of the marginal product of investment. This concept can be viewed in terms of returns to investment required to shift to a higher level of mechanisation.

Given the level of real wages and the rate of profit, an economy will increase the degree of mechanisation if it is

---

[1] This point was recognised at least as early as Adam Smith in *The Wealth of Nations*: 'He [the capitalist] would have no interest in employing the workers, unless he expected from the sale of their work something more than is necessary to replace the stock advanced by him as wages; and he would have no *interest* in employing a great stock rather than a small one unless his profit were to bear some proportion to the extent of the stock employed'. Quoted in Karl Marx, *Economic and Philosophic Manuscripts of 1844* (Moscow: Foreign Languages Publishing House, 1961) 37. Marx follows the quotation by saying: 'The capitalist thus makes a profit, first, on the wages, and secondly on the raw materials advanced by him'. Ibid., 37. It is precisely this point, which the neoclassical reaction to Marx ignored, that breaks the wage–marginal productivity relation.

profitable to do so. If the shift is profitable, then total output will be greater[1] at the higher level of mechanisation. Thus as output per head is higher, with the same labour force, total output will be higher. The additional product resulting from the higher level of mechanisation is the marginal product of the finance used in supplying each man with a more mechanised technique. The value of capital is, of course, in this case indeterminate, for the rate of profit entering into the cost of capital is different, the physical capitals are different, and the real-capital ratio is different. Relative shares are also indeterminate. Thus this approach cannot in any sense be called the marginal product of capital as it is impossible to determine what the value of capital is. Further, there can be no conclusions as to the relation between marginal products and returns to factors:

> The level of rents and wage and the rate of profit are not determined by the marginal products of land, labour and investment. All three are determined together, in a complicated way, by the spectrum of technical possibilities, the supplies of land and labour available to the economy as a whole and the amount of accumulation that has already taken place, and by the level of effective demand for commodities and the rate of investment.[2]

E. ASSESSMENT

The most significant, and surprising, result of Mrs Robinson's analysis may be the 'perverse case' in the choice of technique which recognised this phenomenon as a problem long before the switching controversy became a major issue in the literature. Thus, in addition to providing her own analysis of the problems of economic growth, Mrs Robinson has delved deeply into neoclassical analysis to peruse its usefulness and check its credibility. While Mrs Robinson retains some remnants of the neoclassical approach in terms of allocative efficiency and

---

[1] This example is dependent on all labour remaining employed and thus a greater total output as well as output per head is produced at the higher level of mechanisation.

[2] *The Accumulation of Capital*, op. cit., 311–12.

choice of techniques, she rejects its basic distributional contention on the grounds that it has never defined a rate of profit outside the illusory marginal product of capital.

The basic contention of her work, bolstered by the perverse case, is that the quantity of capital can have no precise meaning unless the rate of profits is known. She thus rejects any theory that attempts to deduce the rate of profit from the quantity of capital as highly circular and based on faulty logic. From this result she concludes that the rate of profit must be determinate if a realistic approach to the factors affecting economic growth is to be made. Consequently, Mrs Robinson chooses to work in comparisons of golden ages, where the rate of profits is constant over time. Even in this type of analysis she has shown that analysis is no simple matter. It is necessary to realise that when capital valuation is possible it rests not only on the mythical golden age construction, but of necessity involves the predetermination of the rate of profits. Mrs Robinson's theory of profits is basically derived from the profits theories of Kalecki and Keynes and rests heavily on the Keynesian assumption that investment is an autonomous act independent from decisions to save. Her system provides both a determinate rate of profit which makes capital valuation possible and a theory of distribution that has the method of profit determination as an integral part.

The most common objection to these types of formulation is in the savings assumptions made about income classes.[1] Mrs Robinson has, however, included both consumption out of profits and savings out of wages in her analysis. In the last chapter, Pasinetti's conclusion showed that the theory of profit determination used by both writers does not alter when workers are allowed to save and own capital.[2] The next chapter

---

[1] See Samuelson and Modigliani, 'The Pasinetti Paradox in Neo-Classical and More General Models', op. cit., and R. Solow and J. Stiglitz, 'Output, Employment, and Wages in the Short Run', *Quarterly Journal of Economics*, LXXXII (Nov. 1968) 53, where it is stated of Keynesian theories of distribution, 'in that theory the distribution of income is made to depend primarily or exclusively on the different propensities to spend and save wage income and profits'.

[2] Analysis of worker's saving appears in *Essays in the Theory of Economic Growth*, op. cit.

will look in greater detail at the effects of the assumption of differing savings propensities for different types of income.

Mrs Robinson's work contains the most detailed approach to the necessity and effect of the determination of the rate of profits on the distribution of income and economic growth. The dual nature of the relation between the rate of profit and the rate of growth is more explicitly outlined in her work than in others. She points out in detail that there is a two-way relation between the rate of profit and the rate of investment such that the latter will be the major determinant of the former but that the former will, through expectations, affect the value the latter obtains. The trade-off between rentier consumption and investment is also outlined as well as the effect on real wages through the distribution of income. The only non-concrete part of the system is in the first dual relation between investment and profit. Animal spirits and expectations in relation to the rate of profit serve as the explanation of investment. This aspect is similar to Kaldor's dynamism and is entirely consistent with the *General Theory*.[1]

The simplifying assumptions that have been retained throughout, the fixed consumption basket and homogeneous labour, are not damaging, while they allow the work to focus on its basic concern: capital accumulation. The valuation of human capital should be susceptible to the same kind of analysis as applied to capital. The composition of the consumption basket, as long as a golden age steady state is maintained, is less crucial[2] than when the profit rate is changing, for with redistri-

[1] J. M. Keynes, *The General Theory of Employment, Interest and Money* (London: Macmillan, 1936): 'Most, probably, of our decisions to do something positive, the full consequences of which will be drawn out over many days to come, can only be taken as a result of animal spirits – of a spontaneous urge to action rather than inaction, and not as the outcome of a weighted average of quantitative benefits multiplied by quantitative probabilities' (161).

[2] See, however, Paolo Leon, *Structural Change and Growth in Capitalism: A Set of Hypotheses* (Baltimore: Johns Hopkins Press, 1967), where, following Italian theoretical research in the 1960s, Leon argues that with increasing output and real income Engel's Law will operate, changing the relative weights of commodities in the consumption basket and thus affecting the profitability of the firms producing the commodities unequally. Leon thus rejects the constant commodity basket assumption and as a result the

bution, demands for particular goods will alter. Even so, such cases defy analysis even with a given commodity make-up of the consumption basket. Trying to deal with all three problems would, indeed, make any one's solution intractable: 'The analysis can be extended to any degree of refinement, but the more complicated the question the more cumbersome the analysis. In order to know anything it is necessary to know everything, but in order to talk about anything it is necessary to neglect a great deal'.[1]

---

assumption of a uniform rate of profit in the system. The book contains many other equally provocative conclusions (but seemingly received doctrine among the Italian academic community) and doubtlessly will provide impetus for further investigation.

[1] Joan Robinson, 'Rising Supply Price', originally published in *Economica*, n.s., VIII (1941) 8, and reprinted in G. J. Stigler and K. E. Boulding (eds.), *Readings in Price Theory* (Chicago: Richard D. Irwin, Inc., for The American Economic Association, 1952) 241.

12 KEYNESIAN MODELS: THE GENERALITY OF THE ASSUMPTIONS

The two main approaches to problems of long-run economic growth have now been presented. The analysis of the two types of basic model – neoclassical and Keynesian – has been based on the propositions concerning the treatment of the rate of profits and distribution theory outlined in Chapters 1 and 2.

Neoclassical writers have questioned the generality of some of the assumptions in the Keynesian models.[1] This chapter will investigate these objections and attempt to indicate how additional considerations can be taken into account.

A. ASSUMPTIONS

The analysis will be confined to conditions of golden age steady growth. There is no technical progress. Firms are assumed to be carrying out investment sufficient to employ the work force which is expanding at a constant rate per unit of time, n. The level of money wages is given.

The ratio of investment in total output that produces growth at rate n will also determine the distribution of resources between available (consumption) and unavailable goods output. The pattern of prices that will rule over time will be determined by the size of the combined income flow (aggregate demand) that meets the flow of output of available goods. Demand in the consumption sector is composed of (a) the wage bill in both the consumption and investment sectors less savings from wages, (b) unearned income less saving, and (c) any direct consumption by firms out of profits. The existing technique of production and the proportion of real resources commited to investment will determine the flow of available goods. The conjunction of these forces over time will establish a pattern of

[1] See Samuelson and Modigliani, op. cit.

prices which, given costs of production, will allow the determination of profit margins and thus profit rates.

The relation between costs of production, demand and profits will depend on the overall investment policies of firms and the consumption decisions of households, given the technique of production. Given household incomes, a higher proportion of investment in total output will mean a higher ratio of money demand to available output. In equilibrium, prices and profit margins would then be higher with the real value of household incomes lower.

To avoid complications of monetary policy the banking system is assumed to supply just the amount of short-term finance that firms require. Since the increase in national income that results from net investment is generated with a lag, firms are assumed to finance net investment in the current period by borrowing from banks. At the same time profit retentions accruing from last period and borrowing from households can be used to repay last period's bank advances. The banks are then increasing the fund of finance each period by the difference between this period's and last period's net investment. Thus the rate of growth of the fund of finance (and the total money supply) is the same as the rate of growth, g. The rate of interest will be unaffected by the actions of the banking system. This will allow the analysis to focus on the conditions that determine the rate of return households receive on their savings when savings are used to purchase financial assets from firms.

Some neoclassical writers have objected to the use of classical savings assumptions $(s_p > s_w)$ or the use of any differential thriftiness conditions attached to wages and profits.[1] To meet this objection the analysis will utilise a social system that may be characterised as a 'property-owning democracy'. There will be no wages class and profits class in the sense that every household draws income from both sources.

The analysis will also include pricing imperfections and the introduction of financial institutions. The former are never treated in neoclassical models and Keynesian models are often

[1] Samuelson and Modigliani, op. cit.; Solow and Stiglitz, op. cit.; and Solow, *Price Expectations and the Behaviour of the Price Level* (Manchester: Manchester University Press, 1969) 41.

accused of omitting the latter. Although Joan Robinson is the only Keynesian writer to introduce these factors explicitly, they will be seen as basic to Keynesian models.[1]

The postulated property-owning democracy is divided into firms and households. Households are faced with two decisions concerning the disposition of their current income.[2] They must initially decide how much to consume. Given the consumption decision, households must decide in what form they will hold current and accumulated savings. This latter decision is normally called liquidity preference and is made subject to the types of assets that are offered by firms and financial institutions. It is assumed that households *do not* hold real assets in their portfolios, nor do they desire or demand such assets.[3]

The firms have to decide the amount of new real assets to produce (or purchase) and the type of long-term finance that will be used. Firms may also purchase placements, but this is assumed to be a secondary consideration used to co-ordinate continuous cash earnings with discontinuous investment projects. Firms are assumed to deal primarily in real assets.

The link between the firms' profits and households' unearned income is thus established through the firms' control over decisions to produce (or purchase) new real assets via the issue of placements to be held in the portfolios of households.

The financing decisions of firms will affect the quantity, return and type of placements held by households. The prices and returns to placements are thus co-determined by prevailing market expectations, the investment and financing decisions of firms, and the consumption and liquidity preference of households. Firms have expectations about the flow of yields on real assets; households have expectations about future returns and prices of paper assets.

---

[1] See *The Accumulation of Capital*, op. cit., bks IV and V; *Essays in the Theory of Economic Growth*, op. cit.; and 'Harrod after Twenty-one Years', *Economic Journal*, (Sep. 1970).

[2] Cf. J. M. Keynes, *The General Theory of Employment, Interest and Money*, op. cit., 166–7.

[3] Oddly enough, this assumption is an exception to most models.

G

B. A SINGLE PROPENSITY TO SAVE

To analyse a system that reflects a single overall propensity to save out of net income, it must be assumed that all net income in the system is paid out to households, i.e. that all profits are paid out as dividends or that the return on bonds equals the return on the value of physical assets. This totally precludes any attempt to approach institutional reality in the financing of investment, but allows the pursuit of the possible logical case of a single propensity to save out of all income. Firms are thus restricted to external finance and always distribute all net profits. Households will then receive the same rate of return on their financial assets as the firms earn on physical assets.[1]

The question to be determined is whether there exists a rate of profits that will make the savings of households out of their total income equal to the given golden age rate of investment. In this particular case the rate of profits, the margins over prime costs, as well as the amount of money income paid out in the system will be a function of the prices set by corporations on their output. The higher the prices set by corporations, the higher will be the margins of prices over prime costs. The rate of profit will then be higher and dividend payouts to households will be higher. At the same time, with a single average propensity to save, the level of savings in money terms is higher but the ratio of saving to income is unchanged. The value of investment goods must also change *pari passu*, for with each higher level of prices and profits, the higher price of investment goods will raise the value of investment goods by the same amount as it raises money savings. When the rate of investment is above or below the given ratio of saving to output there is no set of prices that will equate savings and investment. Since the value of investment increases in step with money savings, if savings and investment are unequal at one set of prices they are unequal at all possible price levels.

On the other hand, if the rate of investment is compatible

[1] Cf. Pasinetti, 'Rate of Profit, etc.', op. cit., where a similar assumption is necessary for his very different conclusions with two propensities to save.

with the given s, then savings and investment will be equal for *any* set of prices and profit rates.[1]

With a given single s, there is only one rate of investment that will generate stable growth. It is the rate set by the given savings ratio. If the value of s is a given constant, there can be no sustainable rate of growth outside that set by the households' saving ratio. There is then only one rate of stable growth bounded by inflation or deflation on either side.

In the case where there is a single propensity to save and all profits are distributed, there is nothing to determine the rate of profits or the prices ruling in the system on the single possible

[1] This proposition can most easily be seen by constructing the following table of variables:

Table 12.1

	Consumption	Investment	Total
Value of output	160	40	200
	80	20	100
Wage bill	80	20	100
Profits	80	20	100
	0	0	0
sW $s = \cdot 20$	16	4	20
cW	64	16	80
sP $s = \cdot 20$	16	4	20
	0	0	0
cP	64	16	80
	0	0	0

The table shows a given split of the system's resources between consumption and investment such that the value of investment output is equal to savings. The top line of each cell shows the system with a positive rate of profits, the bottom line a zero rate. In both cases the value of investment output equals savings $(I = sW + sP)$. Thus in a Harrodian system, once the knife-edge is achieved it will be undisturbed by any pattern of prices or rate of profits.

There does not seem to be any reason why the rate of profits need be restricted to positive values. It may be unrealistic in the context of growth, but negative rates of profits seem logically feasible and consistent.

stable growth path. If the rate of growth is compatible with the given savings ratio, then savings will be equal to investment at any set of prices above cost of production and rate of profits above zero.[1] In order to determine the rate of profits and prices in this type of logical construction, the only recourse is to introduce overt price setting in terms of a corporate degree of monopoly.

The result of an indeterminate rate of profits is the same result as shown above for the Harrod model. The present case shows that the indeterminancy inherent in Harrod's growth formulation exists even when the knife-edge rate of growth is achieved. It is necessary to introduce overt price setting in terms of monopoly power to achieve a determinate set of prices and rate of profit for the knife-edge rate of growth.

Accordingly, with a single savings propensity these additional

[1] Another table can show how this might be possible. Assume the system employs 20 per cent of its available labour resources in producing investment output, but that the single savings propensity is ·10.

Table 12.2

	Consumption	Investment	Total
Value of output	360	40	400
Wage bill	80	20	100
Profits	280	20	300
sW $s = ·10$	8	2	10
cW	72	18	90
sP $s = ·10$	28	2	30
cP	252	18	270

In this case it is still true that the value of investment output (40) equals $sW + sP$ $(10 + 30)$. The degree of monopoly in the consumption sector, however, fixes prices that are over four times the labour costs of production while the investment sector margin is just 100 per cent. This is a system not on the knife-edge but theoretically stable. Prices are determinate but the rate of profit is still not known. It is higher in the consumption sector, but from the table it is impossible to determine its value.

properties of such a system become apparent: (*a*) the equilibrium rate of growth is determined by the household saving ratio (corporations are free to set prices as they like, but they may not be able to achieve the natural rate of growth even if they are willing to carry out the rate of investment necessary to produce it); (*b*) short-period perfect competition will not produce a determinate rate of profit;[1] (*c*) with imperfect competition actual capital–output ratios will diverge from possible full-capacity capital–output ratios, thereby raising capital per unit of output; and (*d*) with firms free to determine prices and profit rates, the inverse relation between capital intensity and profit rates will no longer hold.

The recognition of additional aspects of imperfect competition would allow the construction of a system with a sustainable stability at rates of growth outside the knife-edge. This would require dropping the assumption of uniformity of the rate of profits in the capital and consumption sectors, allowing different rates of capacity utilisation in the two sectors. With a lower fixed degree of monopoly in the capital sector the value of investment would remain constant as prices and profit rates rose in the consumption sector, reducing real consumption and providing the saving necessary to balance the rate of investment. The full analysis of such a system is outside the scope of the present work. Further effects of monopoly are introduced below.

C. A RANGE OF VALUES FOR *g*

It is possible, however, for a system to achieve any one of a range of equilibrium rates of growth. This was first shown by

---

[1] Neoclassical economists are fond of assuming perfect competition in their models with $P = MC$ (and the real wage equal to the marginal product of labour), which implies that all plants are continually working up to full-capacity output, with output limited by sharply rising marginal costs. Under these assumptions gross margins, covering fixed costs and net profits, are determined by the difference between average and marginal prime costs. A higher rate of profit then requires a more intensive utilisation of given plant, and a greater difference between average and marginal prime costs. It is still not possible to find a determinate price level and profit rate unless it is externally imposed or agreed upon by firms.

Professor Joan Robinson, who analysed a system in which the ratio of consumption to income was lower for groups receiving income primarily from profits and higher for income earned as wages. In a comparison of her own work and Harrod's[1] she singles out this aspect as the crucial difference. Retention of profits for finance of investment is given as the primary justi-fication for the assumption of differing proportions of con-sumption in wages and profits income. There is no reason or necessity to limit Keynesian models to wage and profit groups.

Within the property-owning democracy the overall house-hold propensity to save, s, and the retention ratio of firms, r, take the place of savings from wages and profits income that produce

$$\pi = g/s_p. \qquad (12.1)$$

When households save a constant portion, s, of their wages, W, and dividends, D, and firms retain r of profits, $D = (1-r)P$. Total profits are then

$$P = I + \{(1-s)D - sW\}. \qquad (12.2)$$

When households save out of wages just the amount they spend out of dividends, $P = I$ and $P/K = I/K$ or $\pi = g$. This is the Pasinetti result.[2] Where r is lower D is higher and $P > I$ or $\pi > g$. The savings–investment equilibrium

$$I = sW + s(1-r)P + rP \qquad (12.3)$$

produces the modified formula

$$\pi = \frac{g - s(W/K)}{s(1-r) + r}. \qquad (12.4)$$

It is still true that the propensity to save out of profits is dominant over savings from wages,[3] for inspection will show that $s(1-r) + r$ is the overall propensity to save out of profit. The

[1] 'Mr Harrod's Dynamics', in notes to *The Accumulation of Capital*, op. cit., 404–6.

[2] Cf. p. 182, n. 1 above.

[3] This, it must be recalled, is the original contention of Kaldor's claim and Pasinetti's expansion. It is impossible to talk of workers and capitalists within the context of the present models as these classes have been assumed out of existence to meet Samuelson and Modigliani's claim that the Keynesian model requires permanent income classes.

correction is necessary because distributed profits are subject to additional saving above the retention of firms. Even when both s and r enter the determination of the overall propensity to save from profits, it cannot be said that households' saving determines the rate of profits. In that firms, taken together, have a range of choice in determining r, they will have the ability to determine total savings, for they can determine the size of D that enters household income by varying r. As will be shown below, the functioning of financial markets will further ensure that saving will accomodate to the investment decisions of firms.

In the cases presented, a range of possible equilibrium rates of growth will exist, limited at the upper bound by the lowest real income households will accept and at the lower bound by some positive rate of return adequate to encourage firms to carry on the prevailing rate of investment.

D. BOND FINANCE

When households save out of income and purchase placements, the analysis of financial markets must be explicitly introduced into the model. Investment is carried out independently by firms and financed by retentions and borrowing, yet households are free to save as much as they like. There is nothing to guarantee that firms will borrow just because households have savings or vice versa. Determination of the mechanism that will equate savings and investment in the model will require the analysis of both the formation of prices in the goods market and supply and demand conditions in financial markets.

The analysis now assumes that external borrowing is limited to bonds and retains the previous assumptions concerning the actions of the banking system and the golden age rate of investment. The system contains households who receive wages and interest and buy bonds with their savings. Firms carry out investment and issue bonds to fund investment that is not internally financed from retentions. The rate of interest offered on bonds will generally be considerably less than the rate of return expected by firms from investing in real assets. If it were not, a chance fall in receipts would necessitate either bankruptcy or liquidation of assets to meet contractual interest payments on outstanding bonds.[1] This type of uncertainty will effect the rate of return on bonds as well as the degree of corporate indebtedness or gearing.[2]

When the rate of interest on bonds is below the rate of profit, $\pi > i$, then, even when firms issue only bonds, internal retentions equal to $\pi - i(B/K)$, where B/K is the proportion of bonds to capital, will accrue to firms. As bondholders do not even have the feeble control over the corporation that shareholders possess, the managers will be free to use retentions to swell their salaries or provide themselves with palatial offices instead of financing new investment.

When retentions are not used to swell costs, total savings may be written

$$S = s(W + iB) + (\pi K - iB). \tag{12.5}$$

The market rate of interest will determine the return to household wealth and the cost of borrowing to firms. The new issue of bonds by firms and the demand for bonds by households will then determine the level of household income, given the money wage. Financing decisions of firms and conditions in the bond market will thus be of crucial importance to the analysis of factors affecting the possible existence of steady growth.

With a given rate of investment, and a given issue policy by firms, the bond market will settle on a price and interest rate for bonds that will equate the household demand for bonds with the supply as determined by firms.

If the firms are carrying out more investment than they wish to finance internally, they will borrow the difference from households. In equilibrium, household consumption will fall short of income by the same amount that retentions fall short of investment. The savings of households will then be equal to the

[1] Governments of course are exempt from this stricture as they can always tax the bondholders in order to pay them interest.

[2] See *Sunday Times Business News*, 'Crisis in the U.S. Economy: The Worst Yet to Come', 24 May 1970, 47, where it is suggested that the share prices of the most highly geared conglomerates are being discounted for fear of their inability to meet interest payments, much less pay any dividends.

value of bonds issued. The rate of interest is the variable that provides equilibrium by acting on the level of household unearned income, given the household propensity to save.[1]

If saving by households at the ruling rate of interest were greater than the borrowing requirements of firms, there would be excess demand for bonds. The prices of bonds would be driven up and the rate of interest would be reduced. The return per unit of household wealth would then be lower and the cost to firms of a given amount of finance would be lower. This might encourage firms to finance a higher proportion of investment by borrowing.

Equilibrium will be established at the market rate of interest that adjusts household income and thus household savings to the investment determined by firms. (The oft-debated question of whether more or less saving will be done out of a given income when the rate of interest is higher or lower is not under discussion; in this case s is given and assumed constant).

The functioning of the adjustment mechanism can be most easily seen by comparing two systems, alike in every respect, except that in the first system the household propensity to save is higher. In the first system the market price of bonds is higher while the yield on bonds is lower. The return to household wealth is lower. The lower return to household wealth will cause the level of household incomes in the first system to be lower and thus the level of aggregate household savings will be lower, irrespective of the reactions of the subjective desire to save to the rate of interest. The bond market will thus establish in equilibrium the price and return on bonds which will make the aggregate savings of the system compatible with the financing decisions of firms. In both systems the rate of accumulation is the same by assumption. It is a stable equilibrium rate for both, even though households in the first system save a higher proportion of their income.

As long as firms have the will and the ability to undertake the rate of investment necessary to achieve the natural rate of growth, prices in the goods market and in the bonds market will

[1] The mechanism employed in the case of bond finance is suggested by a similar proposition put forward by Kaldor. Cf. Section E below, and p. 190, n. 1.

adjust to make the savings of households compatible with the external borrowing requirements of firms.

Given the resources available in the system, the rate of investment will determine the division of total output between investment and consumption. With a given money wage and propensity to save by households, the conditions in the bond market will determine the level of total income (the rate of return to household wealth) that will produce the equilibrium pattern of prices in the goods market and the equilibrium price of bonds.

E. SHARE FINANCE

To handle the problem of household saving and borrowing by firms when firms use non-contractual shares, an approach first suggested by Kaldor can be employed with some modification.[1] The key to Kaldor's approach is the concept of the valuation ratio,[2] v, which symbolises the ratio of the market value of a firms' shares to the value of its capital, K. The approach can be adapted to serve the assumption of a property-owning democracy.

With share ownership typical of all households, total net income can be written

$$\Upsilon = W + (1 - r)P + rP \qquad (12.6)$$

where r is the retention ratio of firms and P the net profits of firms. Likewise total savings by households and firms is

$$S = s(W + (1 - r)P) + rP. \qquad (12.7)$$

Households are demographically divided by age. Young households save to buy shares which are sold in old age to provide retirement income.

In equilibrium the dissaving of older households will

[1] This in response to some criticisms by Samuelson and Modigliani of Pasinetti's 1962 paper. See 'A Neo-Pasinetti Theorem', in the Appendix to N. Kaldor, 'Marginal Productivity and the Macro-Economic Theories of Distribution', *Review of Economic Studies* (Oct. 1966) 316–19. See also Chapters 6 and 10 above.

[2] First introduced in the theoretical literature by R. L. Marris, *The Economic Theory of 'Managerial Capitalism'* (London: Macmillan, 1964).

balance the savings of new households and provide shares for them to buy. When firms issue new shares the addition to existing shares plus those released by the dissaving of old households will make up the net supply of shares available for purchase by new households.

When some new investment is financed by retentions, capital gains will accrue to existing shareholders as the capital value per outstanding share rises. Thus the capital gains per share are less than the increase in the firm's total market valuation as the increase in the firm's valuation (and stock of capital) is spread over existing shareholders and the purchasers of new issues in relation to the proportion of new net investment financed via new issues.

When the valuation ratio $v = V/K$ (and all firms are assumed to be identically the same in terms of their profit and growth rates), the income to any shareholder is composed of dividends equal to $(1 - r)P$ and capital gains equal to rPv.[1] It is the value of v, given r and π, that assures that the sale of shares plus new issues equals the net savings of new households along the equilibrium path.

If the new issue of shares plus the sale of shares by older households were less than the savings of new households there would be an excess demand for shares in the market. The price of shares would be driven up, and the valuation ratio would be higher. A higher valuation ratio provides for higher purchasing power per share sold in retirement. With a given propensity to consume out of assets in retirement, the dissaving by old households would rise to offset the excess saving of new households. Equilibrium is established when the valuation ratio equates the consumption of retired households with the savings of new households, and the demand for shares by new households with the new issue of shares by firms and the sale of shares by older households.

When firms have the inclination and the ability to carry on the rate of investment that will produce growth at the natural rate, aggregate household saving will adjust to match the external finance requirements of firms. Thus the analysis shows

[1] *Economic Heresies* (New York: Basic Books, Inc., 1970; London: Macmillan, 1971) ch. 8, pp. 117–25.

that the model need not be limited to a single value of g as in the Harrod case once the mechanisms which adjust savings to the prevailing rate of investment are included. There is no need to postulate that firms' intentions to invest and households' intentions to save must be equal. This will be so in the aggregate even though each household may provide for retirement as it pleases. Many intermediate cases can be constructed, including one in which bonds, shares and the banking system are all involved. Further complexity will not, however, change the results and the Keynesian model need not be rejected because of the restriction of the Harrod case. Indeed, the model can allow any desired degree of complexity that increased generality implies without invalidating the essential proposition that as long as the investment decision is independent of saving, the rate of profits and thus distribution will depend on the rate of investment of firms and thriftiness conditions. This conclusion will not change when the assumptions of perfect competition are relaxed in the following section.

F. IMPERFECT COMPETITION

Competitive imperfections can also be introduced into a model that does not assume class divisions by income source.[1] It is not necessary to assume that all demand curves are perfectly elastic and that all firms produce full-capacity output. Assume that there is, along a possible equilibrium path, a normal rate of less than full-capacity utilisation of plant and near full employment. Given the money wage and the market rate of interest, equilibrium requires a pattern of prices that equates the expenditure of households with the flow of output corresponding to the normal rate of utilisation. Individual firms will thus meet small fluctuations in sales by adjusting output around the normal level of utilisation while holding prices constant.

Given household wage income and expenditure decisions, the excess of prices over prime costs of production will vary with the normal utilisation of plant, higher prices and lower average output reflecting a higher degree of monopoly.

[1] For an analysis of degree of monopoly effects on a wages–profits model, see Joan Robinson, 'Harrod after Twenty-one Years', op. cit.

It is easy to see that if there is no saving by households (and thus no external finance) the degree of monopoly will not affect the rate of profit, but it will affect the real wage. When households spend all their income, demand curves have unit elasticity. With just firms and households, $\pi = g/r$. A higher degree of monopoly yields the same money expenditure by households irrrespective of the level of output. Retentions by firms are thus unchanged, irrespective of the degree of monopoly, as proceeds over prime costs are the same.

When prices are higher, output is lower, and the real wage is thus also lower. With total profits constant the share of profits in the reduced output is higher, the share of wages lower.[1] With lower output per unit of plant, the capital–output ratio is higher.

When saving from household income is introduced, households have a reserve to defend their real level of consumption in the face of a higher degree of monopoly. Thus the demand for goods becomes inelastic and the degree of monopoly will affect the rate of profit.

A higher degree of monopoly means a lower real value of household incomes with given money wages and market rate of interest. Lower real income implies lower real saving by households. Thus the reduction in the rate of profit due to household saving is less and the rate of profit is correspondingly reduced by less. Retentions and the rate of profit are then higher. Thus when

$$\pi = \frac{g - s(W/K)}{s(1-r) + r} \tag{12.8}$$

the rate of profit is higher when (W/K) is lower due to a higher degree of monopoly.

When firms are borrowing from households to finance the excess of investment over retentions, a higher degree of monopoly will cause the issue of bonds to be reduced by the amount of increased retentions. Since households' real savings will be lower by the same amount that retentions are higher, conditions in the bond market will be undisturbed as the reduced

[1] Cf. M. Kalecki, *Essays in the Theory of Economic Fluctuations*, op. cit., and *Studies in Business Cycles 1933–1939*, op. cit.

volume of bonds is taken up at the prevailing price. The net worth of households will then be lower over time as household real income is lower.

With a constant cost of capital per unit of capacity at any point on the given growth path, the ratio of capital to output will be higher when the degree of monopoly is higher. In short-period terms this puts to rest the neoclassical contention that the rate of profit and capital intensity are inversely related. With pricing imperfections, a higher rate of profit associated with a higher degree of monopoly implies a higher, not lower, capital to output ratio.

Once the regime of perfect foresight, perfect competition and guaranteed full employment is left, the neoclassical relations between profit rates and capital intensity have very little meaning or application. It is not so much capital scarcity that determines the rate of profit, but the firms' desire and ability to carry out investment and the ability to set prices in relation to the households' desire to consume. Profits exist, not because capital is scarce, but because resources are limited. What is invested cannot be consumed. It might be better said that high profits result from a scarcity of consumption goods rather than a scarcity of capital.

G. GENERAL CONCLUSIONS

The models outlined in this chapter, except the initial case, use differing propensities to save, although not strictly out of types of income or by income class. All cases have been posed in a manner that made such divisions impossible. The type of system considered maintained functional distribution solely in terms of production, paying wages and earning profits. The economic agents, however, were owners of the capital stock and viewed their income as neither wages nor profits, but as a mixed lump of income. By allowing households to own title to capital a limited range of monetary and financial aspects could also be introduced. When households are saving these aspects cannot be ignored.

The system viewed in this way does, however, yield the same general results as suggested by Keynesian writers using formulations that assume specific propensities to save out of wages and profits. The notion raised by the neoclassical critics, that Keynesian models that use these assumptions in some sense require income classes of any nature, permanent or transitory, can therefore be rejected. The results are broadly similar under a wide range of assumptions concerning propensities to save and income class.

The effect of savings assumptions on the independency of investment is highlighted in the initial Harrod prototype case. With a given s and the assumption of a uniform rate of profit, it is indeed true that there is only one possible stable rate of investment and growth – that set by the single savings propensity of households. Thus savings, while not determining, can limit the rate of investment that can be steadily maintained, which in turn limits real income to a single value. The rate of profit is indeterminate unless the short-period characteristics of imperfect competition are introduced.

When the rate of investment is given the status of a variable independent from savings, it will determine real income and the rate of profit when the knife-edge is overcome. The employment of the mythical property-owning democracy shows that the results of the model will be broadly the same whether or not income is identified in terms of wages and profits. The analysis of the capitalistic system in terms of wages and rentier income is just a natural simplification for the Keynesian models, not a logically necessary assumption.[1]

In essence it is not the assumption about savings propensities from wages and profits that is important in the determination of income distribution, but the assumption that the investment decision, and thus the rate of investment, is an independent variable. This is the basic proposition of Keynes's *General Theory* and the foundation upon which the Cambridge Keynesian theory of growth and distribution is based. The distribution that is of prime importance is the division of total output between consumption and investment, irrespective of the number of classes or savings propensities assumed.

[1] In fact Mrs Robinson's assumptions of savings from wages and profits is based on the assumption that savings from retained income exceed savings from paid-out income.

In a system where incomes consist of both wages and profits in varying degrees, all that is necessary for the functioning of the distributive mechanism of the model is either (a) corporate retentions, (b) monopoly effects, or (c) individually differing propensities to save out of undifferentiated incomes. Of course possibility (c) may be achieved by merely postulating that the propensity to save is an increasing function of real income. This type of assumption may be more palatable to critics than the classical savings assumptions, but raises the same type of social implications as distribution will occur between low and high incomes rather than between wages and profits or households and firms. There is nothing to be found in this broader assumption that will ease the neoclassical case for assuming that capital is freely substitutable and malleable.

In terms of determining the rate of profits, the analysis has shown that irrespective of how incomes are treated, savings from overall profits will still enter the formula that determines π. This must be true for any system of production that uses labour and capital to produce output.[1]

The introduction of imperfect competition in terms of plant utilisation and the degree of monopoly has shown that the rate of investment will continue to play the dominant role irrespective of market structure. The direct influence of investment on profits can only be modified by corporate financing decisions and the firm's estimation of its own market's imperfection. In these cases imperfect competition can also affect the capital intensity of production through effects on capacity utilisation and the rate of profit, given the rate of investment.

When income classes and sources are replaced by mixed incomes and household saving is introduced, the model requires consideration of corporate financing policy and financial markets. This increased scope leads to increased complexity; it neither causes the basic model to be rejected nor provides validation for marginal productivity. Assumptions about savings propensities have nothing to say about capital malleability and perfect foresight. They can make malleability unnecessary, but do not provide justification for its introduction.

[1] For a further analysis of a mythical property-owning democracy, see Appendix D below.

But the primary disagreement between the two approaches is not to be found in assumptions about saving or technical malleability. The important difference is in the assumption about investment. If savings determine investment then one is in the neoclassical pre-Keynesian world which produces the confusion between hard productive objects and finance as a logical necessity. The assumption of perfect foresight is simply another way of saying the same thing. Neoclassical theory is simply devoid of a theory of investment. Perhaps that explains the preoccupation with assumptions about savings.

In a Keynesian world investment determines income. Saving determines aggregate money demand, it does not determine investment. Investment will also determine the flow of goods that meets the aggregate demand. The pattern of prices that is established will be such as to make savings equal to investment. Who does the saving is of little consequence in theory (although it may be very important in reality). It is not assumptions about s that matter, but the assumption about the independency of investment.

Appendices

APPENDIX A
The Line of Causality in Meade's Model

The introduction of constancy in the savings assumptions of Meade's system allows the following extension to show the differences in causality between Meade's approach and others more perspicuously. From equation (3.9B)

$$\Delta K/K = S_p \cdot VK/Y \cdot Y/K + S_w \cdot QY/K \qquad (A.1)$$

$$\Delta K/K + S_p V + S_w \cdot QY/K \qquad (A.2)$$

$$k = S_p V + S_w \cdot WL/K. \qquad (A.3)$$

If, as Meade assumes, $S_p > S_w$, and S_w is additionally assumed to be negligible, then

$$k = S_p V \qquad (A.4)$$

or

$$k/S_p = V \qquad (A.5)$$

i.e. the rate of accumulation is set by the rate of profits and the proportion of profits saved. In the case of a given position on a specified production function $V = \overline{V}$, and thus k and S_p must be constant. If, $k > 1$, V will fall as W rises (i.e. V varies as the capital–labour ratio changes) and the rate of accumulation will change at the same rate as the marginal product of capital. That is, given the classical savings assumptions, the rate of profit determines the rate of accumulation. Thus, given the constant value of S (implying a constant value of $S_p(S_w = 0)$), it is the rate of profits, V, as determined by the production function which determines the rate of growth of capital, k. If $S_w > 0$, the increase in W will exactly offset the fall in V (given U and Q constant with constant returns) which, if $k > 1$, will save k from a negative value at the limit of substitution. That is, k will increase by $SwQY$, less its decrease from $S_p VY$, for $SY = \Delta K$ and $k = \Delta K/K$.

In Chapters 8–12, the relation is seen to be reversed and the rate of accumulation and thriftiness conditions determine the rate of profits, quite free from any reliance on the production function and the problems that it presents.

APPENDIX B
The Technical Progress Function Once More

In this appendix several alternative approaches and interpretations of Kaldor's Technical Progress Function will be presented. All initial interpretations are suggested in Kaldor's published work, but they have seldom been analysed in any depth therein.

A. THE NATURE OF TECHNICAL PROGRESS

It is possible to view the nature of capital-saving or using bias in the function. Given a non-linear form of the function such as T in Fig. B.1, point S will have $\dot{P}/P > \dot{i}/i$. This implies that the rate of increase in output per head with the technique at S is greater than the rate of growth of investment per head, $(\Delta O/L)/(O/L) > (\Delta I/L)/(I/L)$, and thus both the capital–output and capital–labour ratios, K/O, K/L, will be falling as the technique is introduced, so that the technique at S is capital-saving. Conversely, at point U on T, $\dot{P}/P < \dot{i}/i$,

$$\frac{\Delta O/L}{O/L} < \frac{\Delta I/L}{I/L}$$

and both K/O and K/L are rising, i.e. the technique is capital-using. Thus, in general, it can be said that all points to the left of N (where $\dot{i}/i = \dot{P}/P$) are capital-saving and to the right capital-using.

It is not possible to associate a rate of profit with either the technique chosen or the level of investment per head from the function. However, taking any point on T where progress is not balanced (i.e. a point other than N), say S, it is still possible for a constant rate of profit to be maintained even though K/O is falling at that point.

At this stage one of the crucial limitations of the function becomes apparent. Time relations have never been specified. This allows for any number of alternative interpretations. Continuous values of I and P, over time, can be viewed as

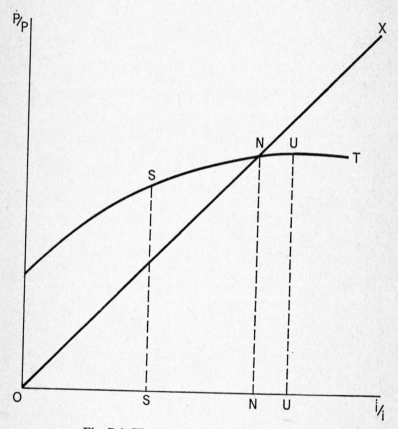

Fig. B.1 The Technical Progress Function

movements perpendicular to the page. From the point S, each time increment off the page, assuming the T function does not shift, will involve a constant rate of profits along the ray emanating from S as long as the *share* of profits falls at the same rate as K/O and K/L fall. Ignoring realistic limits to capital saving, this exercise will yield a constant rate of profits over time. As long as the ray is a straight line, the increase in productivity is constant as is the rate of investment per head. The rate of growth is then constant but the ratio of investment to consumption must be falling, as is the ratio of capital to income. Looking at this in terms of the capital and consumption sectors, the labour employed in the former must be shifted to the latter at a precise rate to maintain stability. To preserve the rate of profits at a constant rate the value of capital must be falling while the rate of accumulation is constant.

Continuous equilibrium of a steady type becomes a very complicated proposition when time is introduced. As it has been shown that such a state is possible outside N, the mechanism by which a system might move towards N must be investigated. Along any ray from a point to the left of N, if entrepreneurs react to the increased turnover of output with *expectations* of a rising rate of profit, they may be encouraged to increase the rate of investment per head. This will pull the ray upwards to the right in the vertical plane above T. The increased investment will tend to offset the fall in the share of profit that would have occurred had the additional investment not been carried out and the rate of growth will increase as will realised profits. Entrepreneurs, thus satisfied, will continue the increase in investment until point N is reached where both the share and the rate of profit are constant with steady growth. If investment is carried beyond point N, expectations will be disappointed and investment cut back.

Unfortunately, in the analysis of time shifts, the value of capital and the rate of accumulation have been lost to sight. Unless the elapsed time between each rightward shift is long enough for the entire stock of capital to be replaced, there will, at any point in time, exist pieces of capital equipment produced at different rates of profit from that ruling in the period. It would then be impossible properly to value the stock of capital in existence and thereby derive a true rate of profit. In such a case there is something to be said for Kaldor's use of the *expected* rate of profit to value new fixed investment. However, this is only valid when the expected rate is the actual rate and is expected because it is the realised rate so that it will give proper valuation of capital. The method is meaningless when applied only to equilibrium existence at point N, but becomes more meaningful in the analysis of the approach to N. This latter approach then depends on the existence of near-perfect foresight. Kaldor, unfortunately, often leads his readers to believe that his adjustments are instantaneous when indeed time is a crucial factor. The only other possible approach to the problem is to assume that the system starts initially from point N.

Shifts in the T curve due to large innovations or increased dynamism will also cause complications. It is clear that (a) the move towards N cannot be viewed as movement from point to point along the curve, and (b) that it is the movements through time that are of interest in determining the possibility of attaining such a position as N. Shifts in the curve over time will cause a *given* rate of investment to yield different positions on the curve to the right and left of N as it shifts up or down or changes shape. In this case the moves to regain N after a shift in T become even more important. Kaldor, in this sense, is right in saying that acceptance of the curve shows the futility of classifying bias. It is possible to obtain conflicting classification from the curve, e.g. all points to the left of N are capital-saving, but a move to the right from S towards N appears as capital-using progress. In this sense only one point on each curve for each time period is relevant.

B. THE OPERATIONAL SIGNIFICANCE OF THE FUNCTION

This leaves the problem of viewing the curve from the point of view of the individual firm or the economy as a whole and the time and technique specification. From the aspect of entrepreneurial needs affecting innovations, the curve holds up quite well. Kaldor's representative firm is limited by labour availability. Thus a high rate of growth will cause a severe shortage of labour and a high rate of investment per head. Firms with low rates of growth may operate within their margin of excess capacity and thus labour strain is not great. These firms may be limited by their ability to obtain finance and thus choose a low rate of investment per head and capital-saving techniques.

While this interpretation applies well to firms, it is hard to translate to the economy as a whole. The curve is given in terms of the rate of change in investment per capita. Thus a high rate of absolute investment and rate of growth, if it is all used to introduce a low investment per head technique, moves only a short distance along the curve. This same rate of investment could also be consistent with points up to N. Thus it is not possible to relate the rate of investment and the rate of profit to the rate of investment per head. There is a rate of profit and rate of investment implicit in every point on the curve, but there is no way of finding what it is. This is expecially crucial when it is the existence of a system at point N which determines the values of these variables due to the investment–productivity link. The basic notion that the faster the rate of installation of new equipment, the faster newer technology can be introduced, is sound, but the further operational significance of the function is limited until (*a*) time relations are specified, (*b*) the micro–macro aspects are linked, (*c*) the pattern of technique introduction is specified (i.e. is only the technique at the point on the curve used or all others before it as well), and (*d*) the relation between the rate of investment and the rate of investment per head is specified. This last relationship is crucial, for unless a constant rate of investment is associated with a certain technique or rate of investment per head, different positions on the curve are possible with a constant rate of profit and investment. As cited above, if all investment is concentrated in the first technique, there is absolutely no reason for the system ever to reach N. If a certain level of N on a given T is reached, it is difficult to maintain constant neutral growth when T shifts over time. Until these relations are properly specified and investigated the Technical Progress Function is unfit to carry the explanatory weight Kaldor places upon it.

APPENDIX C
Technical Progress and Transition

A. NEUTRAL PROGRESS AND TRANSITION

It has been shown that neutral technical progress may exist over time without changing the equilibrium relations ruling in a golden age economy. The actual ingestion of machines available from an autonomous once-over shift in the spectrum of techniques will now be investigated. Calling the technique in use on the existing spectrum of techniques alpha minus and the equivalent technique on the new spectrum alpha, the new alpha technique will be available to firms as replacements for alpha minus plants come due. As the new alpha equipment is introduced, the output of commodities will start rising, for alpha has a higher output per head than alpha minus plant. To provide effective demand to purchase the increasing output, real wages must rise in step with the increase in output per head of labour employed in the production of commodities. This may be accomplished through rising money wages with prices constant, or falling prices with money wages constant.

As the new technique of production spreads through the capital sector, the output of new alpha plants will be increasing at an increasing rate. As output per head in this sector is rising, the labour required to produce a given amount of capacity is falling. The labour thus released may then be transferred to work the rising proportion of newly produced alpha plant which will produce more new alpha plant.

With neutral technical progress, labour time per unit of plant employed is constant while output per unit of labour employed in both sectors (commodities and productive capacity) rises in step. Thus a gradual shift from old alpha minus to new alpha plant will leave the relative amounts of labour employed in the two sectors constant. Consequently relative shares will remain constant and the rate of profits is constant. The real wage will rise with output per man and the value of capital per man (gradually increasing as the ratio of alpha to alpha minus plant increases) will become constant at the new alpha level when all alpha minus plant has been replaced. Accumulation may then continue along the golden age path with the investment sector producing replacements for alpha plants that were first introduced.

The transition is not so smooth, nor the results the same, if there is either an increase in the rate of accumulation or if there is a rise in the rate of technical progress and a new spectrum of techniques becomes available before the most recent has been fully digested into use. Thus the sudden availability of an alpha plus plant before the changeover from alpha minus to alpha plant has been completed may cause an excessive demand on the productive capabilities of the capital sector. This might occur if the capital sector, while still in the process of producing alpha plants to replace its own and commodities producers' alpha minus plant, were called upon to produce alpha plus plant for those producers who already have alpha plant installed. This would be similar in effect to entrepreneurs deciding to increase the number of plants each wants to employ and thus will have effects on the capital sector similar to an increase in accumulation.

The capital sector, with an increase in the demand for plants, will seek more labour. If the capital-goods producers react quickly enough to the change in technique and alpha plus plants are produced to replace still existing alpha minus plants, then productive capacity may increase quickly enough to allow a smaller amount of labour to produce an increased amount of commodities. Some labour will then be available to meet the additional labour requirements of the capital sector. This shift, however, will change the relative amounts of labour in the two sectors. The increased employment in the investment sector will cause profit per man in the consumption sector to rise. Thus real wages will be lower. With a lower cost of labour a less mechanised technique on the new spectrum (beta plus) may be more profitable. There is nothing in the system to guarantee that the system will settle into a new golden age at this new level of mechanisation. Maintaining a golden age is thus seen to be a very tenuous proposition, even when technical progress is neutral. This gives support to Mrs Robinson's judgement as to the mythical nature of golden ages.

B. BIASED TECHNICAL PROGRESS AND TRANSITION

Although it is not possible for a true golden age to exist when biased progress is taking place, the effects can be analysed to a degree and some statements on relative shares can be made. This problem is approached with least difficulty by analysing a golden age economy with a constant rate of profit that is one day confronted with a non-neutral spectrum of new techniques. Thus the new techniques of the same level of mechanisation will have a lower real capital to labour ratio if the new technique is capital-saving. As the new technique is introduced, the value of capital per unit of output and the real capital to labour ratio will fall. If the rate of profits remains constant, the share of profit will be lower with real wages higher. To provide this constant rate of profit the real wage per man must have risen by more than the increase in output per worker due to the superior, biased technique. If new spectra continue to have a capital-saving bias, the economy is in what Mrs Robinson calls a quasi-golden age, with a constant rate of profits and a continually rising labour share in total output. This situation is similar to that outlined in Appendix B for movements over time at points to the left of point N on the Technical Progress Function. There must, of course, be some limit to the extent capital-saving innovation can be carried, and at some point either neutral or capital-using bias will occur. Thus, in Mrs Robinson's view, one thing with another technical progress will tend to be offsetting and thus neutral over the long pull. The results for capital-using bias are similar, only opposite to the capital-saving case given a constant rate of profits.

The existence of biased technical progress also creates some interesting effects on amortisation and replacement decisions which will in turn affect the rate of investment and thus the rate of profits. With a superior capital-saving bias it is possible for the entrepreneur to obtain the same amount of productive capacity as his old plant at less cost with a capital-saving plant. Hence his amortisation fund from the old plant will more than cover the amount needed to replace the old capacity. With a capital-using plant the amortisation fund will be less than sufficient to provide the same capacity. Thus in order to maintain a constant rate of investment and rate of profit, his investment in new plant must be in excess of the amortisation fund. Thus it is very possible for the rate of investment to change when there is bias in technical progress.

For example, in the capital-saving case, if entrepreneurs react by keeping their finance commitment constant and reinvest the whole of the amortisation fund, the rate of capacity increase will rise and there will be scarcity of labour to man the extra capacity. Thus the rate of profit may be reduced as wages are bid up in the scramble for labour. Consequently, the level of mechanisation will be out of phase and entrepreneurs will find it profitable to introduce a more mechanised plant. When the change in mechanisation occurs it will be impossible to judge whether real wages have risen or fallen although they were initially seen to rise.

In the capital-using case, on the other hand, if only the amortisation fund is reinvested the rate of investment will fall and total capacity will fall, and as the output of commodities will thus be lower, the real wage of labour will be lower. This may also induce the introduction of a more profitable technique of a lower degree of mechanisation.

Mrs Robinson believes that in an energetic capitalist system a constant rate of profit is the most likely result in the capital-using case. She therefore maintains that there is likely to be asymmetry in the effects of the opposite types of bias. Capital-saving progress is seen as most likely to result in a lowering of the rate of profit and capital-using progress to raise the real-capital ratio with a constant rate of profit.[1]

[1] Paolo Leon argues, quite persuasively, that the concept of a number of techniques equally eligible for introduction at a point in time is a figment of the neoclassical imagination. He claims that at most one new technique will appear (or be desired by firms) and that the new technique will be

The transition process that any actual economy would undergo with either neutral technical progress or biased technical progress and changes in the level of mechanisation are thus seen to be very complicated. The transition with biased technical progress would be much less smooth than may be, but is not necessarily, possible with neutral progress. It is the golden age concept's greatest usefulness that it enables the analysis of changes that undermine its existence.

---

superior to all others already employed if it is to be adopted. In that entrepreneurs have power to influence the development of techniques (research and development units, etc.), Leon argues that they will seek a single desired technique and not a range with each superior at different combinations of the profit rate and real wage.

He criticises Mrs Robinson, first for assuming that the rate and character of technical progress are autonomous to the firm, and second for assuming that technical spectra have a range of techniques.

This, of course, is true, but does not change the analysis of the effect of changes in the rate or character of technical progress on the relations in the system. The results will be the same when alpha plus succeeds alpha whether or not beta plus, gamma plus, etc., exist or not. Likewise the results of beta suceeding alpha will be the same irrespective of whether beta merely appeared in the course of ongoing research or was determinedly sought after by an entrepreneur faced with an increase in the real wage bill. The same reason must apply for changes in the rate of progress. What Leon desires is a descriptive model, whereas Mrs Robinson's analytical technique can be applied to show results over a wide range of assumptions about the actual generation of technical progress. See Leon, *Structural Change and Growth in Capitalism*, op. cit., 80–8.

APPENDIX D
The Classless, Non-Income-Differentiated Model

The general relationships of Chapter 12 are now approached in a slightly different form.

Assume the economy has no income classes whatsoever. All inhabitants work and all receive some profits income in addition to wages. Wage income is determined in the normal manner with corporations paying wages. No stipulation is made regarding the level of the real wage or the money wage; there may be wage differentials. The managers of corporations are automata who have no life function except as corporate decision-makers. The amount of gross profits, net of amortisation, is free to be distributed in any fashion to the working population. For example, it may be distributed in a profit-sharing scheme, or the government may tax all uninvested profits and give tax rebates to the working population. For present purposes it will be assumed that the total value of capital in the system is represented by a number of equal placements which are distributed across the population in proportion to any particular household's percentage of the prime cost of the output of the existing capital stock. Thus if w_i is the wage of the ith household, its percentage of total placements will be $w_i/w_N = S_i / \sum_{i=1}^{n} S_i$ where wN is the annual wage bill and $\sum_{i=1}^{n} S_i$ is the total number of placements representing ownership if the stock of capital in existence. In essence it makes little difference to the example how the value of capital is apportioned to the population.

It will also be assumed that the system is competitive enough to allow a uniform rate of profit in all lines of production. To avoid some intricacies in the division of capital the labour force is presumed to be constant with neutral technical progress occurring at a steady rate. The rate of growth has long been constant in the past and thus so has the rate of profit; hence there is no problem of a correct valuation of the capital stock at any point in time.

There is one, and only one, propensity to save out of income for the individuals in the system. The only discretionary aspect left open is to the automata of industry who retain the right to make investment decisions and are free to decide whether net investment should be financed externally or by retaining profits (and thus reducing the amount of profits paid out as dividends to individuals). Because of these assumptions there will be only one household income class in the system and only one household propensity to save in the economy.

As the system has been outlined, the total earnings of households are equal to wages paid plus dividends received on shares held. The total amount of income received by households in the system will then depend on the pay-out ratio, r, of the corporations. Thus $r = D/P$ where D is the total dividend and P net profits and there is no lag in dividend payments. Accordingly, as the income paid out is usable for consumption by households, total household received income is

$$E_H = wN + rP \tag{D.1}$$

and the retained profits are

$$R = (1 - r)P. \tag{D.2}$$

Total net income for the system will then be

$$Y = E_H + R = wN + rP + (1 - r)P. \tag{D.3}$$

If the savings propensity of households equals zero, all money saving in the system is done by firms so that aggregate savings equal undistributed profits

$$S = (1 - r)P \tag{D.4}$$

when $h = 1$.

If, however, workers save a portion of their received income, then consumption is

$$h(E_H) \tag{D.5}$$

where h is households' average propensity to consume, and household savings equal

$$(1-h)E_H \tag{D.6}$$

while total saving in the system is

$$(1-h)E_H + (1-r)P. \tag{D.7}$$

Thus total income in the system can be represented as

$$Y = C + S \tag{D.8}$$

or

$$E_H + R = (h(wN + rP)) + ((1-h)(E_H) + ((1-r)P)) \tag{D.8A}$$

and for households

$$E_H = (h(wN + rP)) + ((1-h)(wN + rP)), \tag{D.9}$$

the difference being R, the retained earnings of corporations. From (D.8A)

$$E_H + R = wN + P \tag{D.8B}$$

and from (D.9)

$$E_H = wN + rP \tag{D.1}$$

and

$$P - rP = (1-r)P = R. \tag{D.10}$$

The revised equations show the movement of income in relation to r. Thus it can be seen that the value of R (or r) will affect the value of household effective demand (although not their *total* real income), since corporations cannot, by definition, consume.

The appearance of r in both right-hand terms of (D.8A) and (D.9) indicates that its value will affect both the level of consumption (given h) and savings for households and the thriftiness conditions for the economy as a whole. Taking (D.8) for the economy as a whole

$$Y = cY + sY \tag{D.8C}$$

where s and c are the average savings and consumption pro-

2H

pensities of the entire income generated in the system and will differ from h and $(1 - h)$ depending on the value of r. Thus the higher is the value of r, the higher is the value of c (which is itself lower than h) and the lower is the value of s (which is itself higher than $(1 - h)$). The values of c and h, and S and $(1 - h)$, will only converge when $r = 1$.

Thus when h is of a given value, the level of r will determine the thriftiness conditions for the economy as a whole which will be of a quite different value *from those of households*. The value of r will not of course affect the level of total income for any household but it will limit the amount of its spendable income out of its total income claims.

Thus far it has been assumed that households have no claim on the withheld profits; nevertheless households will receive these withholdings indirectly. To understand this accrual the determination of the value of r must be analysed. Corporations will be assumed to retain the autonomy of making investment decisions. Thus the utilisation of the economy's total resources as determined by corporate investment policy will determine the relations between available (consumption) and non-available (capital) goods output in the system. This decision will, of course, still not affect the money income of the society as all households have titular claim to any income earned in the system. The investment decision will, however, determine the consuming power of the income claims and together with the pay-out ratio will determine the purchasing power of usable income. That is, the two decisions as to the amount of investment and the method of financing the investment will determine the level of effective demand and the amount of consumable output over which it is exercised. It is in these relations that the determination of the rate of profits and its effect on distribution is developed. In general, the value of the pay-out ratio, r, will be less than one in a corporation that wishes to retain a certain amount of certainty as to the availability of finance, irrespective of the conditions that might be prevailing in the money market. Thus, if uncertainty is high, the planning process is long, or the rate of interest is high, the value of r will most likely be small. In a case where there is no shortage of funds in the short- and long-term money markets, then the value of r can be higher. The level of the value of r is then tied to finance conditions and the rate of net investment.

A. ZERO RETENTIONS

If the value of r were unity, irrespective of methods of finance, then the savings propensities of households would set the savings ratio for all income generated in the system. It is the level of household savings that must be accommodated to the level of investment chosen by corporations. In this case the consumption value of total income will depend on the level of investment alone. If the capital sector is a higher proportion of the total output than savings of the total household income, given the level of money wages, total income will be constant but the real value of total income will be lower than if they were of the same proportion. Price levels, margins and profit rates will all be rising with dividends rising by the same amount. If the value of h is constant there can be no stable price level or rate of growth outside that set by the household rate of savings. The effect of $r = 1$ is to recycle the higher prices back in terms of higher dividends and it is impossible to reduce the con-sumption value of income. Thus no matter what the price level or the rate of profits, savings from the system will be constant and the system will be explosive or depressive depending on whether the constant real savings are less or greater than investment. This is again a case similar to Harrod's. It differs in respect to the relation of the division of output into two sectors. Without this specification, any rate of profit will satisfy the level of savings at the precise rate of growth dictated by the value of the savings ratio. It is thus seen that it is necessary for the system to have different savings ratios for individuals and corporations if there is to be a definable rate of profit and stability in the system.

B. ZERO DIVIDENDS

If the pay-out ratio is nil the maximum divergence between s and $(1 - h)$ occurs. In this case there is no profits income included in household incomes, and the wage sets the amount of disposable income and the rate of investment the consumption value of this income. Thus when the rate of investment exceeds the value of $R + (1 - h)E_H$ the amount of money income for desired consumption will be in excess of costs of production plus the previous gross margin on available output and thus margins will rise. As profits rise the level of retained earnings will rise until there has been a sufficient shift in income from households to corporations and the value of retained earnings covers the excess investment. In the event households reduce their savings in an attempt to outbid other households for the available consumption goods, the prices increase and the increase in retained earnings and the rate of profit will be all the greater while the real value of households' money income will be all the lower, but the consumption value of income the same.

On the other hand, if investment falls below $R + (1 - h)E_H$ the level of effective demand will fall, as will output, prices and profits. As long as employment is maintained, real income of households will rise. If not, all values will fall and the level of retained earnings and employment will fall until the level of investment is equal to the value of $R + (1 - h)E_H$ with fewer households employed. The present case with $r = 0$ resembles that of the classical savings assumptions where workers consume all their income and there is no spending out of profits income. Unemployment in the last example is a result of too large retentions in relation to the investment planned by corporations given positive savings by households.

C. HOUSEHOLD SAVINGS, DIVIDENDS AND RETENTIONS

Now consider the intermediate case where the pay-out ratio is at some value between zero and unity and introduce some further complications. Since households are saving, some provision must be made for the disposal of these savings. Corporations seeking to expand investment at a rate greater then the level of their retained earnings at the existing pay-out ratio will have a demand for additional finance. Assume the existence of a fractional reserve bank which accepts deposits from households and pays a rate equal to the ruling rate of profit on these deposits. The bank also lends funds to corporations at this same rate. Alternatively household savings could be taken up by the issue of additional shares by the corporations. Thus a receptacle exists for savings but the existence of the bank guarantees that corporate investment need not be limited by available savings.

Given the money wage rate, available resources and the level of investment, there will be a corresponding division between available and non-available output. If the pay-out rates were higher, the money income of the community would be higher but less than in proportion. The amount of money demand exercised over the available output would consequently be higher and therefore prices, and profit margins, and the rate of profit, higher. The extent of the movement in real income would be to the point where the retentions out of total profits plus household savings balance the level of investment. The consumption value of income of the community is unchanged even though disposable money income is higher, since the amount of available consumption output is unchanged. If the pay-out ratio is higher than the value of the average propensity to save, there can be no stable solution since disposable money income increases faster than savings out of received income and results in spiralling inflation.

D. THE GENERAL EFFECT OF r

Thus r, through its effect on s, will determine the level of money incomes necessary for $I = sY$. Even though households have legal claim to all income earned, there is still distribution of income via prices and profit margins which will act to limit the amount of real purchasing power of a given total money income in the system to the value of available output produced in the system.

It is clear that the value of $1 - h$ will also determine the degree of price change necessary, but given investment and the total level of resources it cannot affect the level of real income or be a factor of determination of the rate of profits. The value of r serves the same function in determining the level of effective demand and the level of profit margins as spending out of profits in the models with wage–profits distribution schemes. A higher value of the pay-out ratio, for any given rate of investment, will affect the same higher level of profit margins and rate of profits as a decrease in the savings propensities of pure profit-earners. If firms link investment decisions to the rate of profit, investment and growth can then be stimulated by raising the pay-out ratio, subject to advantageous conditions in the money markets.

This appendix has thus tried to show in more simple terms the relations between the investment decision by corporations and the consumption-saving decision by households. In the exercise, the overall conclusion becomes apparent. It is not the way thriftiness is defined but the independency of the investment decisions from those of savers, given limited resources, that is the crucial aspect of these type models.

INDEX